Animals and the Environment in Turkish Culture

Animals and the Environment in Turkish Culture

Ecocriticism and Transnational Literature

Kim Fortuny

I.B. TAURIS
LONDON • NEW YORK • OXFORD • NEW DELHI • SYDNEY

I.B. TAURIS
Bloomsbury Publishing Plc
50 Bedford Square, London, WC1B 3DP, UK
1385 Broadway, New York, NY 10018, USA
29 Earlsfort Terrace, Dublin 2, Ireland

BLOOMSBURY, I.B. TAURIS and the I.B. Tauris logo are trademarks of Bloomsbury Publishing Plc

First published in Great Britain 2019
Paperback edition published 2021

Copyright © Kim Fortuny, 2019

Kim Fortuny has asserted her right under the Copyright, Designs and Patents Act, 1988, to be identified as the Author of this work.

Cover design: Adriana Brioso
Cover illustrations © Mine Sübiler www.minesubiler.com

All rights reserved. No part of this publication may be reproduced or transmitted in any form or by any means, electronic or mechanical, including photocopying, recording, or any information storage or retrieval system, without prior permission in writing from the publishers.

Bloomsbury Publishing Plc does not have any control over, or responsibility for, any third-party websites referred to or in this book. All internet addresses given in this book were correct at the time of going to press. The author and publisher regret any inconvenience caused if addresses have changed or sites have ceased to exist, but can accept no responsibility for any such changes.

A catalogue record for this book is available from the British Library.

A catalog record for this book is available from the Library of Congress.

ISBN: HB: 978-1-7883-1818-1
PB: 978-0-7556-4366-0
ePDF: 978-1-7867-3663-5
eBook: 978-1-7867-2657-5

Typeset by Integra Software Services Pvt. Ltd.

To find out more about our authors and books visit www.bloomsbury.com and sign up for our newsletters.

To my dear Mother, Darlene Fortuny
And in memory of "Electric Jim," my Dad.

Contents

Acknowledgments	viii
Permissions and Grant Acknowledgments	x
Introduction	1

Part 1 Land

1. Herman Melville's *Near East Journal* and Ahmet Hamdi Tanpınar's *Five Cities*: Affinities of Culture, Nature, and Islamic Mysticism in Istanbul — 13
2. Nature's Place in Political Romanticism: Selected Poems by Nâzım Hikmet — 37
3. Resourcing Nature: Land Ethics, Poetics, and "Things I Didn't Know I Loved" by Nâzım Hikmet — 61

Part 2 Animals

4. Islam, Westernization, and Post-Humanist Place: The Case of the Istanbul Street Dog — 77
5. Ecopoetics, Dead Metaphors, and Bird Migration: The Bosporus Passage of the European White Stork — 105
6. The Benefits of Doubt: A Sea Turtle and the Ecological Sublime — 127

Afterword	154
Notes	158
Bibliography	170
Index	179

Acknowledgments

This book has traveled so much distance that it is easy to forget all the people and places that have contributed to its inception and production. I have a number of families to acknowledge, the first being my academic family at Boğaziçi University, Istanbul. Foremost, I would like to thank the extraordinary research assistants who made this book possible, namely, Arif Camoğlu and İpek Kotan. Their consistent enthusiasm, diligence, and professionalism have been a gift to me. Other graduate assistants whose contributions I appreciate include Lamia Kabal and Aysun Kan and, in the final stages, student assistant Buşra Bakan. I have been very fortunate to find a home away from home in my professional life. My mentors and colleagues in the Department of Western Languages and Literatures at Boğaziçi University are also some of my closest friends and working side by side with them through the years has been a privilege and a pleasure. Our remarkable students are also a source of energy and hope, and I appreciate daily the work we do together. Many anonymous peer reviewers offered excellent suggestions that improved the text and I send my gratitude out to them.

My family of friends who have helped sustain me through the writing process is a large one. Special thanks to Emine Fişek and Başak Demirhan for the daily nuts and bolts of living. Elif Ünlü, Ethan Guagliardo, and Leila Braverman for every other day. Thanks to my sister Gülen Güler and brother Zafer Sarı. Friends distant but dear include Meg Russett, Ingrid, and Gerard Philippon, Rhonda Roth and the Oxbow Park yoga people. And all the Altman Rd. people, Paula and Herb, Joan and Kerry, Karil and Scott. Special thanks to Hakan Yeşildere.

Lastly, I would first like to thank my superior mother for doing what she does most naturally, supporting and nurturing those around her. She has been a constant source of love and friendship for me and I dedicate the book to her. Our father Jim Fortuny would have liked this book and recognized himself as the early inspiration for all things wild. I thank him profoundly for that. I miss you. I would also like to thank my siblings Jill, Ralph, and Guy for being my people and also my niece Isabelle and all the other offspring who make summers in Oregon a beautiful thing.

Permissions and Grant Acknowledgments

Three of these chapters originally appeared as articles, in slightly different form, in the following publications: "Herman Melville's Near East Journal and Ahmet Hamdi Tanpınar's Five Cities: Affinities of Culture, Nature, and Islamic Mysticism in Istanbul." *Nineteenth-Century Contexts.* 37.2 (2015): 127–145; "Nature's Place in Political Romanticism: Selected Poems by Nâzım Hikmet" appeared as "Nazim Hikmet's Ecopoetics and the Gezi Park Protests." *Middle Eastern Literatures.* 19.2 (2016): 162–184; "Islam, Westernization and Post-Humanist Place: The Case of the Istanbul Street Dog." *ISLE (Interdisciplinary Studies in Literature and the Environment).* 21.2 (2014): 271–297.

The research and writing of four chapters were made possible through grants provided by BAP projects at Boğaziçi University, Istanbul, Turkey: Chapter 2: "Nature's Place in Political Romanticism: Selected Poems by Nâzım Hikmet" (No 7280P, P. Kodu 13BO4P3); Chapter 3: "Resourcing Nature: Land Ethics, Poetics, and "Things I Didn't Know I Loved" by Nâzim Hikmet" (No 10221, P. Kodu 15BO4P2); Chapter 4: "Islam, Westernization, and Post-humanist Place: The Case of the Istanbul Street Dog" (No 6664, P. Kodu 12BO4P1); Chapter 5: "Ecopoetics, Dead Metaphors, and Bird Migration: The Bosporus Passage of the European White Stork" (No 12940, P. Kodu 17BO4P4).

Introduction

Although a Pacific Northwest American with roots in the foothills of the Oregon Cascade Mountains and Willamette River Valley, I have spent a good part of my adult life, and all of my professional life, in Istanbul, a complex and crowded old world metropolis. When one thinks of Istanbul one does not think of nature per se. But it is perhaps this assumption that has fed my desire to think through questions of post-humanism the relevance of Romantic poetics to contemporary green movements, the place of feral animals in cities, the political relevance of public green space, and other similar topics that occupy my writing here. To move back and forth between contrastive environments, one relatively rural to one emphatically urban has been, and continues to be, a constant exercise in revision and adaptation. We work with what we have at hand: "Write what you know," Hemingway frankly advised. When one is lucky, life can deal us a rich if sometimes disjunctive range of experience. And with experience comes something akin to knowledge, or so one hopes.

This book reflects this sometimes uneasy movement between landscapes and cityscapes. It also attempts to negotiate through inclusion the various voices that make up the book's polyphonic world, some Turkish, some North American, some literary, some theoretical. While the primary focuses of the book are selected environments, animals, and literary texts in Turkey, my own background in American literature circulates throughout these discussions. Nature, of course, does not recognize national borders or identity, though biotic life adjusts or reacts to walls erected by humans to contain it or keep it out. In this spirit, the various landscapes that follow come together with diverse cultural or intercultural references and literary and non-literary texts under the auspices of an impartial natural world. They also come together in response to the conviction that work that responds to environmental pressures on the world we live in must engage the local, wherever that may be, as well as the global. If we're lucky, we have access to both.

The transnational worldview at the center of this book has a personal textual history. In a previous book, *American Writers in Istanbul* (Syracuse UP 2010), I traced my own bicultural experience in the writing of canonical writers such as Herman Melville, Mark Twain, Ernest Hemingway, John Dos Passos, Paul Bowles, Nelson Algren, and James Baldwin. Most of these writers only stopped by long enough to fall in love or disillusionment before moving on. Most of these writers only stopped by long enough to fall in love or disillusionment before moving on, all except James Baldwin who made Istanbul one of his alternative homes throughout the 1960s. It was Melville, however, who would prove to be the bridge to the focus of inquiry that occupies the present text: nature. In my chapter on his *Near East Journal* entries dedicated to his visit to Istanbul in 1856, I had argued that his record of the city suggests that there is much about Istanbul that reflects a lawlessness or detachment in the relationship between man and nature, an important theme in *Moby Dick*. While nature is not empathetic in Istanbul, just as the whale is disinterested, man and his monuments nevertheless seem to co-exist stoically within a natural urban wilderness. Melville suggests, I argued, that nature and human culture in Istanbul tend to their own detached, yet synchronic, rhythms. These assessments were based on close readings of the journal notes and my own readiness to read Melville's focus on cemeteries and mosques as indicative of a larger preoccupation with the interconnectedness of cultural monuments and nature and something ineffable, call it spirit, that penetrates both.

One day I received an unpublished English translation of a chapter on Istanbul by the early twentieth-century Turkish writer Ahmet Hamdi Tanpınar from his book-length work of non-fiction *Beş Şehir* (*Five Cities*). The translator was Ruth Christie and the chapter has since been published in *Texas Studies in Literature and Language* (2012). Tanpınar, whose fastidious, lyrical prose was and continues to be too difficult for me to read with ease in Turkish, entered my life like a beloved great uncle. All that I had been trying to sort out in the Melville chapter of my book suddenly had a better, wiser precedent. This is what Tanpınar had to say about trees:

Our great architects never failed to set several cypress and plane trees beside their buildings; the contrast with dense foliage created one of their finest compositions. Some went further and reserved a space in the center of the divine geometry of the courtyard to a mosque or religious school for a cypress or a plane-tree to flourish, for a rose to bloom, for ivy to twine and twist.

(Tanpınar 461)

When an architect or "pious donor" planted a tree, continues Tanpınar, "[H]e knew that a tree entrusted to the earth is a gift of value, a talisman securing a neighborhood, a district, even a whole community and all its religious beliefs" (Tanpınar 461). I've since quoted these passages a number of times in my own writing, including here in Chapters 1 and 2. They never cease to interest and move me. They gather and secure my own disparate observations within the confines of a more trustworthy prose.

This book is a continuation of the journey begun with Melville and then Tanpınar. The first chapter is a comparative one, naturally. Nineteenth-century North American Melville and twentieth-century Turkish Tanpınar proved to have much in common once put into conversation with one another. Of the several correspondences I identify in Chapter 1, "Herman Melville's Near East Journal and Ahmet Hamdi Tanpınar's Five Cities: Affinities of Culture, Nature, and Islamic Mysticism in Istanbul," one is the relationship between nature and culture in the city. According to my reading the spiritual world permeates both, and each writer consistently draws our attention to this immanence in Istanbul. Melville summons the rhetoric of Sufi poets, the language of absence in presence, to account for the enigmatic appeal of the Bosporus. Tanpınar, a student of mysticism, as well as Member of Parliament, frequently draws the reader's attention to the proximity of death to life in the city. As in Melville's journal, this co-existence is manifested in the interplay of architecture and nature.

Moving forward chronologically in terms of the time-line of composition, though out of sequence in the organization of the present chapters, the next project for the present book narrows in on one particular urban creature that appears to negotiate, and with panache, the fine precarious line between life and death in the city that Melville and Tanpınar identify. This discussion, which appears as Chapter 4 in this book, is a foray into the field of Animal Studies.

In "Islam, Westernization, and Post-Humanist Place: The Case of the Istanbul Street Dog," I turn to a creature of the natural world, but in this case a member of the urban wildlife community, the Istanbul street dog. My friend Gülen Güler, an Istanbul-based film producer who was formulating a documentary film project about the dogs, inspired this direction. I found myself pulled more and more into the world of the feral, something I was always attracted to, but had no developed opinions about. The Istanbul street dogs would ultimately be my guides into this unknown territory, a role they often play in peoples' lives here. The research would contribute to Gulen's documentary film about the dogs entitled *Taşkafa: Stories of the Street,* directed by Andrea Luka Zimmerman. John Berger, the writer and public intellectual, would volunteer his voice to the project as narrator.

Other writing projects followed in a similar vein, though not all are included in this book. One article, "Elizabeth Bishop's 'Pink Dog' and Other Non-Human Animals" (*Textual Practice*, 29.6 (2015): 1099–1116), looks at animals in Elizabeth Bishop's poems. The animal around which all the other animals circulated in the article is an urban street dog in Rio de Janeiro. As is the case with Istanbul's street dog population, urban renewal takes its toll on the scavenger in the poem "Pink Dog." Though the poem was not one of Bishop's best, it allowed me a familiar door onto other non-human animals in other, better poems in her oeuvre. And just about then, just when I was solidifying my political argument against the abuses of urban development on marginalized populations, thirty activists set up tents in Gezi Park in the center of Istanbul. They thwarted neoliberal plans to tear out one of the only remaining congregations of mature trees in the city's tired center. They were tear-gassed for their efforts of course, and then we all jumped into the urban wilderness with them.

And this is where the Turkish poet Nâzım Hikmet entered this book. Gezi Park was alive with music, dance, image from digital to spray, and, of course, literature. Poems hung on trees. Hikmet was everywhere. And I started thinking. I had read limited collections of his poems but often felt like a tourist in front of them. They spoke of resistance I had not experienced. Having arrived in Turkey in the post-coup 1980s, been away through the 1990s and living back in Istanbul in relative calm though the early 2000s, I felt Hikmet's poems were not mine. They spoke of injustices I could only comprehend in the abstract. Everything changed for me at Gezi of course. I too was baptized in tear gas and by water cannon. I decided to re-read Hikmet after Gezi was silenced. So many of the poems hanging from trees were about trees and I wanted to get a deeper sense of how nature and social activism functioned together in the work of one of Turkey's most beloved exiled writers. Why was he so relevant to the protests beyond the more obvious appeal to leftist populism? It turned out there were not yet any academic studies on Hikmet that considered nature in his poems in the kind of political terms I was considering.

I eventually began to develop ideas on the place of nature in Hikmet's oeuvre. Like the Gezi Park protesters, Hikmet was labeled romantic, even by those who supported him. But the popular use of the term "romantic" fails to acknowledge the original political edginess of Romanticism in its nineteenth-century literary guise, an adversarial tension that often engages alternative notions of the value of nature. Romantic nature often does not serve human needs alone but is represented as embodying integrity beyond human use-value. In Hikmet's poems cultural heritage is intrinsically tied to the land. This was obvious. What was less obvious was that as I read him with heightened attention, I realized that the nature offered in the poems was not always conceived of in anthropocentric terms. In many of the poems, nature seemed to be honored in its own right, and humans were encouraged to pay attention to its textures and rhythms. I concluded that nature, the literary arts, and sociopolitical protest are fused in the poems and give rise to Hikmet's relevance to contemporary environmental movements in Turkey. The second chapter of this book, "Nature's Place in Political Romanticism: Selected Poems by Nâzım Hikmet," is the result of this inquiry.

My travels around Turkey had taken me to the Hemşin, a lush river valley running between the eastern Black Sea and the Caucasus Mountains. I wasn't prepared for the familiar beauty of the Fırtına River. It was winter and it ran fast and wild, like so many of the rivers in Oregon. It was off-season but Selim at the Fırtına Pansiyon kindly opened his doors to us. It was here that I learned firsthand about the local resistance to the hydroelectric dams being planned along the Fırtına, one of the many environmental movements in the provinces that had inspired and culminated in the urban Gezi protests. I had noticed one exhausted river after another limping into the Black Sea along the coastal road as we drove east from Trabzon. Ragged concrete and rebar walls had battled the river and won. But the Fırtına had been left alone until now. I was introduced to a gentleman who had been leading the movement for years and had become something of a folk figure as well as a television personality. We sat outside his three-story wooden house looking out over the steep divide of the valley. Like his neighbors he considered the Fırtına a living entity and a companion. He and his friends had put themselves in danger to protect the neighborhood from outside developers who considered the river a resource to be harnessed and exploited rather than respected and protected.

The third chapter in this book is the outcome of this trip to the Fırtına valley. I was negotiating the emotional effect the experience had had on me as an academic with activist tendencies. I wanted to translate my visceral response into something useful. I began thinking about preemptive measures rather than stabilizing responses to these engineering projects. What might be done to thwart the thinking that feeds into institutionalized environmental abuse in the first place? This is simultaneously a naïve and ambitious question and especially for those of us who work in the field of Ecocriticism or Ecopoetics. There is not much I could say that has not already been said and then said another way. But as an English professor I had no real choice but to look to the only real arsenal I had some access to and some competency to exploit: language, poetic language to be precise.

In this third chapter, "Resourcing Nature: Land Ethics, Poetics, and 'Things I Didn't Know I Loved' by Nâzım Hikmet," I begin with the familiar idea that the way we talk about nature affects the way we interact with it. When we call land a resource because we are trained to call it so, we conceive of it primarily in terms of its use-value to humans. This training has facilitated support for the rapid proliferation of hydroelectric power plants and dams along the Black Sea coast and throughout Anatolia. The damage to the environment has been extensive, but only local populations whose lives are intrinsically tied to the land and water tend to be keenly aware of this. In order to change the behavior of distant urban populations whose energy needs outweigh their ecological acumen requires some very fundamental changes, changes, I argue, at the linguistic level. I suggest that one way to begin is through broader education in the Humanities. Reading literature and culture expands the critical capacities because they deepen one's rhetorical range. And of all the literary genres it is perhaps poetry that is best positioned to challenge and disrupt the deterministic mythologizing processes that lead to the misappropriation of nature.¹

I turn once again to the Turkish poet Nâzım Hikmet to illustrate this disruption. I focus on one poem, "Things I Didn't Know I Loved," because it is a good example of the ways in which poetry can redetermine the relationship of humans to nature. In this poem the use-value of natural "resources" is undermined. Boundaries and delineations between the human and the elemental dissolve. In my close reading of the poem I work toward the notion put forth by Scott Knickerbocker in *Ecopoetics: The Language of Nature, the Nature of Language*, that poetics can "nudge consciousness to a more ecologically ethical state, which in turn shapes behavior," I suggest that Hikmet's poem reflects a "[h]eightened perception that promotes deep thinking," the kind of thinking that leads to environmentally sound human relationships with nature. And this I conclude is one practical use of poetry.

The fifth chapter turns again to Animal Studies in the form of ornithology. The spring and fall migration of storks over the Bosporus is an event. Those of us who frequent, or in my case, work on the hills that overlook the Bosporus have a front row perch for these stunning passages. For me it begins with an optical illusion. Looking up to check cloud patterns as I often do I'll see what looks like an ellipsis trailing off and away from its sentence. The small dots circle and regroup. They are very high. I feel it before I understand it. Yes, it is May. They've arrived. Some evenings the migrating storks will come very close. I've looked at them nearly eye-to-eye, as they've skirted the hills.

Aware that certain so-called megaprojects have been built or are being built directly on the stop-over sites of these ancient migration routes I wanted to include a discussion of this in this book. Chapter 5, "Ecopoetics, Dead Metaphors, and Bird Migration: The Bosporus Passage of the European White Stork," attempts to respond to this ecological dilemma by bringing together ornithology and poetics. It sifts through the environmental and biological data on the migrations, weighing and considering it alongside selected Turkish poetic texts that engage with migratory storks who pass through Turkey. What I find is that the art and the science reinforce one another. The biannual passage of the European White Stork is as central to local cultural memory as it is to the genetic makeup of the species. It is this convergence, the cultural and the biological, the human and the animal, or in this case bird, that speaks loudly for the conservation of the species and its ancient migration route. Because I adhere to the belief that in order to effectively address environmental problems we must engage the sciences and the arts simultaneously, and in this case within the confines of the same essay, I offer a cross-disciplinary approach to an ecological impasse. As an exercise in applied theory, it touches on current issues in Ecopoetics and Animal Studies.

The final chapter in this book takes a personal turn, much like this introduction. I somewhat forgo the objective "academic" voice that directs the book thus far and veer toward the subjective first person in an effort to look directly, and in as jargon-free fashion as possible, at a solitary encounter I had with a large loggerhead sea turtle off the Turkish Mediterranean coast. In Chapter 6 entitled "The Benefits of Doubt: A Sea Turtle and the Ecological Sublime," I explore the implications of the tradition of the sublime because in retrospect I realized that my response to the sea turtle seemed to conform very closely to this inheritance. Narrowing in on discussions of the sublime and nature in Longinus' "On the Sublime" and Kant's "The Analytic of the Sublime," I note misgivings I have concerning the applicability of these source texts to my experience. I am concerned by the absence of material nature in their paradigms. Turning to Herpetology, the branch of zoology concerned with the study of reptiles that include sea turtles, I look at the way this field might give me substantive ways to think about the fear and awe I experienced in the face of what for me was an inscrutable encounter. I propose a synthesis of these seemingly discordant approaches to nature, one philosophical/aesthetic, the other scientific, in the form of the "ecological sublime," a reading of the sublime informed by Ecocriticism. I close this chapter with notes on sea turtle conservation on the south coast of Turkey and the possible role of the sublime in conservation education.

The ranging title, *Animals and The Environment in Turkish Culture: Ecocriticism and Transnational Literature*, reflects the various intellectual and experiential currents that have fed into its conception. These currents include three waves of Ecocriticism beginning with habits of seeing and reporting pervasive in the 1990s when creative writers and English professors partial to environmental ecology first joined forces under the loose guise of *The Association for the Study of Literature and the Environment* (ASLE). Post-humanism and cross-cultural and transnational approaches to nature characteristic of second- and third-wave Ecocriticism respectively also make up these currents.[2] The inclusion of both land and animals, though separated for the sake of editorial symmetry, stems from a desire to present these "fields of study" as mutually suggestive and mutually inclusive, a cross-disciplinary approach to research and writing the Humanities creates space for.[3] And much in the way that land and animals are better read within the context of the other, so are literature and culture bound by a similar interdependence. While the primary geographical focus is Turkey, the biotic issues are global. And while the majority of the literary texts examined are Turkish, the ecocritical concerns are not confined to specific national cultural production but appeal to matters international in scope. The reader need not be versed in Turkish literature and culture in order to engage with the ethos of the discussions. The reader familiar with Turkish literary arts and culture may find a disseminated, globally relevant way to consider familiar local literary texts, landscapes, and animals.

My professional preoccupation with nature and literary, cross-disciplinary, and cross-cultural entanglements began and came of age in Istanbul. Nothing in my early formal education prepared me for the immense impact this city and country would have on my intellectual life. Histories tend to tell us of the humans who write them. But there are also natural histories to tell, and not only those that the vocabularies of scientists can do justice to. Istanbul is rife with the possibilities of vegetation and wildlife. Where trees are allowed to mature, or better yet, are tended and fostered and protected, marvelous things happen to human structures. Where dogs, migratory birds, and turtles are allowed free passage, humans experience modes of being that deepen and enhance their own. They are also less alone. When city planners, architects, engineers, and the ministries that empower them strive to respect the dignity of the natural beings their schemes share space with, people and places prosper. These are not excessive Romantic conceits. They are historical facts. Turkish writers and even American writers who have come to Istanbul have been telling us this for years and years. There is, perhaps, a "divine geometry" that can exist between the man-made and the natural. Call it beauty, call it truth, call it what you will. I will close this introduction by agreeing with Tanpınar that the symbiosis, whatever form it takes, is a gift to be honored, something this book attempts to do.

Part One

Land

1

Herman Melville's *Near East Journal* and Ahmet Hamdi Tanpınar's *Five Cities*: Affinities of Culture, Nature, and Islamic Mysticism in Istanbul

When Herman Melville came to Istanbul in 1856 on an eight-month Old World tour, he recorded his observations in sketches and fragments, extracts of which would be edited by Howard Horsford and published by Princeton University Press one hundred years later under the title *Journal of a Visit to the Europe and the Levant October 11, 1856–May 6, 1857*. Melville's "pilgrimage" to the Old World was not an extraordinary undertaking in 1856. The writer's interest in the Near and Middle East reflected an occidental trend in the late eighteenth and nineteenth centuries on both sides of the Atlantic inspired by, among other things, archeological discoveries in the Near and Middle East and a developing interest in comparative religions and philology. Islamic civilizations that shared geography with ancient Christian cultures were of particular interest in America's engagement with the region due, in part, to the founding typological narratives that conceived of North America as the chosen land, the New Jerusalem in the popular Christian conscience.[1] A surge in American Protestant missionary activity in the Ottoman Empire in the nineteenth century led to an output of narratives by and about Americans in Ottoman lands, narratives that often reflected what Ussama Makdisi calls "the apotheosis of American exceptionalism" (Makdisi 178). It was a moment in mission history, he writes, when "American rationalism, racialism and evangelism fused together" leading to a self-portrait of the United States as an "unproblematic land of liberty," particularly, it might be added, when compared to the untidy deep history of the eastern Mediterranean (Makdisi 178). *Knickerbocker Magazine*, one of North America's most important literary and critical journals of the time, carried articles on the Near East as a subject in nearly every issue starting in January of 1836 (Finkelstein 10, 19).

Although Edward Said suggested in 1978 that "the American experience of the Orient was limited," compared to the "layer upon layer of interests, official learning, institutional pressure, that covered the Orient as a subject matter and as a territory in the latter half of the nineteenth century" in England and Europe, he nevertheless allowed that "[c]ultural isolatos" like Melville, along with the "ubiquitous" American missionary, took some interest in the Orient (Said 192, 290).[2] Travelers east were expected to share their journeys through letters and journals, more famous travelers via public lectures. As Howard Horsford notes in his 1955 introduction to the journals, Melville's recordings of his impressions tend to be typical of most travel journals of the period: entries are cursory, sometimes merely lists of words: the rough material of more polished narratives to come. But what distinguishes Melville's journal notes from those of travelers with amateur literary ambitions, or evangelical objectives, not surprisingly, is the power of his writing to inscribe so much with so little rhetorical effort. While many entries recorded during his visit to Istanbul, especially those recorded on his first days, are characterized by the confusion and disdain one often comes across in writing about the city, past and present, the journal becomes simultaneously a series of meditations on the enigmatic nature of reality familiar to readers of *Moby-Dick*.

Like Ishmael, Melville in Istanbul is never only a witness to empirical phenomena as he wanders the streets and cemeteries, or sails along the Bosporus in a caique, "[c]ushioned like an Ottoman" (*Journal* 103).[3] He too has his eye out for intimations of things inscrutable, an interest that predates his voyage to the Near East, a preoccupation emerging as much from his lifelong conversation and struggle with Christianity, as from his former travels and his deep reading in various world mysticisms. Nathaniel Hawthorne would make the following note of the traveler who began his Old World tour with a visit to his mentor in Liverpool in 1856:

> Melville as he always does, began to reason of Providence and futurity, and of everything that lies beyond human ken … It is strange how he persists … in wandering to and fro over these deserts … He can neither believe, nor be

comfortable in his disbelief; and he is too honest and courageous not to try to do one or the other.

(Hawthorne 432–433)

While Melville travels to and through Istanbul in the wake of national interest in the region, he also journeys receptive to ways in which Turkey would answer to his impasse with the ineffable.

Approximately one hundred years later the Turkish writer Ahmet Hamdi Tanpınar (1901–1962) would breathe life into the interstices of Melville's sketchy Istanbul text. As Tanpınar wandered through the backstreets of Istanbul toward the middle of the twentieth century, nearly thirty years after the official end of the Ottoman Empire, he gathered the data and produced a prose that fleshes out Melville's text in a style that recalls the rhetorical vigor and agility of his American predecessor. Tanpınar's collection of long essays entitled *Five Cities* (*Beş Şehir*), published in Turkish in 1946, and still unpublished in English in full at the time of this writing, looks carefully and artfully at five Turkish cities: Ankara, Erzurum, Konya, Bursa, and Istanbul.[4] And while no evidence exists of a direct intertextual relationship between the two Istanbul texts, there are third texts and contexts they share, enough so that remarkable affinities arise in the writing of the mid-nineteenth-century American and the mid-twentieth-century Turk. Both writers are invested in projects of national identity building and their respective representations of this in writing are conflicted; both writers are at odds with Western constructs of progress; both write under the influence of a European Romantic tradition which grew out of the eighteenth-century Enlightenment and was in part a reaction to that century's enthrallment to the unlimited possibilities of human reason; and both took a particular interest in Islamic mysticism in the form of Sufism in their efforts to account for their distrust of, and dissatisfaction with, modernity.

The 2007 winner of the Nobel Prize for Literature, Orhan Pamuk, in his memoir *Istanbul: Memories and the City*, acknowledges his debt to an earlier generation of Turkish writers who wrote with particular care about Istanbul's past, or, rather, the presence of the past in post–Second World War Istanbul. He focuses on two writers in particular, the poet Yahya Kemal and the novelist and essayist Ahmet Hamdi Tanpınar whom he respectfully refers to as his "melancholic" literary predecessors. Pamuk spends much time discussing the difficulties of translating the Turkish word *hüzün*—suggesting, as it does, a contradictory feeling of pleasant sadness in connection with an unrecoverable past. And in order to demonstrate the nuances of this word in Turkish he turns to Tanpınar's books which, he says, capture the full spectrum of the word *hüzün*, from its historical, political, and social depths, to its emotional and psychological reaches. Tanpınar's books

> offer the deepest understanding of what it means to live in a rapidly westernizing country among the ruins of Ottoman culture, and who shows how it is, in the end, the people themselves who, through ignorance and despair, end up severing their every link with the past.
>
> (Pamuk 209)

Yahya Kemal and Tanpınar's generation of Turkish writers were born Ottoman Turks and lived through the final years of the empire. Both witnessed the War of Independence led by Mustafa Kemal Atatürk (Tanpınar was twenty-two years old when the Turkish Republic was officially founded in 1923) and both writers were involved in the acceleration of the Westernization and nationalization projects and processes that followed. A novelist and a regular contributor to arts and literary publications, Tanpınar was a professor in the Faculty of Letters at Istanbul University, the oldest academic institution in Istanbul. He served as a deputy in the National Assembly from 1942 to 1946 and also for a time in the Ministry of Education. Of the six novels and four collections of non-fiction, *Five Cities* and the canonical novel *Huzur* (*Peace* or *A Mind at Peace* according to a recent translation) were the only two books published in his lifetime. *Five Cities* is a remarkably lyrical and polyphonic voyage into contemporary Turkey's distant past.

If Orhan Pamuk focuses primarily on the elegiac *hüzün* that permeates the Istanbul chapter of *Five Cities*, he complicates his own Romantic attachment to his literary forefather by contextualizing the political project behind Tanpınar's text. Post-Ottoman Turkey, like the United States in Melville's nineteenth century, was determined to fashion a national identity and cultural production that could supersede former imperial influences: the Ottoman legacy in the case of Turkey, Britain in the case of the United States. The famous reforms introduced by Mustafa Kemal Atatürk that included changing the alphabet from Ottoman script to Latin script led to the desired *rapprochement* of Turkey to the West, but also served to sever modern Turkey's relationship to its scriptural past, thus much of its cultural heritage.[5] Less dramatic, because so universally practiced, but perhaps even more problematic was the new Republic's collective project to create an origination myth or genealogy with the new nation as its latest and inevitable manifestation. But a dearth of material on the Steppes of Central Asia and the nomadic and oral traditions that left no written traces of the "original" Turks led to a crisis of identity even before that identity could be fully established. The simultaneous and conflicting nationalist program to cleanse the Turkish language of foreign elements led to a further crisis of letters. Talat Halman notes that the language reforms in post-Republican Turkey would lead to "the most extensive vocabulary change registered in any language in modern times": "in 1920 the written language consisted of 75% Arabic, Persian, and French words, but by 1970 words of Turkish origin had risen to 80% and borrowals reduced to only 20%" (Halman 3).[6] As a writer and a scholar Tanpınar would become directly involved in this vastly complicated project. Lacking other stories to tell, as well as a common language in which to tell it, these writers rewrote Turkey's cultural past by "rehabilitating" its Ottoman heritage. Thus, Pamuk argues, as Tanpınar and Yahya Kemal wandered through the ruins of Istanbul and wrote about the melancholic beauty of its neighborhoods, their aims were simultaneously aesthetic and political. "They were picking through the ruins looking for signs of a new Turkish State, a new Turkish Nationalism: The Ottoman Empire might have fallen but the Turkish people had made it great" (Pamuk 250).

Pamuk's assessment of this aesthetic-political quest is certainly correct: the literary result of this search far exceeded the "utilitarian rhetoric" inevitably churned out by state-sponsored literary projects (Pamuk 250). Unlike many of his predecessors and contemporaries who either "praised or condemned the process of westernization," Tanpınar attempted to remain objective, argues Olgun Gündüz in "Ahmet Hamdi Tanpınar: A Unique Figure in Turkey's Westernization Quest": "He endeavored quite openly to understand and articulate the split people went through as an outcome of this phenomenon" (Gündüz 19). His dialectical approach to the representation of cultural transformation partly accounts for the quality of the writing. "Indeed, one of Tanpınar's literary achievements is his narrative aestheticization of the anxiety of a society on the verge of permanent yet uncertain change," suggests Erdağ Göknar in "Ottoman Past and Turkish Future: Ambivalence in A. H. Tanpınar's *Those Outside the Scene*" (Göknar 5). Focusing on Tanpınar's third novel that takes place in Istanbul after the First World War, Göknar argues that the "tone of Tanpınar's novels might be characterized as part lament for the loss of a late-Ottoman cultural past and part anxiety about the future of Turkish national society" (Göknar 3).

> Unable to rely on a disintegrating past or on a foreseeable future, the Istanbul society under occupation in *Those Outside the Scene* can seek deliverance only at the greatest cost: either by forsaking the past for the "new" (in the form of the national) or by accepting the compromise of Western rule in the form of occupation, mandate, or colonial authority.
>
> (Göknar 5–6)

Tanpınar's aesthetic treatment of this sociocultural ambivalence, his ability to represent in complex terms "the psychological dilemma of a people whose identity has been transformed as a result of rapid sociocultural change" is what marks his fictional and nonfictional prose (Göknar 3). The insipid or hackneyed language of nostalgia that is the hallmark of nationalist propagandas worldwide would give way to a patriotic "poetics of the past" in the subtle hands of Tanpınar (Pamuk 113).

History has criticized both Melville and Tanpınar for various, often conflicting, allegiances. Tanpınar has been accused of being a reactionary, a writer too entrenched in an Ottoman past to serve the future-oriented nationalist project. He has simultaneously been criticized for entertaining Machiavellian nationalist interests, co-opting and then romanticizing an Ottoman legacy in the service of the State. Pamuk suggests he was both and neither: Tanpınar's "melancholy of the ruins" made him seem to be a nationalist "in a way that suited the oppressive state" (Pamuk 113).[7] Tanpınar found a discourse that allowed him to voice criticism of the progressive reforms dictated by the Westernization process with a certain impunity. Hasan Bülent Kahraman, in his article "Yitirilmemiş Zamanın Ardında: Ahmet Hamdi Tanpınar ve Muhafazakar Modernliğin Estetik Düzlemi" ["In Pursuit of Time Not Lost: Ahmet Hamdi Tanpınar and the Aesthetic Dimension of Conservative Modernism"], suggests that Tanpınar's ambivalence is a studied one.[8] He quotes from Tanpınar's collection of autobiographical essays, published posthumously in 1970 under the title *As I Lived*, to support this claim: "According to the right, I am opposed to them in favor of a leftist ideology. For the leftists, however, I am a supporter of the right, if not the fascists, because I talk about Turkish music, the call to prayer, and our own history" (Tanpınar qtd. in Kahraman 623). This statement, according to Kahraman, highlights Tanpınar as a "conservative reformist": he is against the "internationalism or globalism" of the left when it denies Turkish local culture (Kahraman 624). It will also be seen that he, in turn, protests the right by questioning, among other things, his own religious identity as a Muslim (Kahraman 624).

Melville too has been characterized by his critics as both a political reactionary and an iconoclast as he responded in his writing to the effort, ongoing since the revolutionary period, to distinguish and elevate an American narrative above and beyond its European roots. The *Pequod* is often read as a petri dish for an experiment in American Democracy. More recent criticism reflecting a transnational trajectory in American Studies has reconsidered the rhetoric of Manifest Destiny in Melville's fiction as a "cosmopolitan vision of national identity," rather than one of "superiority in isolation," as noted by earlier critics, however (Marr 140). Timothy Marr, in "Without the Pale: Melville and Ethnic Cosmopolitanism," notes that although Melville is associated with the Young Americans, a group of New York critics who rallied for a distinct, post-colonial American culture and thus "privileged the United States as the earthly location for a multicultural paradise that drew upon the whole world for an American legacy," the writer nevertheless protested "the fatal embrace" of American interests abroad (Marr 140, qtd. from *Typee* 28). Melville was highly critical of the "Protestant missionary enterprise," for example, argues Marr, because "he believed that Christianity rested on an unearned superiority and was itself in need of salvation" (Marr 143).

Basem L. Ra'ad, in *Hidden Stories: Palestine and the Eastern Mediterranean*, goes further, suggesting that Melville, along with Mark Twain, was one of the harshest critics of "sacred geography" in nineteenth-century American letters (Ra'ad 79). Both writers, he argues, "point to the need for the US to revise its potentially destructive identification with the Old Testament model, which it used during the colonial beginnings to construct a national myth" (Ra'ad 64). While these writers are given little attention in Said's *Orientalism*, neither were the kind of travelers to the Holy Land who were "biblically obsessed and pre-disposed to hate Arabs" (Ra'ad 83). Both writers satirize modern Old World tourism and emphasize the geopolitical necessity of "unlearning all that has been given to people to know about Palestine" and the inscribed geography known as the "Holy Land" (Ra'ad 85).[9] Referencing the same "fatal embrace" in *Typee* as Timothy Marr, Emory Elliot in "'Wandering to-and-fro': Melville and Religion," notes Melville's "early disillusionment with the Christian, capitalist, imperialist project and in particular the use of religious rhetoric and proselytizing as a weapon of such destruction" (Elliott 178). In a similar transnational vein, Markus Heide has argued in "Herman Melville's 'Benito Cereno,' Inter-American Relations, and Literary Pan-Americanism" that Melville's "focus on dark spots in American history" is "not limited to the national history of the United States but acquires a hemispheric dimension" (Heide 8). Heide notes that critics like Eric Sundquist and Gesa Mackenthun ("Post-colonial Masquerade" and *Fictions of the Black Atlantic*) have shown that "Melville's fictions treat 'domestic' issues such as slavery and expansionism, but they also concern themselves, however, with colonialism and imperialism in a way that goes beyond the national context, with implications that position the United States in a global economy and in international networks and postcolonial struggles" (Heide 8).

While early critics admired what was often read as a positivist symbolic melting pot in Melville's literary rendition of the "many in the one" on the high seas, life on board Melville's various ships is nevertheless fraught with problems. Ahab, the Pequod's charismatic dictator whose energy is the novel's driving force, as well as the source of the ship's destruction, is a transgressive antihero without whom there would be no story. Melville's vision of the United States in *Moby-Dick* tests the resilience of multicultural democracy in the face of various forms of centralized authority. William Spanos, in *The Exceptionalist State and the State of Exception*, examines the narrative of the young US democracy as radically departing from "Old World" forms of political hegemony. In the context of Melville's last, unfinished novella, *Billy Budd*, Spanos sees an "ironic insight into the arrogant, optimistic, and to use one of [Melville's] favorite words to characterize the forwarding linearity of its practical imperative, unerring–and eventually, self-destructive exceptionalist ethos of the American national identity" (Spanos 4). Citing an 1852 review that asked the critical community to "freeze" the writer of *Pierre* "into silence" for what Spanos calls Melville's "deeply penetrating ontological, moral, cultural and political criticism of an America structured in domination," Spanos goes on to argue that the exceptionalist discourse coming out of America was indeed unexceptional in that it reiterated earlier British and European colonialist ambitions (Spanos 39, 38). Jared Hickman suggests in "The Theology of Democracy" that in *Moby-Dick* Melville was posing the question of whether a democracy steeped in the "antidemocratic terms" of Calvinist monotheism could possibly become democratic itself (Hickman 25). Hickman places Melville in the company of pragmatists such as John Dewey and William James, "both of whom recognized that if 'God' was not in the first place democratized, then -ironically- the more fervently one sacralized a democratic order, the more antidemocratic it could become" (Hickman 3). Focusing on what he calls moments of ironic Christian hyperbole in the rhetoric of Ishmael (rather than Ahab), Hickman suggests the "absolutist ideal of power" embodied in Melville's intimations of a Calvinist God threatened to "only derail genuine democracy and provide further warrant for various forms of imperialistic domination" (Hickman 25).

The journey of Melville's reputation, like Tanpınar's, or, it could be argued, any writer of what is believed to be of national or international consequence, has gone through various reincarnations. Much like the case of Tanpınar in Turkey, Melville has been called a reactionary, a visionary, or, more recently, a cosmopolitan apologist, depending on what readings of national identity the canonical writer appears to reject or endorse in his literary texts. And like Tanpınar, Melville was at times silenced by the critical community for views that failed to endorse contemporary orthodoxies, whether secular or theological.

Tanpınar's discursive attitude toward superimposed forms of Western-style democracy has been the basis of much criticism, particularly in the mid-twentieth century and later during periods of heightened nationalist and secularist opinion. At the turn of the twenty-first century there were many who were uncomfortable with what was perceived of as Tanpınar's Islamic sympathies. "I am not on the side of the reformists," Tanpınar claims in *As I Lived*. "I believe in Allah. Still, I do not know if I am a true Muslim. Nevertheless, I wish to die believing in the religion of my mother and father and I do not forget that my nation is Muslim, and I wish it to remain so" (Tanpınar qtd. in Kahraman 624). Like his mentor Yahya Kemal, argues Kahraman, Tanpınar's Islamic sympathies concern more the notion of "cultural muslimness" or Islam as an organizing principle that helps to maintain a sense of community for the nation, rather than as an orthodoxy (Kahraman 624). "Because Kemalism dispelled muslimness as a tool for collective consciousness," Tanpınar can be considered at odds with the secularization and Westernization project. Rather than orthodox doctrine, Islam for Tanpınar is an "aesthetic category," one that is not "bound by a religious institution," but is rather "a sociological reality" that functions as a vehicle for transmitting cultural values (Kahraman 624).

It is certainly true that a negative perception of the legacy of Westernization, including policies and dictums central to Atatürk's reforms, dominates the pages of the Istanbul chapter of *Five Cities*. A certain dramatic irony is evident in the early sections of the Istanbul chapter that focus on the positive interpenetration of European and Ottoman life.

> Istanbul's past was a fusion of great and small, significant and insignificant, old and new, local and foreign, beautiful and ugly, even vulgar, the result of a melting-pot of innumerable elements ... Every import that passed through customs became part of Islamic life. The English mohair worn by a senior judge, his lady's headscarf made in Lyon, a desk in the French style inscribed with Ottoman calligraphy, a lamp of Bohemian workmanship, all became "Islamized."
>
> (*FC* 8)

These "converted" European fashions lead to a fusion that Tanpınar enjoys from a historical distance. "Fusion," however, turns to confusion in the wake of the Tanzimat period (1839–1876) when Western-style social and political reforms were introduced during the reigns of Sultans Mahmud II and Abdülmecid I.

> While the remnants of Mahmud II's era, the high officials, pursued their customary lives discussing poetry and politics, listening to saz music, drinking coffee and smoking their pipes in their spacious domestic hall reserved for men, among friends, guests, flatterers, intercessors and hangers-on, the new generations educated in Europe who had become used to a French way of life, gradually adopted a new life-style. And Beyoğlu, Janus-like, entered city life looking both backward and forward.
>
> (*FC* 42)

As the centralized power of the Ottomans becomes more and more defused, the cultural exchanges between the Empire and Europe began to reflect the shift in power. No longer in a position to actively convert the imported fashions to suit Ottoman forms of Islam, a younger generation under the influence of faster foreign lifestyles is instead seduced, suggests Tanpınar. And this new passivity in the face of the West leads to the loss of venerated traditions that, in turn, lead to the loss of family fortunes in what is represented by Tanpınar as a cause–effect relationship. This marks the beginning of the end of what Tanpınar repeatedly refers to as integrated Ottoman culture:

> From Abdülaziz there was no longer any stability in Istanbul life. From the palace downwards every well-known inhabitant of Istanbul, every vizier who owned large mansions … who on nights of Ramazan, received for dinner a hundred uninvited guests, were all living in debt, a little ashamed of themselves before the community and an Istanbul that had lost its means of production and had cast its future to the winds by imitating Paris, center of the world's market. At every turn of the rubber wheels of the fine carriages made at the Bender factory, the age-old Empire came a little closer to its predestined Fate.
>
> (FC 43)

Tanpınar's criticism of westernization simultaneously advances the notion of a pure Turkishness, unencumbered and unsullied by interloping influences. He appears to invert the rhetoric of European Gothic Romance in many of his commentaries concerning the negative influence of a tarnished West on an innocent "eastern" Istanbul.

> Between the Nişantaşı quarter with its few remains from the days of Abdülmecid, and the Kasımpaşa quarter that was still living in the time of Güzelce Kasım Pasha, a new milieu sprang into life and proceeded to seduce the authentic citizens of Istanbul.
>
> (FC 42)

This "new milieu" positioned in binary relation to an original local culture feeds into contemporary identity politics in post-Republican Turkey. Like Herman Melville's fluctuating experimentation with American exclusivism and inclusivism, Tanpınar too walks a fine ideological line, creating fuel for critics and apologizers alike. But Tanpınar, like his friend the poet Yahya

Kemal, reserved the right to criticize the policies of Westernization, despite the danger of doing so, even when, at one point, there were "student movement[s] against teachers who betrayed the nationalist cause" (*FC* 40). Though Tanpınar would become a canonical writer in the latter part of the twentieth century, he, like Melville, faced unofficial forms of censorship in his own lifetime. And if the occident often functions as a foil for problems with Tanpınar's oriental Ottomans, the orient, whether Polynesian, Near or Middle Eastern, functions as a filter through which Melville sifts his ongoing argument with the West. When asked to be "western" by a Turkish nationalist project, Tanpınar turned to an "eastern" legacy. And when asked to be "eastern," that is something distinct from the West, something authentically Turkish, Tanpınar would look to Western Orientalism for the literary records that would help him rehabilitate the cultural history of his nation (Pamuk 115). And in their bid to challenge the reigning ideologies of their respective time and place, Tanpınar and Melville converge directly in the discourse of Romantic Orientalism.

Like his fellow Romantics at home and abroad, Melville was disturbed by the effects of Western materialism on collective and private man. Having directed philosophy to a radical level of skepticism, the eighteenth-century positivists had abandoned many forms of metaphysical inquiry, save a certain perfunctory space reserved for Christianity. In America, turn-of-the-century strains of traditional Christianity, even liberal Unitarianism, had failed to engage the imagination of many, especially of many in the arts. The majority of studies, past and present, focusing on questions of religion in Melville's work have focused on his engagement with Calvinist doctrine, particularly in the case of *Moby-Dick*.[10] Criticism venturing beyond the immediate perimeters of the Bible has tended to read Melville in the context of Platonism. Arthur Versluis, in *American Transcendentalism and Asian Religions*, suggests that Ralph Waldo Emerson and Melville represent the cultural opposition between the Neoplatonist and Gnostic lines of Christian sensibility respectively. As more recent studies have shown, however, Emerson the Transcendentalist, and the inveterate outsider Melville would take a serious interest in non-Christian philosophies in the face of what had become for them a spiritual silence at home. The rise of interest in Oriental studies in the late eighteenth and early nineteenth centuries, and in comparative religious studies in particular, had opened doors to alternative systems of belief that would become more than subjects of intellectual study for these writers.

Melville may have been skeptical of Emerson's positive enthusiasm for metaphysics, but while he ridicules Emerson in an 1849 letter to his friend Evert Duyckink, where he concludes an irreverent diatribe on the "transcendentalisms, myths & oracular gibberish of Emerson ... this Plato who talks thro' his nose," he also confesses that he prefers such a "fool" as Emerson to a wise man: "I love all men who dive ... I'm not talking of Mr. Emerson now–but of the whole corpus of thought-divers. That have been diving & coming up again with bloodshot eyes since the world began" (*Portable* 378–379). Melville's own attraction to the metaphysical was as troubled and dark as it was profound, and his relationship to the Transcendentalist movement and interest in the Eastern poets and their metaphysics is a complex one.

The New Historical response to the Cold War reading of Melville by F. O. Matthiessen and others in *American Renaissance*, a ground-breaking study that dominated English studies after its publication in 1941, led to a rereading of Melville that had focused on his complicity with antebellum US individualism and imperialism. The New Historical approaches, in their turn, often suspended other possible ways of reading Melville's internationalist writing, however.[11] Some transnational studies since the turn of the twenty-first century have picked up where nineteenth-century ethnographers left off and focus again on the historical East in the fiction and poetry of Melville. Rather than relegating Near or Middle Eastern references to the proverbial dustbin of orientalist tropes, references to world religions other than Christianity are of interest again to scholars. Focusing on the poem *Clarel*, and building on earlier arguments by T. Walter Herbert Jr. that map the break-down of theocentric thought in *Moby-Dick*, David Watson, in "Melville, Interrupted," writes that "[L]ike many other American travelers to Palestine—including Mark Twain..., Melville tells of American pilgrims returning to the origin of their Judeo-Christian belief system within the territory of the Ottoman Turks and other Muslims" (Watson 2). "This encounter becomes an occasion," in critical studies in Melville, "to connect America, Europe, and the Middle East into a syncretic transnational matrix in which belief systems are woven together to illustrate the 'intersympathy' of the planet's 'creeds'" (Watson 2). Jenny Franchot, in *Melville's Traveling God*, in turn, looks at how Melville engages aesthetically and allegorically with the hybridity of world religions, including Christianity.

While many of these transnational readings engage with historicized sites of contact, they tend to elide the possibility of Melville engaging non-ironically with other faiths, including Islam, however. Franchot argues that faced with the "emptied" and "exhausted anthropological wonders" he comes face to face with in his Middle East travels, Melville concludes his narrative poem *Clarel* with a renouncement of the "illusion of travel, into which one can journey and lose the burden of unbelief and the self" (Franchot 183). Although Watson notes the same rocky and empty landscape in Palestine, he rejects the interfaith matrix suggested in readings like Franchot's, suggesting rather a secular community ethics in the poem and in Melville's personal life; "Clarel enters into a transnational community," but it is one that is "irreducible to religion and creed as it is to the terms of the nation-state" (Watson 25). The pilgrims are joined at the end of the poem, but rather "simply together, schematized and constellated by the same pre-figural landscape opened by the retreat of faith" (Watson 28).

Dorothee Finkelstein's 1971 study of Melville's reading in Orientalism, much of which was standard for cultivated Americans in the nineteenth century, suggests that Melville traveled east of Athens many times in his mind both before and after his actual voyage to the Levant in 1856. Of the many Near Eastern texts available in the library of the Albany Young Men's Association, which Melville joined in 1835 at the age of fifteen, was a 1772 edition of the *Gulistan* by the Persian Sufi poet Sadi, translated by Sir William Jones (Finkelstein 42–43). This collection of poems, whose German translation by Goethe had profoundly influenced the European Romantic movement, would directly impact the American literary scene when Emerson's poem "Saadi" was published in the *Dial* in 1842, helping to popularize the Sufi mystics in America (Finkelstein 44, 92).[12] David Scott offers short but good readings of Henry David Thoreau's important engagement with the Persian Sufi poets Hafiz and Saadi of Shiraz in "Rewalking Thoreau and Asia: 'Light from the East' for 'A Very Yankee Sort of Oriental.'" He notes that although Thoreau was not necessarily drawn to the Prophet Muhammad or the Koran, it was "Sufism, the esoteric mystical side of Islam" that moved him (Scott 22). Like Finkelstein's reading of Melville, Scott offers a close reading of Thoreau's specific references to mystical Islam in his poetry and prose, and in doing so illustrates the depth of Thoreau's understanding of Sufi metaphysics. Wai Chee Dimock argues in

"Hemispheric Islam: Continents and Centuries for American Literature" for a decentering of American literature by "map[ping] it against the coordinates of hemispheric Islam" and agrees with Timothy Marr, in "opening up 'broader planetary latitudes,' and summoning up those 'displaced yet looming' specters that have haunted 'the Americas since their first 'discovery'" (Dimock 47–48). While Dimock's reading of a sample of Emerson's translation of Hafiz underestimates Emerson's deeper understanding of mystical Islamic poetry, like Finkelstein she emphasizes the direct, rather than ironic, relationship between American Transcendentalism and Sufism.

Ahmet Hamdi Tanpınar and his contemporaries received a portion of their education in pre-Republican Ottoman culture from the European Romantics, the French Romantics in particular. Though this aspect of his "education" is perhaps exaggerated, Tanpınar himself laments that his search for Ottoman aesthetic responses to, for example, the Bosporus Straits as an aesthetic subject, yields only abstract results: "The absence of prose and painting and the fact that our poetry is only an aesthetic game, throws real life into the shade" (*FC* 47). "Eastern stories are repetitive and self-consuming," Tanpınar writes in "Şark ile Garp Arasında Görülen Esaslı Farklar" ("Essential Differences Observed Between East and West") collected in *As I Lived*, "which means they were not able to utilize their rich content and background. Whereas in Western stories, it is life and the individual the writers foreground in their works" (*Lived* 26). In this absence of a historical and utilitarian approach to representation in the art of the East, Tanpınar thus turns to the French for information about the material Ottoman world. The Romantic movement and its signature attraction to the dilapidated and abandoned, a reactionary rejection, in great part, of urban modernity, offered Tanpınar and his like-minded contemporaries a discourse which suited their hermeneutics of loss. Gautier's melancholy descriptions of Istanbul, which, Pamuk notes, were meant as praise, greatly influenced Yahya Kemal and Tanpınar according to Pamuk (Pamuk 94). But while the French Romantic travel writers would focus their melancholy orientalist eulogies on famous monuments, Tanpınar and his friends would also lament the old back neighborhoods and intimate corners of the city. Pamuk suggests that Tanpınar and Kemal's interest in historical quarters under modern economic duress, and "the poor, defeated and deprived Muslim population" that lived in them, were not necessarily the places where the writers lived themselves: "Only outsiders can see Istanbul's neglect as picturesque" (Pamuk 257–258). But just as this reading of poverty as picturesque had served French Lamartine, English Wordsworth, and American Thoreau in their respective critiques of modernity, Tanpınar also resurrects a cultural past that Turks could hold on to, and be held up by, in times of modern stress.

Tanpınar's Romantic approach to Istanbul becomes more transcultural when we consider the moments of mystical rapture that permeate his discourse in the Istanbul chapter of *Five Cities*. Where Melville often invokes oriental rhetoric in his most philosophical moods—Plato is "divine," but "Zoroaster whispered me before I was born," says the traveling narrator of *Mardi* in the context of artistic inspiration—Tanpınar's "oriental" references are at once culturally inherited and adopted, innate, and learned (*Portable* 350). Tanpınar was a student of mysticism, as well as member of parliament. In the time of Suleyman the Magnificent, Tanpınar notes, statesmen, "the council chamber," as well as the army and even ordinary people belonged to a dervish sect (*FC* 26). The Conqueror himself "nourished a love" for the "more or less separatist" religious orders (*FC* 26). Islamic mysticism in the form of Sufism becomes, it can be argued, an important point of reference for both writers.

Moby-Dick reveals a more than superficial engagement with tenets of mystical Islamic and suggests that Islam had already become more than a mere foil for Melville's various arguments and experiments with Christian ideology. While it might be tempting to bypass the various non-Christian references and go directly to third-century Neo-Platonism, one of the nebulous sources of both Christian and Muslim mysticisms, this circumvention reduces the complex trans-religious play of the novel. Timothy Marr, writing on "Islamicist moments" in Melville's work, focuses primarily on the territories of the Americas in "'Out of This World'-Islamic Irruptions in the Literary Americas." He suggests that Islamic difference in Melville offers an opportunity for freedom movements in the Americas, "a variety of unincorporated spaces that lie beyond the full control of continental systems of cultural power" (Marr 2). In Marr's argument, Islam remains a trope in Melville's work, but one that takes on cosmopolitan dimensions and works to globalize domestic reforms in the United States. "Islamic difference provided transcultural resource," he argues, "for representing the rebellion against race-based systems of American slavery" (Marr 19).

Jean-François Leroux, by contrast, offers a more direct application of Islamic tenets, not as tropes for sociopolitical movements in the Americas, but as philosophical or spiritual positions in their own right. He suggests in "Wars for Oil: Moby-Dick, Orientalism, and Cold-War Criticism" that Fedallah in *Moby-Dick* be read not as the purely evil and oriental influence that he most often is, but rather as a dark mirror to Ahab's monomania, "motivated," as the Parsee himself is, by "revenge on Ahab's infidelity" (Leroux 15). Fedallah's is a "woe and even a wisdom similar to Ishmael's and Ahab's," suggesting that as with the Christian Gnostics and Sufis, good and evil are "inevitably and intimately linked in manifest creation": "what seems to be evil comes from God too, and must therefore be good" (Leroux 16). Ahab's "infidelity," in this context, comes from his denial of this theological dialectic. Leroux's reading of Fedallah suggests that Melville, like Thoreau, had a keener understanding of the complexities of mystical Islamic cosmology than is often noted, even by apologists.

Jeffrey Einboden's study of Ihsan Abbas's 1965 rendition of *Moby-Dick* into Arabic furthers even more the idea that Melville had an invested understanding of the Islamic sources he was employing in his novel. The translation undertaken by the Palestinian scholar, Einboden argues, functions to "remap the coordinates of his US source, charting alternative geneologies for *Moby-Dick* protagonists and motifs" while "excavating the novel's own transnational origin" (*Nineteenth-Century* 7).[13] Abbas himself argues, however, that the American writer relied on Western Orientalists and writers like William Jones and Thomas De Quincey for his "Islamic borrowings" (Abbas qtd. in Einboden, *Nineteenth-Century* 104). However, like Wai Chee Dimock in "Deep Time: American Literature and World History" and Dorothee Finkelstein earlier, Einboden illustrates elsewhere the extent to which nineteenth-century American writers had direct access to and were actively engaged in primary source Islamic materials, albeit in translation. Though Dimock and Einboden focus primarily on Emerson, both note the physical circulation of mediaeval mystical poetry in New England libraries. Emerson's relationship with Islamic texts was a lifelong engagement. He would translate seven hundred lines of Sufi poetry in his journals from 1846 on, and write the preface for the first American edition of Saadi's *The Gulistan* in 1865 (Dimock, *Deep Time* 768). This interest in Islam implies for Einboden a "resistance to Anglo-continental influence, seeking alternative genealogies and trajectories for an emergent American identity" (Einboden, "Early American Qur'an" 2).[14]

Tanpınar saves his direct references to the Dervish Orders of Istanbul for the latter pages of the Istanbul chapter of *Five Cities*. Couched within his critique of Western influences on the "authentic" citizens of Istanbul, Tanpınar switches mid-paragraph to "the finest memories of our past," Sultan Abdülmecid's era "when the Mevlevi convent was built in Galata" (*FC* 42). Tanpınar includes these orders in his idealized sketches of Istanbul authenticity, the "local traditional ways of life" that continued according to Turkish memoir writers such as Çaylak Tevfik Bey (*FC* 42). Tanpınar's depiction of pre-Tanzimat, pre-Westernized Istanbul emphasizes the aesthetics of the city's cultural past, suggests Berna Moran in "Bir Huzursuzluğun Romanı Huzur" ("*Peace*, A Novel of Anxiety"). What Tanpınar indicates by the repeated use of the phrase "our way of life" throughout his oeuvre signifies "a question of taste for Tanpınar," one that privileges forms of art, tradition, entertainment, ritual, and drama, that are "authentic" because they are "received not from outside," but rather "molded and experienced with no intended imitation or artificiality," "like a work of art" (Moran 302).

Despite the steady encroachment of Western modes of living, including a taste for the new and untried, life continued in some sectors of Ottoman Istanbul as it always had, writes Tanpınar,

> in the rooms and halls furnished with their low divans and armchairs covered in red velvet and sofas hung with tassels and fringes, where they drank coffee and smoked pipes, and where they passed long evenings exchanging witticisms and reciting lines of poetry or discussing politics ...; at Ramazan communal prayers were held and in dervish convents ritual ceremonies were observed.
>
> (*FC* 42)

Rather than exotics living in the midst of the quotidian, the mystical communities are represented here as integral to high culture as coffee and contemplative pipe smoking. They are involved directly in the aesthetic and communal cultural landscape of the city. Tanpınar devotes a subchapter in the Istanbul chapter of *Five Cities* to the Mevlana Order in Istanbul. "Anatolia had always been the mother of sects and religions" and by the seventeenth century "the Melami had found favour in Istanbul" (*FC* 26). The mystical sects of Asia Minor, of which Sufism is only one, were often oppressed by conservative Sunni groups, he notes. And in 1925 a law would be passed under Ataturk that would close all *tekkes*, or convents of the mystical orders of Turkey. This ironic historical development which joins the agendas of orthodox Islam and Turkish nationalism attests to the alluring power of these orders in Turkey on into the twenty-first century. Near the conclusion of the Istanbul chapter Tanpınar offers that if he had been alive in the time of Merkez Efendi [1463–1551] "I might have been one of his dervishes" (*FC* 63).

It is in the context of the loss of a cultural past that Tanpınar alludes to the loss endemic to desire, a recurrent theme in Sufi literature.

> In the divine wisdom of these men who followed their ideals in silence, I am searching for a lost world. I yearn to reach their heights, but failing, I turn to poetry and literature. I want to drink from the cup of music; the cup empties, my thirst remains, for art is, like love, thirst-making, and can never be assuaged.
>
> (*FC* 63)

A passionate rhetoric linking the divine and the aesthetic, associated in Western letters with the Romantic tradition in poetry, echoes more directly here the linguistic and philosophical legacy of Saadi, Rumi, and Yunus Emre. Some Turkish scholars argue that while Tanpınar's writing may be suggestive of Sufi mysticism in both content and style, his is nevertheless "closer to idealist philosophy and spiritualism in the Western sense of the term" (Birlik 2). It can be argued, however, that Tanpınar's inclusion of Mevlana so centrally in the Ottoman inheritance in *Five Cities* is part of his project to rehabilitate the present via the past. It could also be said that the depths of Tanpınar's mysticism or nationalism need not be gaged in mutually exclusive terms. Moran suggests that what Tanpınar strives for in his writing in general is not a return to the past, but rather "applying [the past] to ground the new" (Moran 304). The marked reference to the Dervish orders in the concluding pages of the Istanbul chapter suggests that, in this text, Mevlana, like other aesthetic organizing principles, is meant to be considered not as a relic of the past, but as part of the ground on which the new, the future is to be based.

Finkelstein devotes a subchapter to cataloguing Islamic references in Melville's work, most of which are mystical in nature. As Tanpınar directly adopts and adapts the rhetoric of his literary forefathers, Melville, in a bid to engage his Islamic sources beyond the superficial trappings of occidental orientalist discourse, allows his prose to expand into poetry whenever his subject gravitates toward Eastern mysticism or the divine. Thus, it is perhaps the texture of each writer's prose, the poetic turn their language takes when the subject at hand tends toward immanence that suggests the most important affinity between the two writers. Like Melville's narrator in *Moby-Dick*, Tanpınar too seems to position himself as a witness to the vital relation between appearance and reality. As Tanpınar fleshes in Melville's Istanbul sketches with the history and culture necessary for a comprehensive sense of the monumental city, he often comes to similar abstract and rhapsodic conclusions about a detail of architecture or landscape.

As both writers, one Turkish, the other American, walk the backstreets of the city in search of their respective Istanbuls, both writers inscribe a dialectical relationship between nature and architecture that in turn gestures toward the divine. Though critics often note Melville's disappointment with the landscapes and scenery of the "Old World," and it is true that the *Near East Journal* descriptions flatten out when he enters Egypt and become more and more bleak the closer he approaches Palestine, Melville's treatment of Turkey, and Istanbul in particular, is colorful and energetic. Observations often begin with a concrete detail that functions as a conduit toward the abstract. This tendency characterizes both writers' work in general: in *Moby-Dick* Melville again and again offers empirical facts of whaling or life at sea as the objects of philosophical, often Platonic meditation. Tanpınar's novel *Huzur* is an extended exercise in the dynamic interrelationship between the concrete and abstract central to mystical Islam. Throughout the Istanbul sections of the *Near East Journal*, Melville's observations of the cityscape are offered in terms of vegetable imagery.[15] Architectural details, particularly of dilapidated structures, maintain an organic relationship with the natural world that persists in the city. And these symbiotic relationships often culminate with reflections on the divine. Trees are of special interest to Melville: "Cedar & Cyprus the only trees about the capital.—The Cypress a green minaret & blends with the stone ones ... The intermingling of the dark tree with the bright spire expressive of the intermingling of life & death" (J 94). Tanpınar, who also devotes much of his chapter to the trees of Istanbul, likewise notes their compositional relationship to the surrounding architecture, though he is able to offer a more learned context. His observations also lead to the signification of these material details in metaphysical terms.

> Our great architects never failed to set several cypress and plane trees beside their buildings; the contrast with dense foliage created one of their finest compositions. Some went further and reserved a space in the center of the divine geometry of the courtyard to a mosque or religious school for a cypress or a plane-tree to flourish, for a rose to bloom, for ivy to twine and twist. In fact, an old Turkish garden, such was its style.
>
> <div align="right">(<i>TSLL</i> 461)</div>

When an architect or "pious donor" planted a tree, "[H]e knew that a tree entrusted to the earth is a gift of value, a talisman securing a neighborhood, a district, even a whole community and all its religious beliefs" (*TSLL* 461). For both writers, therefore, the relationship between nature and culture in the city is never inert. The spiritual world permeates the material world and each writer consistently draws our attention to this immanence in Istanbul.

The proximity of death to life in the city, thus their co-existence, is manifested in this interplay of architecture and nature. Visiting the ancient walls of the city, Melville notes "[T]hese walls seem skirted by forests of cemetery—the cypress growing thick as firs in a Scotch plantation. Very old—a primal look—weird. The walls seem the inexorable bar between the mansions of the living & and the dungeons of the dead" (*J* 87). The cypresses of the cemetery and the city walls come together and form a point of existential contact. Tanpınar inscribes this same interpenetration within the Sufi notion of absence as presence, and the association of the ecstasy of union with a higher power and the sadness of exile. Attempting to describe the experience of the music of Ismail Dede (1778–1846), "this Dervish of the tender soul," Tanpınar writes, "[W]ith Dede we emerge from a country of mystical longings where death is seen as an eternal union of lovers. His tree of death grows up in the real world like the ancient trees that appear lofty and solitary here and there in Istanbul, in the gardens by the Bosporus, on the hills of Üsküdar!" (*FC* 58). Nature and culture are the evident and symbiotic signs of things invisible and they abound throughout the pages of both writers' texts.

The Bosporus, "a mysterious channel of such a nature that moments experienced on one side are tasted as memories on the other," is another primary subject of meditation for both writers (*FC* 44). Like so many writers that came to Istanbul before him, Melville is drawn to the metaphorical potential of the waterway separating the European continent from the Asian continent. In an unpublished poem entitled "The Continents," Melville reads in the divide a desire for union beyond life and death: "Even so the cleaving Bosporus parts/Life and Death.—Dissembling hearts!/Over the gulf the yearning starts/To meet—infold!" (*J*, Editor's footnote 104). In the poem Melville summons the rhetoric of the Sufi poets, the language of absence in presence, to account for the sublime appeal of the Bosporus. In another place he describes the Bosporus as "Magnificent! The whole scene one pomp of art & nature. Europe & Asia here show their best. A challenge of contrasts" (*J* 93). Proceeding with a conceit in which the two shores "advance" and "retire," and where neither is "willing to retreat from the contest of beauty," Melville offers a variation on the theme of exile and desire that threads through the poems of Saadi, Hafiz, and Mevlana (*J* 93).

Tanpınar concludes the Istanbul chapter of *Five Cities* by denying his nostalgia for past eras, however. The conclusion functions as a volta, a reversal in the narrative that performs the shifting emotional complex of pleasure and pain suggested in the notion of *hüzün*. He writes, "I couldn't live for more than ten minutes even in the Istanbul of Suleyman the Magnificent" (*FC* 63). The aesthetic value of the city, he goes on to explain, is in its accumulated beauty, "the experience of four centuries behind us, and two different world views between us" (*FC* 63). He attempts in the final lines to offer a negotiated past, one that does not deny contemporary political and social gains, one that allows Eastern and Western traditions to infold into one another. Tanpınar's conclusion, like Melville's final notes on the city, attests, however, to the value each writer ascribes to the aesthetic traces of the past so vital to the present glory of Istanbul. As Melville sails at sunset on December 18, 1856 around Seraglio Point on his way to Alexandria via Smyrna, or modern-day Izmir, he takes a final look at the intermingling of nature and culture that has dominated his Istanbul notes: "Glorious sight. Scutari & its heights, glowed like sapphire … As a promontory is covered with trees, terraced up to its top, so Constantinople with houses. Long line of walls.—Out into the Sea of Marmora" (*J* 105). Tanpınar leaves the reader with his own hermeneutic struggle with the past: "I run from mirage to mirage ... lips I don't recognize talk to me with voices I don't recognize, in endless signs, but I understand nothing they say" (*FC* 63). But like Melville he goes on to suggest that what we can take of Istanbul into the future is the poetry the city offers the discerning heart: "The only reality is the desire within you. Try not to let the fire go out" (*FC* 64). And this poetry that permeates the city offered the Turkish writer and the American writer a sense of what an integrated future might mean.

Though nearly a hundred years separate the two Istanbul texts, the affinities are strikingly alive. While this has much to do with particular parallels in their respective historical moments, certain positioning within their contemporary cultural contexts, there exist echoes not so easily defined by materialist theories of literary influence or circulation. The strength of their literary production stems from things less tangible. Both were outcasts at the center of storms, neither completely of nor out of the worlds they were born into. The agile boldness with which each writer crosses back and forth over the fine lines of separation between historical and ahistorical time, physical, and abstract space is made evident in their writing on Istanbul, a city that, true to its reputation, invites reflection on the inscrutable.

2

Nature's Place in Political Romanticism: Selected Poems by Nâzım Hikmet

In June 2013, a small group of environmental activists put up tents in one of the only remaining public green spaces in the heart of Istanbul. Private financiers with the backing of the conservative ruling party dedicated to neoliberal economic development and without a proper public mandate had positioned bulldozers to begin the construction of a shopping complex couched in the faux-historical trappings of an Ottoman barrack. First the trees were to go, and with them, according to the activists, something vital to the well-being of the city. When the Turkish writer Ahmet Hamdi Tanpınar wrote in 1946 that "[O]ur great architects never failed to set several cypress and plane trees beside their buildings" and that when an architect or "pious donor" planted a tree he knew that it was "entrusted to the earth" as "a gift of value, a talisman securing a neighborhood, a district, even a whole community," he was speaking deep from within a tradition of honoring urban nature (Tanpınar 461). Cities and nature, the man-made and the organic, are conceived of as mutually inclusive, rather than mutually exclusive, designs in his discussion. Rather than landscaping, or decorative supplements to manufactured structures, trees are essential to the physical, aesthetic, and even spiritual health of a population.

In Turkish, the root of the word for citizen (*vatandaş*) is *vatan*, which also means homeland or soil.[1] Thus, in Tanpınar's native Turkish, the citizen is etymologically connected to the land. Civic space that competed with and took complete precedence over the geological environment denied the very etymological roots of its terminology. The Latin root of the word "citizen," *civis,* was first used in the phrase *corona civica,* or civic garland. A garland of oak leaves and acorns was given to a person who saved another's life in ancient Rome. Soil and trees thus play a seminal, though sometimes forgotten, role in the very language we use to talk about public space, Turkish or English. After a decade of excessive development, and the concomitant growth of a new, disproportionately moneyed elite, various shades of middle-class prosperity, and a sizeable group of the predictably disenfranchised, activists put their foot down in Gezi Park. They were doing their civic duty. They were protecting the homeland.

The initial demands were limited and practical: stop the construction, nothing more, nothing less. Entrenched city officials, unused to citizens making such unorthodox and publicly visible demands on authority, scratched their heads for a few days. When it was clear that the occupiers would not leave, the police were sent in to clear the tents. The sweep was violent: tents were torched and the passive resistors were physically assaulted. The city was shocked by the violence and within twenty-four hours thanks to social media, and to the local news that ignored or censored the event, thousands of citizens came to Taksim Square. The Gezi Park protests had begun in earnest.

For approximately two weeks Istanbul experienced something extraordinary. Politics and the arts—visual, literary, musical, multi-mediatic—came together in the defense of nature. The confluence was certainly one manifestation of the urban environmental protests going on all over the world, especially since the 2011 Occupy Wall Street movement in New York City, where protests against social and economic inequity merged with environmental activism in Zuccotti Park. But demonstrations against environmental abuses are common in Turkey.[2] And the scale of the Gezi gathering was extraordinary even when compared to international and national precedents. The park became an intensely fluid space where thousands of people from various backgrounds and with various grievances came together to protest and party, but mostly to wait, day and night, under the open sky, under the trees. Musical performances and dance performances erupted spontaneously, or with limited arrangement. The atmosphere was carnivalesque. A lending library was set up and the people, mostly the young who were not visitors but full-time occupiers, read to pass the hours.

It is no surprise that the Turkish writer Nâzım Hikmet became one of the central voices in the movement. His books along with those of other Turkish and foreign writers circulated in the free library.[3] Quotations from the poems hung from trees. Having been censored, jailed, and eventually self-exiled for his political beliefs and his ability to make those beliefs at once accessible yet aesthetically sound in his poems, his posthumous presence made sense. While Hikmet is perhaps best known for his communist and humanist allegiances, his poems are also steeped in the physical landscape of his homeland. In his poems, politics, aesthetics and the environment are syncopated fields of contact. And herein lay an important justification for his presence. The Gezi Park protests demanded a new kind of attention; one another generation of citizens, both for and against the demands of the young protesters, were unused to experiencing on such a scale. They were asked to think poetically about politics, think environmentally about poetry, think politically about the environment, and all at once. This cross-fertilization was not easy, even for the willing.

By day three some supporters were already questioning the protests. Despite their committed and passionate support for the original occupiers, some of those involved, either directly or indirectly, over the age of forty were uncomfortable with the ambiguous nature of the organization. They were concerned that the lack of central governance in the horizontal power-sharing model favored by the original occupiers could never give rise to a legitimate political movement or party. The extemporaneous performances were inspired, but for those who had survived or weathered the violent ideological struggles of the late 1970s and eventual military coup of 1980, as well as the various coups or imagined coup attempts since, Gezi struck them as naive.[4] With no center, the communal effort could not hold. By day three doubts concerning the viability of the movement were being expressed in concerned whispers. How could such an amorphous body expect to become a lasting political entity? Where were the leaders? It was unrealistic, impractical, unsustainable. It was, in short, romantic.

Romantic as an adjective, and in universal popular usage, has come to mean something diametrically opposed to realistic. It signifies something longed for, realized in dreams only. It exists in the "if only" world of the conditional future, "if we could, we would." Romantic is a word as overused and abused in popular usage, however, as other, equally maligned adjectives such as "democratic" and "liberal." Contrary to the common application, the term Romantic, romantic with a capital "R," signifies a complex network of references that refer to much more than escapist abstraction. It denotes primarily a historical moment and period of writers and artists in the late eighteenth and early nineteenth centuries that generated legacies well into the present. From the earliest known conception, and through its various manifestations and reconfigurations, the notion of the Romantic has been directly rooted in the elements, in soil and vegetation, water and air. And these narratives concerning Romantic nature, whether in poetry or prose, have also tended to have political objectives. While skeptics of the original Gezi Park protesters referred to them affectionately, but doubtfully, as romantic, it can be argued that they were perfectly correct, even if they underestimated the significance of the qualifier, with a capital R.

The political revolutionary roots of nature writing have historically tended to be of two kinds. The first, more obvious, because more common, is an approach to nature, sometimes combative, sometimes nostalgic, that conceives of it primarily as a human resource. In this case nature is not a resource to be exploited in the pecuniary sense of the word, but its worth is conceived of primarily in human terms. The loss of rivers or trees are fought or mourned for because they serve human needs, whether biological or emotional. There is another strain of nature writing with revolutionary political roots that is less human-centered in its approach to nature, however. This approach can be called the Romantic approach. Nature in the classical Romantic tradition can be seen less as an abstract object of study than a subject to be considered in its own non-human, often even biochemical, terms.[5] When there is struggle or lamentation, it is often in the name of the intrinsic value of nature itself, rather than its use-value to humans. The pantheistic tradition, or the location of divinity in the natural world, can be referenced to explain this tendency. But it doesn't completely. As a cultural invention, pantheism is necessarily human-centered in its logos, despite the power it invests in the natural world. In texts that may be considered Romantic in the sense put forth here, the material details of nature are described and catalogued in organic readings that often take the form of prayer. Itemized nature takes the form of blazons in the traditional sense in which each detail that lends to the whole is valued and often adored in and of itself. It is an aesthetics derived from a richness of textural diversity and mysterious symbiosis.

While Nâzım Hikmet may have advised the reader in the refrains of his poem "Letter to My Son" to "believe in," "grieve for," and "rejoice in" "people above all," nature is as necessary to the heart of the poem as it is to his oeuvre as a whole (*Poems* 167).[6] In Hikmet's poems, nature is a center, a place of certainty from which the world of experience radiates, a world often corrupted the further it moves from its origins. "Believe in seeds, earth, and the sea/ ... Rejoice in the earth's blessings/ ... I'll die far from my language and my songs,/ my salt and bread" (*Poems* 167–168). Although an ardent Marxist-Leninist all his life, Hikmet's poetry avoided, for the most part, the aesthetic limitations endemic to much political poetry, earnest leftist verse included. One reason for this is the place Hikmet assigns and sanctions to the natural world. If Marxist materialism, a social-philosophical inheritance of the Enlightenment, tends to conceive of nature as a resource and in terms of its use-value, even as it rejects this tendency when applied to human communities, Hikmet avoids this shortcoming by muddying the proverbial industrial waters with organic matter. Propaganda does not subvert art; the message does not overtax the messenger.

The great-grandson of Polish and German Huguenot aristocrats seeking refuge in Istanbul, and the grandson of pashas on both sides, Hikmet's family was one example of Ottoman cosmopolitanism at its most discerned. His father was the governor of Diyarbakır, Aleppo, Konya, and, finally Salonika, as well as a writer of poetry. His paternal grandfather, Nâzım Pasha, with whom he lived during his childhood, was particularly important in his life. A follower of Mevlânâ Celâleddîn-i Rûmî, Nâzım Pasha would put his grandson to sleep with verses from the *Mesnevi*, rather than lullabies (Konuk Blasing 27).[7] Hikmet would later challenge the Sufi mystic in his poem *Rubaiyat*, in which he playfully attempts to apply dialectical materialism, mostly in the form of physical human love, to the *rubai* form and the metaphysical concerns therein, "The world you saw was real, Rumi, not an apparition, etc./Endless and uncreated, it's not the work of the Prime Mover, etc." (KB 117). His experiences outside under the stars, whirling with his grandfather who was the leader of his dervish group, may have partially served to launch the complex esteem for the natural world that would surface in his poems later. He recounts his early sense of awe under the open sky in his late autobiographical novel, *Life's Good, Brother*: "I had to follow the rhythm of the songs and whirl ... and pretty soon I'd get caught up in it and start spinning like a top ... And all this was at night, outdoors, under the stars. It was all amazing. My eyes would be fixed on the stars spinning above me." (qtd. in KB 29).

Nâzım Hikmet would become interested in communism in his late teens, travel through Anatolia noting the difficult conditions of the rural population, and then travel to Moscow in 1921 at the age of nineteen to witness the fruits of the revolution first hand. He would remain a communist for the rest of his life. His communism would never be party communism per se, however, a fact that brought him trouble from the left that held his class background against him and found him erratic and non-doctrinal, even as the right persecuted him for his political leanings. His poems would challenge institutional power and avoid confusing the state apparatus with the nation as an organic concept. As an international Marxist, his voice could be simultaneously local and transnational, and with equal passion. In her biography of Hikmet, Mutlu Konuk Blasing notes that both Louis Aragon and Stalin's daughter would refer to him as a Romantic Communist, presumably for the way in which he took the revolution personally and believed, "naively," that it would be realized, and soon, in Turkey (KB 65,68). Yevgeny Yevtushenko, the Russian writer, suggests that in his later years in exile in Russia, Hikmet would become "a uniquely entrancing living anachronism from the [r]omantic period of the twenties and a belated tragic witness to the epoch of the Great Betrayal of Hopes," or, in other words, Russia under Stalin (KB 201). In both cases Hikmet is associated with the unrealized, perhaps unrealistic: the Romantic as nostalgic.

Despite, or perhaps due to his aristocratic roots, Hikmet was committed to the idea of writing as common labor. This is also a Romantic concept. William Wordsworth in the prose "Preface" to the *Lyrical Ballads*, a manifesto, of sorts, announces, among other things, the cultural objectives of the new poetics he and Coleridge were embarking on. He argues that poetry must shed its exceptionalist allegiances: "poets do not write for poets alone … the poet must descend from his supposed height, and, in order to excite rational sympathy, he must express himself as other men express themselves" (Wordsworth 173). This revolution in poetic expression would join rural labor and the forces of science in a new democratic partnership:

> If the labors of men and science should ever create any material revolution, direct or indirect, in our condition, and in the impressions which we habitually receive, the poet will sleep then no more than at present, but will be ready to follow the steps of the man of science, not only in those general indirect effects, but will be at his side, carrying sensation into the midst of the objects of the science itself. (171–172)

Emerson, and then his protégés Thoreau and Walt Whitman would carry this cross-fertilization of labor, science and the arts even further in their writing in the American Romantic tradition. Hikmet would advance this same Romantic project in his Turkish poetics by not only insisting on the inclusion of the rural and its practices in the urban and urbane, but by presenting them as necessary parts of a healthily functioning whole.

As a modernist poet, Hikmet was forever yoking and fusing the high and the low, the colloquial and the highbrow, the archaic and the modern. He combined folk traditions in Turkish verse with the Ottoman Divan tradition, meaning, in the case of Turkish modernism, that he mixed the spoken and the written.[8] This was common enough in global modernist projects, but in doing so in the Turkish case, Hikmet challenged the new language reforms instigated by Atatürk by including the Arabic and Persian used in everyday speech, even as he helped usher in the new Latin script. Konuk-Blasing in her close study of Hikmet's stylistics suggests that Hikmet's hybrid diction was not just modernist experimentalism, but also lessons in the enormous changes speakers and readers of Turkish were expected to master: his poems "sounded out" the new writing, she argues; they were lessons "in the conversion of Turkish into a phonetic, syllabic system of writing" (KB 78).[9] This gives Hikmet's modernist poetics a particular kind of urgency and cultural clemency. It would also give his poems an unprecedented popular appeal. Recordings of his poetry readings surpassed pop-music sales (KB 93). They were broadcast over loudspeakers in public spaces. As ardently as Whitman wrote for and of the masses, his poems were initially too experimental for most readers to penetrate. Emily Dickinson, his gifted contemporary, found the poems hysterical and vulgar. It was perhaps not until Robert Frost, the first American poet to truly earn the title laureate, one crowned with laurels for public service, that an American poet gained the same level of public appeal as Hikmet did in the twentieth century. Both Frost and Hikmet wrote personally and intimately about nature. Frost embedded subtle indices for reading the interconnectedness of biotic species, including human species. But Hikmet's poems wedded his nature with bold calls for social change. Hikmet's art, like Thoreau's, threatened to obstruct with civil disobedience government policies that abused nature. This is one reason among many that he became dangerous.

The fact that both Thoreau and Hikmet acted as posthumous muses for recent environmental movements in the United States and Turkey, respectively, can be traced to their common inclusion of nature at the center of their sociopolitical protests. Thoreau rarely wrote of one without the inclusion of, or without reference to, the other. Hikmet allowed the political and the environmental to occupy the same poem, or make incursions into the other's non-exclusive territory at various junctures. Both writers insist that land is not valuable as a human resource only. When the use-value of land takes precedence over its inherent value in a culture, nature writing becomes political and polemical.

A survey of Hikmet poems most recently translated into English reveals a number of examples that focus primarily on nature.[10] These poems can be roughly placed into four categories: Anatolian nature poems, poems of land and resistance, nature in exile poems, and Istanbul nature poems. These are constructed categories, of course, and are to be considered in conjunction and as interlocking. Because the poems all rotate around the common center of nature, more often than not these categories reference each other simultaneously. Poems that celebrate or lament Anatolian land or landscapes are perhaps the most common in Hikmet's oeuvre. The Anatolia that he experienced as a child, and later on in his travels, and even later through the stories of fellow prisoners from rural Turkey, is a constant in the poems. While the integrity of the natural landscape is often the primary focus, there are secondary intimations that line the interstices of the verse at every turn: the very sovereignty of Hikmet's nature functions as a call for human communities.

Before embarking on an examination of selected Anatolian poems by Hikmet, it is important to note that his focus on rural Anatolia was not unique among Turkish writers in the early twentieth century. There was during this time a general expansion beyond Istanbul as the dominant locus of literary representations of Turkey. Hikmet's was one of a number of voices directly responding to the sociopolitical changes resulting from the breakup of the Ottoman Empire and the nationalist movements that ensued. In 1918, the Ottoman writer and intellectual Halide Edip, for example, had already begun urging Turkish nationalists in "Let Us Mind Our Own House" to turn their attention to rural Anatolia in order to begin the process of healing the homeland after the devastation of the First World War. Land is central to the nationalist discourse in a 1917 article published by Edip in *Vakit*: "Many of its children today have the conviction that the only attractive fields of activity for them lie in their own country, ruined and gutted as a consequence of many wars … A mere handful of our young men can be saved from the firebrand of war. The country can be saved only if these young men remain here and decide to work uninterruptedly" (Edip qtd. in Köroğlu 102–103). Hikmet, therefore, was in many ways taking part in a general trend in Turkish literary arts.[11] Much of the writing of the period was done in service of nation building. It can be argued that Hikmet avoided the sentimentalism and other perils of rhetorical simplification that characterized much of the literature of the period, however. This can be attributed partially to the transnational scope of his experimental poetics, what Duygu Köksal in "Domesticating the Avant-Garde in a Nationalist Era: Aesthetic Modernism in 1930s Turkey" identifies as Hikmet's cosmopolitan and anti-imperialist, leftist internationalism.[12] Hikmet's representations of Anatolia, even his earliest, are complex partly because he avoids reducing the land to allegories in the service of nationalist tropes.

In one such early poem, "First Look at Anatolia," written in 1921 when he was nineteen, a trek into a mountain range on the Black Sea near Kastamonu inspires this lyric whose trajectory is reminiscent of Wordsworth's own youthful trek through the Alps recorded and rhapsodized in the two long poems *The Prelude* and *Lyrical Ballads*. As the town of Inebolu recedes in the first stanza and the horizon opens the higher two friends climb, the poem moves from town, "the minaret just a stroke, the mosque a dot," to "the Anatolia of our dreams" (*Beyond* 245). There are no clear sociopolitical overtures yet in this early poem.[13] Here we see a youthful essay into a descriptive pastoral mode colored with intimations of the sublime: the marked grandeur of the landscape suggests a mighty force behind the miniature coastline. The force is not personified, however. It is not a metaphor for the human will or power of imagination. It is simply there, "a wonderful country," in all seasons. The young poet has found his Romantic subject in the sense that the landscape is not merely picturesque, nor simply a repository for human feelings, a popular misunderstanding of the goal of Romantic aesthetics. He praises the scale of the land and the diversity of the climate. This is poem enough. Here, Anatolia exists for and of itself; it is simply, but by no means simplistically, Anatolia, *Anadolu*, "full mother," the motherland. This Anatolia exists, as yet, beyond the concepts of empire or state.

Many of Hikmet's prison poems conjure up rural and wild Anatolian scenes and details, as if cataloging will ensure their survival in his imagination—the only mode of transportation he would have for a good portion of his adult life in Turkey. The official persecution of Hikmet began in 1930 when he was accused of abandoning the Turkish War of Independence and becoming a Bolshevik. The American Ambassador at the time enters Hikmet and his "iconoclastic campaigning" in a report, deducing that his popularity proved there was a "powerful communist readership in Turkey" (KB 94). He was labeled a traitor, imprisoned, released, and then blacklisted in 1933. He would be arrested again in 1938, tried in a military court and sentenced to fifteen years in prison.

The poems written from prison that highlight human struggle often present that struggle within Anatolian landscapes that offer relief or diversion through contrast. In "Istanbul House of Detention," for example, the poem opens with references to war and violence. Part two opens immediately, however, with, "I'm wonderfully happy I came into the world:/I love its earth, light, struggle, bread" (*Beyond* 80). After a mingling of references to social struggle, the beloved (the addressee in the poem) and the earth, section three takes flight as if out the window of the prison where the poet is detained. The "I" of the poem travels over Anatolia and records what he sees both from a bird's-eye view, yet simultaneously at range close enough to note, in synesthesiac detail, the palpable characteristics of things. The effect is both vast and intimate. The abundance of its herds and produce is recorded in waves of descriptive catalogues:

> My country:
> goats on the Ankara plain,
> the sheen of their long blond silky hair.
> The succulent plump hazelnuts of Giresun.
> Amasya apples with fragrant red cheeks,
> olives,
>   figs,
>   melons,
> and bunches and bunches of grapes
>   all colors,
>
> (*Beyond* 82–83)

The staggered free verse lines perform the soaring action of the flight. The effect is much like that of a later 1947 poem, "On Ibrahim Balaban's Painting 'Spring'" in which the speaker in solidarity with a fellow inmate who paints a remembered Anatolia from prison records in language, and in similar staggered form, the indigenous richness of the motherland:

> Here, a stork
>   just back from Egypt.
> Here is a deer,
>   creature of a more beautiful world.
> Here, eyes, see the bear outside its den,
>   still sleepy.
> Haven't you ever thought of living
> unconsciously like bears, sniffing the earth,
> close to pears and the mossy dark,
> far from human voices and fire?
>
>   (*Poems* 127)

Here too animals native to Anatolia metonymically present a real world beyond the constructed confines of prison walls. Both the painter and poet attempt to recreate the instinctual integrity and physical autonomy of the animal life in this reality.

Anatolia is central to Hikmet's poems of land and resistance, but the engagement with the land in these poems is more pointedly sociopolitical. In "About Mount Uludagh," another prison poem, Hikmet experiments with animism and personification.

> For seven year now Uludagh and I
> Have stared each other in the eye.
> It hasn't budged an inch
> and neither have I,
> yet we know each other well.
> Like anything living, it can laugh and get mad.
>
>   (*Poems* 129)

The poem is a casual study in biodiversity. The mountain near Bursa in northwestern Turkey is given agency, an agency that is particularly compelling because it is the subject of all the verb action of the poem, until the final volta which abruptly displaces one being for another as the subject of the poem. Uludagh (*Uludağ*) does not function as a symbol, a nexus of compressed meaning out of which radiates the abstract but private signification of the poem. It means itself first and foremost and the first three stanzas are dedicated to establishing its hermeneutic autonomy. The mountain has moods, "like any living thing." It has stormy nights and mild mornings. Only after establishing the mountain's free agency will the writer shift the controlling subject to the human and allow nature to perform a poetic function. A man from the mountain, "having/butchered his neighbor at the altar of sacred property," will come "like a guest" to the prison "to do fifteen years in Cell Block 71" (130). *Uludağ* now becomes a complex foil to human imprisonment in the final stanza. The freedom of the mountain is contrasted with the imprisonment of the poet-observer who can only watch, though not entirely passively, from within the confines of prison: "It hasn't budged an inch/and neither have I." There is dark humor in the standoff; the speaker seems to mock his own helplessness in the face of this other power. Mountain dwellers, however, duped by the myth of ownership that will lead to a better life in which "lady skiers sipping cognac/are flirting with the gentleman skiers" kill one another to possess an acre of the peak's slope (129). The "message" is hardly subtle. But the poem is successful because before adjusting itself to deliver the final critical thrust, it has prepared us for the absurdity of the enterprise by establishing the mountain forcefully as an animated subject. Thanks to this preparation, objectification in the form of ownership appears appropriately futile in the end.

Perhaps the most famous poem of land and resistance is the long poem *The Epic of Sheik Bedreddin*, another poem written from Bursa prison. It is a dream vision in which the poet witnesses and records the ideals and events that led to a fifteenth-century peasant uprising against feudal landlords in Western Anatolia led by a Turkish mystic and Islamic scholar, Sheik Bedreddin. Considered a heretic by the Muslim authority, Sheik Bedreddin "translated his belief in the immanence of God into political action and advocated a kind of socialism, declaring the oneness of all people and religions and calling for the abolition of 'the laws of nations and religions' as well as private property" (KB 103). The multi-ethnic uprising consisting of Turkish, Greek, and Jewish peasants would be defeated by the Sultan, and Sheik Bedreddin hanged. Hikmet introduces the poem by anticipating how he, as a materialist, will be mocked for recording a tale tinged with the esoteric. He embodies the mockery in the figure of a "Professor of Islamic Studies from the Theology Faculty," and in doing so counters potential criticism by associating it with the conservative establishment (*Beyond* 52). During the course of the poem he will ground the action in tactile representations of the Anatolian landscape. In the course of this grounding process he localizes the mystical and the sociopolitical in nature.

The poem opens with descriptions of a poisoned Lake Iznik, a symbol of the state of the land under feudalism: "The flesh of their fish is tasteless,/malaria rises from the reed-beds/and the lake people die/before their beards turn white" (*Beyond* 54). In the three-year interval after the uprising and before the rebellion is finally crushed by the Sultan, life returns, and the poem launches into one of the many catalogues celebrating the return of fecundity.

> The land that one step behind us is weeping
> has begun to laugh before us like a child.
> Look at the figs like huge emeralds,
> branches weighed down with amber bunches of grapes.
> See the fish leaping in the wicker traps,
> their wet scales gleaming, glistening,
> their flesh white and tender.
> "Look," I said,
> 'Human beings here are as fruitful as earth, as sun, as sea.
> Here sea and sun and earth are fertile as human beings.'
>
> (*Beyond* 57)

In the concluding lines of section five, human beings and sea, sun and earth function as mutually referential metaphors in a chiasmus of syntax and sense. Both and all are connected by equivalent fertility. What affects the land affects humans and vice versa. And both respond positively to land policy in which those who act as rightful stewards, rather than overlords of land, share the harvest.

The next sections recount the buildup to the final battle. As Sheik Bedreddin's followers watch and wait for the Sultan's forces, they also gaze on the land that is the source of life, and also the source of resistance. A refrain repeated three times emphasizes the role of earth as a benevolent but calibrated mother; she is also the mother of those who will fight to protect her:

> The gentlest, harshest,
>   thriftiest, most generous,

most,
    loving,
greatest, most beautiful woman:
              EARTH
        was soon
            to give birth.

(*Beyond* 57)

The multiplicity of favorable qualifiers suggests the sacred names that accompany the name of the Prophet. But at the same time, the adjectives are scattered across the page as if in direct defiance of traditional usages of lyrical refrains and religious rhetoric. Here, free verse does triple-duty as it often does in the poems of one of its earliest practitioners, Whitman: it defies distinctions between the devotional, the political, and the pastoral.[14] The poem makes a brief prosaic nod to social materialist theory: "But all this is the inevitable result/of historical, social and economic laws!" (*Beyond* 64). The quoted, exclamation-topped phrase is structured as a modern intrusion into the text, however. The first-person narrator's answer is conflicted:

> Don't tell me, I know!
> My mind bows to your truth.
> But my heart
> does not follow such language.
> It says
> "O crippling fate,
> O treacherous wheel of fortune."

(*Beyond* 64–65)

It is as if an older, deeper, more Eastern sense of *kader* or fate lingers in the Marxist poet's troubled heart.

The death of Sheik Bedreddin and his followers is represented metonymically through fallen fruit: "This is no pear what will break from its stem/even if bruised it won't drop from the branch," proclaims the mystic warrior (*Beyond* 68). His physical death is not so much transcended as blended with the landscape. The followers' deaths are more directly violent, yet still expressed through organic similes: "Bare necks split like pomegranates,/like apples dropping from a green branch/heads fell one after another" (68). Even in death, the rebels return metaphorically to earth. When the battle is over and "tens of thousands" are dead, the land is returned "as fiefs to the lord's servants" (68). When the victorious army of the Sultan passes "[w]ith their colourful banners and plumes and their drums and song and dance" they pass through land that is "ravaged," through winds "like the air in a rotting orchard" (68). The land under feudalism, under private, undemocratic ownership returns to a state of corruption. The final pages of the epic rally back and forth between poetic stanzas and prose sections, the language of class struggle, and finally an elegiac conclusion that dissolves and distances the action with the refrain, "Rain falls softly" (72). The poem ends with the story told by a cellmate about the concealment of the corpse of Sheik Bedreddin and theories of mythic resurrection. Rebirth is put forth as an organic process, however, rather than a purely metaphysical one: "When we say Bedreddin will come again we are saying that his words, his eyes, his breath, will come back again though our midst" (76). It could be argued that Hikmet achieves a fusion of the material and esoteric: the historical mystic figure has dissolved into the land that will continue to inspire freedom movements. His message and the land are one. It is a call to continue the revolution. *The Epic of Sheik Bedreddin* would be the last poem published in Turkey in Hikmet's lifetime.

Nâzım Hikmet's incarceration eventually evoked international condemnation. A campaign to free the Turkish writer was begun in Paris in 1949 by Tristan Tzara with Paul Eluard, Pablo Neruda, Pablo Picasso, and Jean-Paul Sartre among its members (KB 188). In November of 1950 Hikmet was awarded, in abstentia, the first International Peace Prize in Warsaw along with Neruda, the American Paul Robeson, Picasso, and the Polish film director Wanda Jakubwska. In April of 1950, Hikmet, already in poor health, went on a hunger strike. In July 1950 the newly elected Democratic Party released him under a general amnesty and under popular pressure. Denied a normal civilian's life, silenced and persecuted by the authority, and ultimately fearing for his own safety, Hikmet decided to leave Turkey in June of 1951 and go to Russia. Escaping by small craft into the Black Sea he eventually boarded a Romanian freighter. His dramatic journey to exile, the material of folklore, is legendary. The Turkish Parliament would revoke his citizenship, and Hikmet would never see his homeland again.

There are a number of poems written in exile that locate a kind of spiritual sustenance in the land, albeit not Hikmet's own homeland. The allure of the land observed from a train window or physically experienced transcends the arbitrary borders of states in these poems often written in transit as Hikmet took advantage of his new freedom by traveling extensively throughout Europe and the world for the remainder of his life in exile. In a short untitled poem written in 1958 in Arkhipo-Osipovka on the Black Sea in Southern Russia, the poet enters gradually into an emulsive fusion with the natural elements above, below, and around him.

> This year, early fall in the south,
> I steep myself in the sea, sand, and sun,
> in trees
> and apples as if in honey.
> At night the air smells like harvested wheat–
> the night sky meets the dusty road,
> and I blend with the stars.
>
> My rose,
> I've gotten so close
> To the sea, sand, sun, apples, stars.
> Now it's time I got lost
> in the sea, sand, sun, apples, stars.
>
> (*Poems* 216)

In the original Turkish only one verb "*bulanmak*" is used to describe the present continuous action of the "I" in the first stanza, testament to the versatility of the language and Hikmet's pleasure in evocative, lyrical repetitions. To "steep" and "blend" turn to "get used to" (translated here as both "get close" and "get lost in") that could also be read as a pun on "acclimatize" in the original Turkish. The speaker adjusts to the climate until he becomes the climate. A cliché takes on epistemological ramifications when taken literally. When home is everywhere, one is never in exile. The final verb goes one step further, however. The speaker will finally "get lost" in the "sea, sand, sun, apples, stars." He will relinquish his own subjectivity and disappear into his environment, both at its most vast, "stars," and at its most humble, "apples." Like other poems written in exile and about nature, this quiet poem does not present this disappearance as tragedy. Rather, death is indistinguishable from life, and is distinguishable from neither matter nor paradise.

The long poem *Straw-blond*, a travel poem of sorts, was written in 1961 on trains going through "Warsaw-Krakow-Prague-Moscow-Paris-Havana-Moscow." After a furious staccato journey through geographical space and historical time, world events, dream visions, and romance, the poem's penultimate reference is to Istanbul. The reference takes the form of a tree:

> I've heard there's a chestnut tree in Paris
> the first of the Paris chestnuts the granddaddy of them all
> it came from Istanbul the hills of the Bosporus and settled in Paris
> I don't know if it's still standing it would be about two hundred
> years old
> I wish I could go shake its hand.
>
> (Poems 254–255)

The poem will conclude with a championing of labor, as well as reference to a troubled relation with a woman. But the poem ultimately circles back to the poet's origins and these origins are encoded in a nature that transcends national boundaries. Whatever the nostalgia, or patriotism, or origination myths suggested here may be, they are offset by a trans-nationalist vision of a tree. Istanbul, the "forbidden city," is alive in Paris and the gesture the speaker offers this transplanted deciduous being is one of hospitality and camaraderie: he would like to "shake its hand." The poem offers yet another example of the nature that functions as a center of reference in Hikmet's poetry. Though one travels far and wide with the speaker in exile in the poem, it is a tree that takes him, and thus the reader, momentarily home.

Trees are central to the fourth category of Hikmet's nature poetry, what I have called his Istanbul nature poems. These poems may or may not be written from Istanbul, but they often evoke the city through its native urban sentinels, its historic trees. "To Chop Down the Plane Tree" is an allegorical poem written in exile. The violence done to trees is to be read as violence done to the country. The chopping down of a plane tree by striking at its roots is compared to setting fire to the base of a house, an eagle unable to fly due to a broken wing, the inability to think due to a knock on the head. The poem is simple. The exegetical structure is relatively transparent; the tree functions as an uncomplicated metonym for land and people:

> These are the roots of the country;
> The sap rising to the branches
> is hidden in the roots,
> The founders of hope,
> the wings of freedom,
> the wisdom of the people.
>
> (Beyond 185).

In this organic conceit, the roots of the tree are the roots of the country. The processes are the same: everything depends on healthy taproots, on deep-seeded and secure foundations. Those that destroy professionally know that if they strike at the roots of a tree, a culture, they bring down the whole structure. Sap, the life-blood of a tree, is hidden in the roots; hope, freedom and wisdom, the life forces of a people, are concealed in the recesses of a culture, its grass-roots. Hikmet continued to criticize authoritarian government, both in Turkey and in his adoptive Russia. He championed rural labor and socialist values even as he became disillusioned with Stalin's manipulation of communist ideals.

Furthering the sociopolitical allegory, the poem goes on to describe how the disasters represent "one of the truths of our time": the abused state of the country.

> So often, in so many places, the root was axed,
> the sap failed to rise,
> the branches withered,
> the wing was broken
> wisdom killed
> the people driven to the slaughterhouse.
>
> (*Beyond* 185)

Trees and people come to a mutual conclusion in the allegory. As an ancient literary device, allegory has historically been used as cover for potentially incendiary, thus dangerous, content. And in this thinly concealed example, the poem offers a scathing critique of authoritarianism "in many places," meaning both home and abroad.

An untitled poem from the long poem *The Epic of the War of Independence* that begins with the line "Galloping full-tilt from furthest Asia," a well-known poem in Turkey, also summons trees to signify, through allegory, a human condition. But this time the image is not a defeated, but a hopeful, one. The poem begins with a nod to the Eastern roots of early Turkic peoples:

> Galloping full-tilt from furthest Asia,
> craning its mare's head to reach the Mediterranean;
> this land is ours.
>
> (*Beyond* 82)

The claim in Hikmet's poem is not so much nationalistic, thus paternalistic and possessive, as it is a declaration of independence, however. The mare, a metonymic referent to early Turkic nomadic tribes in the Central Asian Steeps, and by association, kumis or mare's milk, a staple of their diet, is presented as traveling at break-neck speed as if compelled to run west for water. The journey from east to west has been arduous and dangerous:

> Blood-soaked wrists, teeth clenched, feet bare
> and earth like a silken carpet;
> this heaven, this hell is ours.
>
> (Beyond 185)

The violent adjectives suggest, among many things, torture and poverty. The line encapsulates the history of ancient migration, the battle to remain, and, finally, the fruits of the struggle. The knotted images in Turkish carpets, particularly silk carpets, are abstract depictions of flora and fauna, earth's plenty. The third line in the first stanza is repeated and adjusted accordingly: if in this region human history is hell, nature and nature rendered in art are heaven. The speaker owns both. This is not reductive, de-historicized, patriotic nationalism.[15] Turkish people are not lauded as victors in a great empirical campaign. There has been much suffering and there has also been much beauty. Each renders the other meaningful, meaningless.

The third tercet takes the short poem in a decidedly socialist direction and brings the history of the region to the current historical moment:

> Never again let labour be enforced,
> let no man exploit another;
> this cry is ours.
>
> (Beyond 185)

What began as a story of immigration and struggle in the first tercet now becomes a polemic against feudalistic and capitalistic forms of exploitation. The refrain now becomes a "cry," a protest. The final tercet binds the various threads of the poem into a figure of democratic pluralism. Hikmet offers an organic image that underscores the natural logic of such a political structure.

> To live free and single like a tree
> and in fraternity like a forest;
> this longing is ours.
>
> (Beyond 185)

The notion of "the many in the one, the one in the many" was central in the writing of Emerson and Thoreau, both of whom protested against the abuses of capitalist economics in the mid-nineteenth century. A new American democracy was to allow for plurality within unity, the collective well-being of individuals. It is a clever chiasmus and a common trope. The tree is also often used as a primary example of symbiotic relationships in nature, how all parts function in service of the whole, just as the whole can only be understood as a sum collection of its parts. What renders Hikmet's use of the tree as a signifier for political pluralism unique is the power the trope gains in its placement in the poem: a story that rushes in four tercet stanzas with the dynamism of a galloping horse from the early Middle Ages in Central Asia to the mid-twentieth-century Mediterranean culminates in a stable, yet biotic, image. The raucous culmination of history is located in a tree and the forest of which it is an allied member. The refrain is adjusted to accommodate the next and final metamorphosis of what belongs to us. The allegory of the tree and forest, the citizen and the nation, "freedom" and "fraternity" is not yet realized, however. For now it remains in the realm of possibility. For now what is "ours" is "this longing."

The final tercet of "Galloping full-tilt from furthest Asia," along with the entirety of another Istanbul nature poem, "The Walnut Tree," was central to the ethos of the Gezi Park protests.[16] The walnut tree in this poem is located in another urban park, Gülhane Park, on the grounds adjacent to Topkapı Palace, central command and home of the Ottoman Sultans for approximately four hundred years. Gezi Park is located in the center of the modern city, above and beyond the boundaries of Byzantine and Ottoman city walls. Yet the poem about a tree in Gülhane Park reads like a harbinger for what would take place in Gezi Park fifty-six years after the poem was written while Hikmet traveled in exile to Balçık, a coastal town on the Black Sea in Northwestern Bulgaria. In this poem, the speaking subject merges grammatically and biologically with a tree. The opening stanza presents the fusion with the immediacy of metaphor, rather than the approximation of simile.

> My head is a foaming cloud, inside and outside I'm the sea.
> I am a walnut tree in Gülhane Park in Istanbul,
> an old walnut tree with knots and scars.
> You don't know this and the police don't either.
>
> *(Beyond* 197)

The identification is at the elemental level. The subject is air and water. He is also earth, both as body, "head," and tree. This is pantheism as animism and origin myth. The knots and scars are autobiography: both the tree and the man expose their stories, wear them in plain sight. But people can't read them and this is a both a curse and a blessing. Illegibility means invisibility, thus absence to those he loves; but it simultaneously provides camouflage against those he fears, or distrusts.

The title as refrain returns to launch the main stanza. Now the similes begin in earnest.

> I am a walnut tree in Gülhane Park.
> My leaves sparkle like fish in water,
> my leaves flutter like silk handkerchiefs.
> Break one off, my darling, and wipe your tears.
>
> (*Beyond* 197)

The comparatives compound: the leaves in motion are like other things in nature, like fish; like other things in culture, like silk. The beloved is directed to experience this fusion by wiping her tears with a leaf. Roles are switched. A natural entity performs the function of a cultural artifact. Leaves then become the controlling subject in the remaining lines of the main stanza as Hikmet experiments with cross-animism.

> My leaves are hands—I have a hundred thousand hands.
> Istanbul I touch you with a thousand hands.
> My leaves are my eyes, and I am shocked at what I see.
> I look at you, Istanbul, with a hundred thousand eyes
> and my leaves beat, beat with a hundred thousand hearts.
>
> (*Beyond* 197)

As if offering a lesson in reading, the speaker begins a rhythmic exegesis. But unlike traditional exegesis, Christian and Muslim, the hermeneutic process does not start with literal things in the material world and move on to allegory in the abstract moral world. Here the world is not transcended or left behind. The tree is embodied in the human, the human in the tree. The speaker is a tree with hands and eyes as numerous as leaves: the tree is the speaker with hands and eyes as numerous as leaves. Classical definitions of personification fall short: the human does not control or inform the action of "inanimate" entities; rather, the human and the botanic animate each other in the conceit.

Once this cross-animation has been established, and thus the integrity of those involved, the poem then ventures into the realm of affect. If the beloved appeared to be a single person at first, she now expands to signify a city. The poem and the synergetic relations between humans and nature are extended to an entire population and environment. The poem becomes a vast love letter "touching" a city and its inhabitants, human and plant. But the subject is "shocked" at something his "hundred thousand" eyes see. And in response to the unspecified confusion or disturbance, the leaves become hearts that beat in unison, the one in the many, the many in the one. In the end, the poem becomes another argument for pluralistic democracy signified by a tree. The final couplet repeats the refrain, which, in the end, takes on new potential.

> I am a walnut tree in Gülhane Park.
> You don't know this and the police don't either.

The problem is twofold. The city is not aware that the lover is present in the trees. And neither are the police. Again, the first is a curse, the second a blessing. There are messages in trees, but they must be deciphered. Though the messages may be read as leaves of paper on which poems are written, a form of mythologizing or immortalizing the self, the messages can also be read as vital information concerning the physical and even spiritual interpenetration of humans and land, here in the form of urban nature.[17] This is a reading of citizenship and *vatan* to which capital driven political authority is blind.

Life imitates art sometimes. And this may have been the case in Istanbul in June 2013. When activists kept vigil over four hectares of "knotted and scarred" urban trees, they were insisting on the free rights of fellow citizens. The gesture was simultaneously practical and metaphorical. Urban environments require, will eventually insist on, diversity: oxygen and nitrogen, systole and diastole. Earth will send creepers and shoots through the least permeable surfaces. Concrete is no exception, despite the proud dreams of old-school city planners. Grounding their movement on this practical fact, the gesture of the activists also functioned in the realm of the allegorical. Saving the trees meant saving an ethos. These two poems by Hikmet existed at the center of that ethos like the words, eyes and breath of Bedreddin. To honor the trees was to honor a cultural inheritance, an inheritance that, in turn, sanctioned the honoring of nature. The relation was circular and dynamic. The activists were doing their civic duty with poems in their pockets.[18]

Nâzım Hikmet, like Ahmet Hamdi Tanpınar, reserved a special place in his writing for urban nature. Like Tanpınar, Hikmet shared with readers what he understood about the essential role of trees to the physical, aesthetic, and spiritual health of a population. Hikmet applied this knowledge to political pluralism and harnessed nature as a resource for social change. This is, of course, a Romantic enterprise. A land ethic that encourages humans to honor nature first in its own right and then to learn to live according to its rules and rhythms, that insists that a sustainable land ethic is synonymous with intelligent political policy has its roots in the Romantic tradition. Simplicity and living simply in close proximity with the natural world, both physically and conceptually, means resisting the forces of excessive capitalist industry that threaten nature as well as humans. Hikmet insists that land is not valuable as a human resource only. When the use-value of land dominates its intrinsic value in a culture, nature writing necessarily becomes political and polemical. Whether the historical moment is nineteenth-century New or old England, or Istanbul and Anatolia in the first half of the twentieth century, or world cities in the globalized early twenty-first century, the literary project is the same: politically charged literature goes green. It becomes, in essence, Romantic.

3

Resourcing Nature: Land Ethics, Poetics, and "Things I Didn't Know I Loved" by Nâzım Hikmet

The use of the phrase "renewable energy" is a tricky one. It is an umbrella term that covers various types of "clean energy," itself an equally precarious noun phrase. Solar and wind energies fall under it, and technically so do hydroelectric dams. When we say fossil fuels, we do not necessarily envision buried combustible geologic deposits of organic materials. It's just petrol. When we say renewable energy, we do not immediately imagine the destruction of green river valleys. The term "renewable" has positive connotations: we think of spring, resurrection, the eternal present.

The language we use to talk about a subject, or object, directly affects the way we perceive and interact with it. This is something the Sapir-Whorf Hypothesis proposed in the early twentieth century and post-structuralist literary and cultural critics have since rightly insisted upon. Roland Barthes in his formative study *Mythologies* famously pointed out that the fundamental principle of myth is the transformation of history into nature. Nature, in this sense, is the prehistoric creation that predates or transcends human constructions. In this sense myth is naturalized and dehistoricized speech. It is the emptying out or erasure of the historical and ideological variables and contexts that give rise to phenomena. Myth naturalizes the unnatural.

Not only do the words we assign to phenomenon participate in the reassignment of phenomenon to myth, we also tend to trust our own rhetorical creations so completely that we forget to question or test their validity. Meaning formation is habit-forming. Once we have invited a definition into our private lexicon and lived with it for a certain amount of time, we take it for granted that it is real. So, for example, when we are trained to call hydroelectric power clean and renewable we tend to believe it is. Governments looking for vast energy sources, employment opportunities, and votes, and the industrial and corporate sectors they contract with know this. Or at least the spin doctors who sell it to the public do. George Orwell in his infamous 1946 essay "Politics and the English Language" famously referred to this rhetorical elasticity as a process "designed to make lies sound truthful and murder respectable, and to give an appearance of solidity to pure wind" (Orwell 120).

This is certainly the case in Turkey now as current development continues on its upwardly mobile trajectory. Despite the mythologizing rhetoric of corporate and government communiqués, hydroelectric power plants (HEPPs) and dams on rivers along the Black Sea coast, as well as 1,700 or so other projects throughout Anatolia, have had dire effects on the environment. The natural terrains that concrete has replaced are somewhat renewable, but it would take a hundred years without human presence for nature to begin to reclaim its own. And in the meantime, species dependent on natural water flow will have disappeared. There is nothing clean about it. When protestors at Gezi were speaking out against the destruction of inner-urban trees, they were in fact resisting a larger pattern of deforestation. They were implicitly protesting a national spike in land and water abuse.

Hydroelectric power is presented, or better, forced on the public in the guise of a renewable energy source. The Doğuş Group, a large holding in Turkey that has HEPPs in numerous areas throughout the country, including one within the Wild Life Protection Zone in the Artvin Province thirty miles inland from the eastern Black Sea coast, is one example. The following "Corporate Policies" statement defines their principles and responsibilities concerning the protection of the environment and the minimizing of waste:

> A great portion of the Artvin Dam and HEPP, especially the reservoir area and the Artvin-Erzurum state highway, is in Çoruh Valley Wild Life Protection Zone. There is *no construction activity* [italics mine] in the Integral Protection Zone *that has great importance for wildlife*. The construction does not have a negative effect on the chevrotain [mouse deer] species in the area; on the contrary, it is *proved by observation* that these species go on with their daily lives near the construction areas. (DOEN)

This statement makes no mention of local civil initiatives including protests and the development of a twentieth-century local folk song tradition that laments the damage done to water, trees, plants, and animals by what is considered government-sponsored corporate greed. The language of the statement is careful to not to perjure itself: construction activity might affect wildlife, but the effect has "no great importance." The harm done disappears into the relativity of comparatives and faux scientific discourse: something vaguely called "observation" "proves," apparently conclusively, that the effect is indeed not great. This is classic modern mythologizing.

There have been local protests for years against the HEPP projects throughout Turkey. Some of the more recent include a November 5, 2015, protest when the Ministry, despite legal objections, gave the "go" to three different HEPP projects to be built on Karpuzçay (Çenger Deresi) in Antalya, claiming that it would do no harm to the environment (Haberler). On January 8, 2016, villagers protested the HEPP to be built on the Çona River in the province of Osmaniye in central Turkey. Presenting themselves as keepers of the land, they demanded that "their green remain green, their water untouched" (Anayurt). On January 30, 2016, villagers in Adıyaman in south-central Turkey protested the HEPP to be built on the Kahta River (Adıyaman). On March 13, 2016, a group of three hundred in Mecidiyeköy, Istanbul, protested an HEPP to be built in Munzur in eastern Turkey, home to the Munzur Valley National Park, one of the richest floral regions of Anatolia (Munzur). On April 9, 2016, villagers closed the road between Amasya and Tokat in northern Turkey in protest of HEPP projects to be built on the Yeşilırmak, a river that flows from the southeast through Amasya and Tokat and enters the Black Sea at Samsun in the north. They sued the authorities but construction ensued leading to the demolition of forests of trees (Amasya).

In many cases ministries in Ankara overrode local legislation to stop the construction of the HEPPs. On 13 March 13, 2016, for example, a group of fifty in Erzincan in northeastern Turkey protested HEPPs to be built in Kemah and Tunceli. They reminded the public that even though the state council decided to stop the projects, the Ministry of Environment and Cities approved the projects to proceed (Erzincan). In rare cases projects have been stopped. On February 3, 2016, a court decision was made regarding the Alara Valley and Uçansu Falls near Alanya on the Mediterranean. Seven HEPP projects were canceled (Alara). However, despite these courageous, because sometimes dangerous, efforts, it has often seemed like too little, too late. This is because the exploitation and manipulation began long before the bulldozers arrived. It began on the page.

Euphemism, obfuscation, and metaphor are powerful rhetorical tools. They are particularly powerful when it comes to representing nature in terms that make it easy to exploit. One practical proof of this is that those who market environmentally dubious projects are well versed in the power of mystification that these tools provide. They know that if things were called precisely what they are, only the boldly cynical would buy or sell. Though, one could argue, this might describe enough of the moneyed population for business to continue as usual. One particularly effective way of selling out nature is to focus the language we use to talk about it on its human use-value. Land is conceived of as a resource. Translations and interpretations of our various creation myths have created the foundational narratives that reinforce this way of thinking: in the King James Bible's version of Genesis, for example, man is given dominion over creation. After he is told to be fruitful and multiply he is also told to replenish and subdue the earth. Christian history shows us that more emphasis has been placed on dominion and subjugation, rather than replenishment, however. Humans prefer to be the commanding subjects when sentencing nature.

At the onset of the rise of the post–Second World War American economy, the conservation activist Aldo Leopold wrote the now-canonical collection of essays *A Sand Country Almanac* (1949) warning readers of the imminent dangers of rapid economic growth to the environment. "The fallacy the economic determinists have tied around our collective neck, and which we now need to cast off, is the belief that economics determines *all* land-use. This is simply not true" (Leopold 225). This statement comes at the end of the book that argues for radical changes in the way Americans conceive of their relationship to the land. If advances in the sciences have anything to teach politicians, he argues, it is that co-habitation, rather than competition, is a more sustainable model for the relationship between species and the environment that supports them: politics and economics, in this model, can be conceived of as "advanced symbioses in which the free-for-all competition" is "replaced, in part, by cooperative mechanisms with an ethical content" (Leopold 202). This extension of ethics to ecological evolution reflects the extension of social responsibility to economics: "An ethic, ecologically, is a limitation on freedom of action in the struggle for existence." What philosophers call humanist ethics, ecologists call "symbiosis."

More than a half a century after Leopold wrote his groundbreaking text, it can be argued that the land relation in advanced and emerging economies is still almost wholly economic, "entailing privileges but not obligations" (Leopold 203). Land is still conceived of primarily in terms of its use-value to humans, even when the intentions are honorable. This is because the language we use to talk about land continues to affect how we categorize it and thus how we interact with it. The American Indian biologist and writer Robin Wall Kimmerer offers an interesting discussion in comparative grammar that confronts this deterministic fact of language. In her short essay "Learning the Grammar of Animacy," Kimmerer notes that in the native language of her ancestors, Potawatomi, a language she is struggling to learn before it dies, nouns and verbs are classified as "animate" or "inanimate." There is no differentiation between the animacy of human beings and natural beings in Potawatomi. Only human creations, a table, a car are classified as inanimate. Thus, when one speaks of a tree or a river, one uses the same syntactical features one uses for humans. She compares the example of "a bay" in English and Potawatomi: "A bay is a noun, only if water is dead. When 'bay' is a noun, it is defined by humans, trapped between its shores and contained by the word. But *wiikegama*, to *be* a bay, the verb releases the water from bondage and lets it live … The language is a mirror for seeing the animacy of the world" (Kimmerer 173–174).

English and languages influenced or in step with its materialist legacy make clear, concrete distinctions between the living and the dead. Humans are animate and so are animals, though lacking human forms of consciousness and language; the animacy of animals is considered less valuable or legitimate. Nature in its non-animal form is non-gendered in English, and even when it is gendered in Romance languages, the gendering is arbitrary and so cannot be considered a reflection of a "humanizing," thus legitimizing epistemological condition. Nature is an "it." It is also silent in post-industrial culture. Building on Michael Foucault's demonstration of the deterministic relationship between social power and privileged speakers, Christopher Manes in his early essay on literary ecology, "Nature and Silence," argues that this silence is the result of the shift of nature from "an animistic to a symbolic presence," particularly tied to the privileging of human reason in Western culture (Manes 17). In the course of this process, nature in our discourse has turned from a "voluble subject to a mute object" (Manes 17). It no longer speaks for itself. It is spoken for. Power companies claim the legal rights to this ventriloquism.

At this point in post-industrial history it is naive to suggest that we might return any time soon to a far-reaching animistic ontological conception of being. What we can perhaps attempt, however, is a gradual recalibration of the language we use to talk about the natural world. Change in behavior requires change in the language we use to talk about something. Sensitizing people, especially students, to the ways language inform their conception of the environment and how this is linked to definitions of progress, especially in fast-track developing economies, is a very important concern in our present historical moment. Students going into the applied sciences are in particular need of this kind of awareness. Their decisions and actions will have the most direct impact on the environment. Literature and language majors, unless they go on to law school or advertising, will have less practical bearing on the fate of ecosystems in, say, the river valleys of the Kafkas Mountains.

Instruction in the humanities can provide the beginnings of critical exposure to the source of human degradation of the environmental: language. Reading literature and culture can indeed expand the critical capacities because they deepen one's rhetorical range. And of all the literary genres it is perhaps poetry that is best positioned to challenge and disrupt the deterministic mythologizing processes that lead to the misappropriation of nature. Poets across cultures have always labored to redefine or rescript the relationship between humans and nature. Because poetry gives voice to things that are silent or silenced in the rational, prosaic world, it is a particularly "useful" medium for exposing people to alternative ways of talking about nature, ways that may work for, rather than against, its very existence. Poetry is, of course, difficult. But its very difficulty is part of its practical function. When readers work a poem, allow their minds to dig and stretch, push and plunder, things happen. Meaning evolves. In an essay that applies neuroscience to the demands the poetry of the late Early Modern poet John Donne makes on the reader, the English novelist A. S. Byatt in "Feeling Thought: Donne and the Embodied Mind" argues that "the pleasure Donne offers our bodies is the pleasure of extreme activity of the brain" (Byatt 248). To grasp the leaps and linkages Donne's poems offer, the mind must "fire in every direction it can" (Byatt 252). This stimulation of the cerebral cortex can be said of the poetic function in general and poems that engage with nature in particular. Poems that ask readers to conceive of nature in unexpected ways can expand the mind's capacity for making connections between what may seem like disconnected entities. The meaning of nature in poems may even breach its human confines. How we think about our relationship to our environment can shift. How we talk about it hesitates in the face of gross assumptions. And this hesitation that can open doors to redefinition may eventually influence how we act.

"Things I Didn't Know I Loved," by Nâzım Hikmet, is an example of a poem that does this kind of work. In this poem the relationship of humans to nature is redetermined because the use-value of natural "resources" is undermined. "Use" becomes obsolete as an operative term in the depictions of beings in nature. Boundaries and delineations between the human and the elemental are thwarted. The subject/object positions that these players inhabit are inverted and destabilized, leading to new ways of conceiving of each. Dead objects are reanimated; controlling subjects are relegated to vehicles of tenors in the metaphorical logic of the poems. In the end meaning expands beyond the predetermined confines of human-centered hermeneutics.

"Things I Didn't Know I Loved" is a later poem written in exile in Moscow in 1962. It is characterized by repetition, refrain, and bold declaratives. The poetic-prose style of the casual free-verse lines is Hikmet's modernist hallmark, his great contribution to Turkish poetics. The *mis-en-scene* is one we often see in Hikmet's later poems: a train window, often in Eastern Europe: "It's 1962 March 28th/I'm sitting by the window on the Prague-Berlin train" (Hikmet 261). Train windows were a frequent setting for Hikmet's poems once he had left the confines of prison or the restrictions and threats of surveillance that dominated his post-prison existence in Turkey.[1] On the surface, the poem is a playfully disinguous list of things the speaker claims to have never known he loved, coming as it does at the end of a long career of praising, in prose and poems, the multifaceted, variegated beauty of the existence of the items in this very list. Short irregular stanzas visit earth, rivers, sky, trees, flowers, the cosmos, snow, sun, clouds, moonlight, and rain. Night both begins and concludes the poem, encapsulating it like a vibrant living planet in cold, but not unfriendly, space.

The first two stanzas test the validity or honesty of his metaphors and declaratives. The voice that takes us on the journey in the poem puts immediate pressure on his process of naming and on the terms he employs to describe his relationship to land:

> night is falling
> I never knew I liked
> night descending like a tired bird on a smoky wet plain
> I don't like
> comparing nightfall to a tired bird
> I didn't know I loved the earth
> can someone who hasn't worked the earth love it
> I've never worked the earth
> it must be my only Platonic love
>
> (*Poems* 261)

Rejecting as he offers what he suspects is a tired, thus inaccurate, metaphor, Hikmet not only refuses to consume this particular metaphor easily, but alerts the reader to a way of reading in general terms. Neither the night, nor the bird, is naturalized into the other. He "doesn't like" these casualties of metaphor. Though metaphors can open up the possibilities of a tenor, or a subject that will be compared, they can also confine or distort it in the service of its "use-value" to a speaker. In stanza two, Hikmet applies this same logic to his own projections onto the land: how can I talk of loving something in which I have only an abstract investment? Labor is associated with adoration. Both require ritualistic observation. But the speaker is mindful that there is a difference between invested labor and disinterested love. A Platonic, thus abstract, love for the land is not the same as concrete, hard-earned love. Like his later reflections on moonlight in stanza thirteen, "the falsest, most languid, most petit-bourgeois," his Platonic love for the land threatens a kind of capitalist exploitation of natural bodies. In Marxist terms, the land and the moonlight are not for sale. Their value is measured in terms of mutual exchange between a devoted observer and an unrestricted observed. Neither the earth nor the moonlight is made to conform to human-centered metaphors. Their "use-value" exists beyond false declarations of devotion and sentimental appropriation.

The poem presents a symbiotic vision of the relationship between the human and nature. Like trees, humans are products of specific geographies, for example:

> I didn't know I liked tress
> bare beeches near Moscow in Peredelkino
> they come upon me in winter noble and modest
> beeches are Russian the way poplars are Turkish
>
> (*Poems* 262)

This is not reductive personification. It is poetic bioregionalism. Trees are "noble and modest" tenors with people for vehicles in similes that create reflective relations between local nature, tree or human. Trees are given agency; "they come upon" the speaker and impress him with their individual characters. When "flowers come to mind" after a boyhood memory of a Ramazan night in stanza seven, the "poppies cactuses jonquils" blend with his first kiss in Kadikoy (*Poems* 263). Though these leaps and juxtapositions may feel like free association, they are in fact grounded in a certain symbiotic logic. Humans do not take precedent over nature in these comparisons and parallels; they do not compete for dominance on the page. Human qualities blend with qualities in nature; human experience turns to nature in search of adequate expression: "fresh almonds on her breath/I was seventeen/my heart on a swing touched the sky" (*Poems* 263). The stanza concludes with a final reference to flowers: "friends sent me three red carnations in prison" (*Poems* 263). The sudden, solemn non sequitur grounds the flower conceit in political history, like the earlier sound of a prison beating that links, spatially and conceptually, the "blue vault" of the sky and the transnational trees in stanza four (*Poems* 261). If abstract human joy turns to nature to lend it formal shape, so do human sorrow and the sociopolitical injustices that lead to it. Creating a signifying medium for human feelings is an old function of poetry. Images from nature furnish an ancient form of political symbolism. What Hikmet does is harness and then free these traditions, allowing human love and social repression to circulate within and throughout the biotic. The effect is not sentimental escapism, but, rather, a tableau of collective events. Like Leopold, and other advocates for nature, Hikmet offers a series of cooperative or coproductive visions of the human relation to the natural world.

What these symbiotic relations between humans and nature do in the poem is something poetry concerned with nature often can do: it reanimates what is considered dead in an anthropomorphic worldview. As illustrated by Kimmerer, Hikmet too "releases" natural phenomena from "bondage," allowing bodies other than human to "live"; the language in the poem becomes "a mirror for seeing the animacy of the world." In stanza ten, the speaker adds "stars" to his accumulating catalogue of things he didn't know he loved (*Poems* 263). The year is 1962. He is in Russia where the race for space is well under way. Although it will be another four years before the unmanned Russian space vessel Luna 9 will land on the moon and send back the first close images of its remote surface, and seven years until man himself will step on the moon, Hikmet attempts to draw the stars closer through metaphor:

> I have some questions for the cosmonauts
> were the stars much bigger
> did they look like huge jewels on black velvet
> or apricots on orange
> did you feel proud to get closer to the stars
>
> (*Poems* 263)

By inscribing the unfamiliar through the familiar, in this case jewels and fruit, Hikmet uses modest metaphors to lend reality to remote space. Stars are not dead objects in a void. They have color and texture, perhaps even taste. There are echoes of Whitman in the reference to pride (as indeed there are echoes of Whitman throughout this poem and Hikmet's mature oeuvre in general). "Have you felt so proud to get at the meanings of poems," asks Whitman in "Song of Myself." Like Hikmet's question, Whitman's is rhetorical and affirmative: pride is not a sin here, but rather the pleasurable result of difficult accomplishment. Synapses have been fired. Poems like planets require extreme lines of approach. Once reached, they become part of our imaginative life.

Hikmet insists, however, that the abstract stars become identifiable planets; just as intangible, nonliteral space becomes the physical "cosmos." Yet he references current debates in political art to conflate, thus dissolve divisions between the representative and the non-representative.

> I saw the colors photos of the cosmos
>   be upset comrades but nonfigurative shall we say or abstract
>   well some of them looked just like such paintings which is to
>   say they were terribly figurative and concrete
> my heart was in my mouth looking at them.
>
> (*Poems* 263)

The cosmos (as in Whitman's poems) cannot be confined to human social theory. Neither bourgeois aesthetic appropriation, nor proletariat popularization can account fully for the complexity of cosmic bodies. Hikmet offers a short ekphrastic remark, appealing to a visual work of art to animate the cosmos for the reader of the poem. The cosmos can be and can't be reproduced. They exist both with and beyond human ken. And because of this existential volatility they are both cautionary tales and relativizing models for human life.

> they are our endless desire to grasp things
> seeing them I could even think of death and not feel at all sad
> I never knew I loved the cosmos
>
> (*Poems* 263)

The cosmos adjusts human conceptions of time. Thus, they are presented neither as distant dead metaphors, nor inanimate orbiting objects. They are alive and humans are involved in their existence.

Whether the poem engages in questions of the "use-value" of nature, the symbiotic relationship between nature and humans, or the reanimation of dead nature, one underlying constant in the poem is that the poem transports its subject beyond the confines of human-centered hermeneutics. Poems encourage us to reread the world we thought we knew. In the penultimate stanza, the speaker "confesses," "I didn't know I liked rain" (*Poems* 264). And what follows is a liquefying of the human body and, or a solidifying of water into a travel capsule, as the speaker merges with the element of water.

> whether it falls like a fine net or splatters against the glass my
> heart leaves me tangled up in a net or trapped inside a drop
> and takes off for unchartered countries I didn't know I loved
> Rain
>
> (*Poems* 264)

Neither the human, nor the elemental, is left in isolation. Each is measured and mixed in the other's composition. And language that relegates all creation to human-centered purposes, be they practical or metaphorical, cannot account for this formula. "[A]nd here I've loved rivers all this time," the speaker announces in stanza two (*Poems* 261). Rivers, like the cosmos, embody obscure messages for humans, even as they exist beyond human forms of signifying.

> whether motionless like this they curl skirting the hills
> European hills crowned with chateaus
> or whether stretched out flat as far as the eye can see
> I know you can't wash in the same river even once
> I know the river will bring new lights you'll never see
> ....
> I know all this had been said a thousand times before
> and will be said after me
>
> *(Poems* 261)

Hikmet nods to another Greek philosopher, this time Heraclitus, the pre-Socratic champion of paradox and flux. He substitutes the verb "step" with "wash" in "no man ever steps in the same river twice," adding connotations of the cleansing powers of river water to the ancient maxim. Rivers, in this stanza, are represented as shape-shifting, yet constant. They are there whether witnessed by humans or not. They are not Berkeley's trees that fall only if and when perceived by humans. Like the cosmos, rivers are "eternal" sources of wonder and contemplation for humans.

The poem concludes with an acknowledgment of the speaker's indebtedness to nature as a material resource, as well as an aesthetic, emotional, and then ultimately less definable resource.

> I didn't know I loved so many things and I had to wait until sixty
> to find it out sitting by the window on the Prague-Berlin train
> watching the world disappear as if on a journey of no return.
>
> *(Poems* 264)

He is still *en route* in the last lines, but finally the poem takes a metaphysical turn. There have been many nostalgic moments in the poem, but these focus on a childhood memory, "holding his grandfather's hand" on the way to "the shadow play/Ramazan night in Istanbul" (the third person pronoun an acknowledgment that it may be fact or fiction) or youthful adventures like being stopped by bandits, "on the red road between Bolu and Geredé"/"when I was eighteen." (*Poems* 262). Nostalgia is relegated to the human history in the poem, however. Nature and all the things he loves in it continue with him into the dark. Like the "sparks" that "fly from the engine" ("I didn't know I loved sparks"), the things he loves in nature are intensified in their magnificence when set against the uncertainty of death that the poet, now sixty, acknowledges and welcomes (*Poems* 264).

Aldo Leopold suggests that "[a]n understanding of ecology does not necessarily originate in courses bearing ecological labels; it is quite as likely to be labeled geography, botany, agronomy, history, or economics" (Leopold 224). And, one might add, poetry. Arguing further against "thinking about decent land-use as solely an economic problem," he implores the reader to "[e]xamine each question in terms of what is ethically and esthetically right, as well as what is economically expedient" (Leopold 224). He then offers one of the more powerful declarations in the text: "A thing is right when it tends to preserve the integrity, stability, and beauty of the biotic community. It is wrong when it tends otherwise" (Leopold 224–225). Hikmet's poem, "Things I Didn't Know I Loved," works toward such a land ethic. "We should not underestimate … the power of literature to affect behavior, even if that process is impossible to measure with precision," argues Scott Knickerbocker in *Ecopoetics: The Language of Nature, the Nature of Language* (Knickerbocker 5). Knickerbocker goes on to make a strong claim for the power of language to open our eyes to the ethics and aesthetics of nature, and, in turn, change human behavior. Like Emerson and Thoreau who championed philosophy in the defense of nature, Knickerbocker illustrates in his discussion of the poems of Emily Dickinson the ways in which poetry encourages wonder and thus facilitates an ensuing respect toward nature. Poetics can "nudge consciousness to a more ecologically ethical state, which in turn shapes behavior. A poet crafts language that, if successful, inspires, startles, or coaxes us into knowing the world with revived senses" (Knickerbocker 17–18). Hikmet in many of his poems, including the one discussed here, reflects the kind of "[h]eightened perception that promotes deep thinking" (Knickerbocker 18). He constructs metaphors that do not succumb to sentimental myths of nature. Nature is grounded and animated. Humans are bound to nature, just as nature includes humans in its various rhythms.

It is much more difficult to exploit a living body than dead matter. When a river is conceived of as alive, "a valuable subject" rather than a "mute object," it is no longer simply a renewable energy source vulnerable to destructive engineering methods that subjugate rather than replenish. Exploitative and destructive methods of land use driven by economic determinism alone may evolve toward cooperative mechanisms that honor land ethics. A symbiotic approach to the needs of humans and the needs of the land they inhabit requires a cultural effort activated by a heightened community-wide understanding of the value of the natural world. This understanding and the language that rouses it, finally, are important contributions poetry and nature-conscious poets like Hikmet have to offer the material world.

Part Two

Animals

4

Islam, Westernization, and Post-Humanist Place: The Case of the Istanbul Street Dog

In one narrow street (but none of them are wide) I saw three dogs lying coiled up, about a foot or two apart. End to end they lay, and so they just bridged the street neatly, gutter to gutter. A drove of a hundred sheep came along. They stepped right over the dogs, the rear crowding the front, impatient to get on. The dogs looked lazily up, flinched a little when the impatient feet of the sheep touched their raw backs—sighed, and lay peacefully down again. No talk could be plainer than that.

Mark Twain in Istanbul, The Innocents Abroad, 266

"That one there … " [points to a street dog off-screen] "she's a Sufi. She eats her food but hides her rice; I think she's feeding a rabbit or a hedgehog. She's a mystery. She has a secret."

Serdar, Taşkafa: Stories of the Street[1]

An animal on the edge of description

Defending the "radical, plural otherness" of animals, Paul Shepard in the early pages of *The Others: How Animals Made Us Human* suggests that animals, and especially marginal animals, resist our cognitive efforts to define them: "Categories defined by human observers inevitably collide with animals at the edges of categories. … In this way they [the animals] exemplify change and attitudes toward them reflect feelings about ambiguity and transformation in a larger sense" (Shepard 282, 59). Referring to the human repulsion to bats, Shepard notes how their status as part bird part mammal offends our sense of recognizable order. "Being paradoxical or 'out of place' means discord, a wrenching of the cosmos, as when a wolf pack invades the village or a bear wanders into the city" (Shepard 59). Anthropologists have shown that "what is culturally unclear" is also "perceived as unclean" (Shepard 59).

Marginal, ambiguous, paradoxical, dirty, the Istanbul street dog, neither domestic pet nor wild being, satisfies Shepard's definition of an animal on the edge. But like other feral canines in other non-Western European and North-American urban centers, the Istanbul street dog is nonetheless a common fixture. He or she vies for food and space with other inhabitants of the streets: cats, nocturnal rats, various scavenger birds, the urban derelict, members of the poor.[2] If a dog is most often defined by his use-value to man—a guardian of property, a herder of livestock, a hunter of game and illegal substances, a status symbol, a pet—the Istanbul street dog, serving no clear or tangible purpose to modern man, lacks a concrete definition. Roaming outside and beyond the traditional lexicons and taxonomies of civilized society, the feral dog belongs to another place and another time. She disarms the tourist who takes photos of her alongside other exotic artifacts of the city. American-born residents of Istanbul, like me, struggle to make room for her in our own imported frames of reference. Local people do not agree on her status. She is at times rounded up and "disappeared," but just as often fed and talked to. She is an enigma, and like all enigmas she must endure various forms of affection and abuse, because as the American poet Marianne Moore writes of the bat, the wild horse, and the flea, in the long version of her poem "Poetry," more often than not, "we/do not admire what/we cannot understand" (Moore 266).

Lisa Sideris in *Environmental Ethics, Ecological Theology and Natural Selection,* like Shepard, defends the place of otherness in the natural world. Putting pressure on her colleagues in the field of ecotheology, Sideris argues that theological approaches to ecology can and must incorporate innovations in evolutionary science in order to honestly negotiate apparent randomness in nature, most particularly for her thesis, the place of suffering in the animal world. Ecosystem theories embraced and recirculated by ecotheologians give privilege to harmony, cooperation, and balance in nature, an understanding of natural processes that is naïve and outmoded, she argues. Darwinian evolutionary theory and more recent but related systems such as chaos ecology, process thought, and field theory replace old-fashioned organic models and, in doing so, reduce the hazards of unscientific approaches to nature.

Unsatisfied with what she sees as the healing and redemption agendas in secular and theological ecological agendas, respectively, Sideris, citing Charles Birch and John Cobb in *The Liberation of Life: From the Cell to the Community*, argues that process thought, which draws on modern physics and chaos theory, rejects the idea of creation *ex nihilo* and posits instead the notion of creation out of chaos. Life in these terms becomes an ongoing process and "conditions of discord in nature generate 'new responses' in all life forms which, in turn, create novelty" (Sideris 109). Field theory physics, which posits, in short, that events cannot exist apart from a field, underscores the fact that interdependence in Darwinian evolutionary theory is not "a solution to strife but a *source* of it" (Sideris 221). Life and death need and feed on one another and ecotheory that does not take into account the necessary give and take, the inevitable "brutality" in nature, risks reducing or demoting what is unstable and ambiguous to levels that are palatable to humans because they are safe for them.

Both secular and theological naturalists in the West make strong and complementary cases for post-humanist, anti-anthropocentric approaches to nature. "Values can be generated by humans without necessarily being centered on them" (Sideris 204). "The human species," argues the American theological ethicist James Gustafson, "is always the *measurer* of all things," but this does not necessarily imply that we are the "measure" (qtd. in Sideris 204). Serra Tlili, in *Animals in the Qur'an*, offers a similar ecotheoretical critique of human-centralism in Islam. She argues that while Muslims hold "ambivalent views about the psychological natures of nonhuman animals and generally share the idea that the latter are inferior to humans," this position is not grounded in a close reading of the Quran (Tlili 3). Tlili suggests that the problem lies in a misunderstanding or misinterpretation of the "nuanced" language of the holy book, not the book itself (Tlili 8). The lives of animals are not given a more centralized position in these readjustments of classical humanism, Christian or Muslim: the objective is not to "devalue" humans (Tlili xi). The aim is to "place them amidst a natural order that God seems to value greatly" (Tlili xi). In cases both East and West, animals are given a new freedom, at least within the ecotheoretical discourse, to wander according to inclinations humans may or may not follow.

These post-humanist positions give us generative, unsentimental ways to think about interspecies relations, and encourage us to think of humans' lack of respect for the integrity of fellow creatures as "speciesism," ecotheory's version of fascism or racism applied to the animal world. The Istanbul street dog, however, like all feral, intercity animals, continues to complicate and thus exert pressure on the terms employed in the anti-humanist debate in ecotheory, particularly in the West. Whether studies in the field criticize or accommodate the differences between domesticated or wild animals, they tend to offer no real space for those beings that do not fit into either category. Urban street animals, and in our case, the Istanbul street dog, neither friendly in the usual sense of the word, nor working, nor wild, remains, for the most part, outside the field of discourse despite fashionable revisionist notions of animals or animal alterity.[3] Like their cousins, the wolves who invade the village, they threaten to cause discord because they are out of place and thus culturally unclear. A consideration of the historical Istanbul street dog offers ways to think about how theoretical categorization continues to hinder applied post-humanism when it comes to an animal on the edge.

A historical case

Associated cross-culturally with travel and death, dogs have herded the dead or ruled the underworld in ancient mythologies from Central Asia to Classical Greece to Ireland. Shepard notes that from the beginning of recorded time a tension existed between the "civilized associations" of dogs as the first domesticated animal in human history and the "degraded state" of the original dogs in the wild (Sideris 63–64). The tension plays out in our stories of the dog as both working companion or servant and potential master in death, suggesting that the narration of man's oldest intimate relation with an animal resonates with primal uncertainty from the outset.

Alongside the history of dog as "man's best friend" runs another history of dog as taboo, especially in some forms of Islam. If Neolithic Middle Easterners exploited the dog in the herding of livestock, Ancient Middle Easterners rejected the dog as polluted. Zoroastrians in ancient Persia made a virtue of the dog's habit of digging up graves and eating the dead by including them in burial ceremonies. Some scholars suggest that the Islamic taboo against dogs that persisted in the early Islamic period had political–historical roots in the power struggles between Persians and Arabs. Honored by Zoroastrianism, a religion that was an obstacle to the spread of Islam, the dog became a site of cultural struggle and finally a casualty of Islamic colonialism. Much like the snake in Egyptian mythology, the deity of a preexistent religion became the demon of an ascending one. The dog in this anthropological argument suffered a classical fate.

Though dogs in classical Arabic literature were often portrayed as symbols of honored virtues like self-sacrifice, Islam in the form of Shiite Orthodoxy tended to deem the dog unclean, making the touching of a dog an abomination, thus forbidden or *haram*. The hound might accompany the Prophet as royal hunter, but in daily life, up to the present day, physical contact with dogs is avoided by many orthodox Muslims and those who are influenced by their views. It is an interesting twist to the ancient history of canines in Persia that in 2011 legislation was being debated in the Iranian parliament concerning the criminalization of dog ownership. The bill proposed that not only were dogs "impure and dangerous" and posed a public health hazard, but that the current popularity of dog ownership with the upwardly mobile classes posed "a cultural problem, a blind imitation of the vulgar culture of the West" (Moavenii).

Many practicing Sunni Muslims in Istanbul dislike the idea of contact with dogs and especially their saliva. It is argued by some, however, that the cultural source of this loathing can be traced to exegeses and opinions of the Quran called *Hadith*, not the Quran itself. The Quran mentions dogs five times, and rather than described as *haram*, they are depicted as guardians or conduits of grace. The story of the "Seven Sleepers" (*Surah* 18, verse 9–26) takes place in Ephesus, in western Anatolia, during religious persecutions in the third century AD. It is a story shared by Muslims and Christians alike; however, a dog named Kitmir is central to the Muslim version. Although the seven men attempt to drive the dog away fearing his barking will reveal their whereabouts, Kitmir is granted human speech by God in order to direct the men to hide in a cave and sleep. The dog remains on guard for 309 years after which time the men awake and safely return to the living. According to Muslim tradition, Kitmir is granted admission to heaven upon his death (Coren). The story, in both its Christian and Muslim versions, with or without the dog, is associated with persecution: the Christians by the Romans, and Mohammed by the Jewish

Elders of Medina. In the case of Islam, a dog becomes an instrument of grace and a symbol of loyalty.

Human–hound relations are thus fraught with ambiguity in the Islamic traditions of Istanbul's historical and cultural inheritance. A popular Turkish idiom recounts that an angel will not enter the house that harbors a dog. Serra Tlili in her ecotheoretically informed study of animals in the Quran argues that despite opinion to the contrary, Islam does not condone speciesism. Like current ecotheological critiques of humanism and human-centralism in perceived notions of dominion in the Bible, critiques like Sideris', Tlili offers a contemporary ecotheological assessment of speciesism in contemporary Islamic practices. She sees a "correlation between the exaggeration of humans' status, which has peaked in modern Islamic thought, and Muslims' deteriorating attitudes toward nature in the last century or so" (Tlili xi). She argues that "human classification systems perhaps do not correspond to divine ones" and that the need to draw lines between human and nonhuman animals "may originate from human limitations and conflicting interests" that the exegetes would agree "do not apply to God" (Tlili 151).

In Istanbul, there is another popular cultural given that exists alongside taboos against dogs, however. It too is based on the widely honored Islamic sanctity for life. It is common to hear the person who moves away from a passing dog on the streets defend the right of that same animal to life. Another popular story based on the Quran says that although Mohammed initially supported the Governor of Medina's edict to kill stray dogs due to hygienic concerns, the Prophet changed his position, claiming canines were also God's creatures and that only God was permitted to take the life of one of his own. He claimed further that canines were useful to humans as guard dogs, hunting dogs, and shepherd dogs, though some argue that he granted that stray black dogs may be the devil in disguise and were therefore to be avoided (Coren). This claim is challenged by those who argue that black dogs also constituted a "community" (*ummas*), the elimination of which would leave a "deficiency (*khalal*) in nature" according to the Prophet Mohammed (Al-Khattabi qtd. in Llewellyn 241). Many contemporary Turkish people, religious or otherwise, refer to the street dog as a living soul: it is often observed that "*Onu da Allah yarattı*" (God created him/her too); or that "*O da bir can*" (He/she's a living soul too). The street dog's status as a living being, and this includes black dogs, is what leads many in the general public to set out food for them and not refer them to the municipality that may take them away to worse conditions than the streets, or more likely extermination. This does not mean that they are treated kindly by all. Animal abuse is a serious fact of urban street life in Istanbul.

The conflicted Islamic attitudes toward feral dogs are grounded in what Tlili calls the disjuncture between popular and nuanced readings of the Quran: despite "sufficient evidence in the Quran that non-human animals are considered moral, rational and even accountable beings," such readings have "limited impact" on most quotidian conceptions of the status of animals, "with the notable exception of the celebrated topic of animals as signs of creation" (Tlili 139). Ironically, however, it may be that it is partially this conflict that has led to both the persecution and the safeguarding of the Istanbul street dog, the evidence of which continues to play out on many urban streets. The distant yet tolerant, or, in many cases, nurturing side of traditional attitudes toward feral dogs has often helped them survive the ambiguity. It is another paradoxical turn in the long history of the Istanbul street dog that Turkish people, in general, do not wish to be held responsible for the worst cases of canine abuse. The first known large-scale effort to eradicate them was rumored to have been instigated not by the Orthodox Muslim community, but by a foreign resident (some say an Englishman, some a Frenchman) who formally complained to local authorities that the street dogs were a hazard to modern life.[4] Though the story has an air of folklore about it, members of the foreign community in Istanbul as well as many Western-minded Istanbulers, particularly in the Pera district where the embassies were located, complained that, among other things, the dogs slept in the tracks of the new tramway and caused accidents. At various times, starting in the early nineteenth century with the first organized eviction under Mahmut II (Sultan from 1808 to 1839), the dogs were rounded up and shipped to deserted islands off the coast of Istanbul in the Sea of Marmara. A second deportation to the islands took place during the reign of Abdülaziz (1861–1876). The final mass exile was ordered in 1910 during the Constitutional Period, simultaneously serving the business needs of a French industrialist who exported the island dogs as leather, bone meal, fertilizer, and oil to Marseille (Hür). Some 80,000 dogs were sent to the islands and died there in this last exodus.

There were negative responses from other residents of Istanbul to these organized expulsions of the dogs. Ümit Sinan Topçuoğlu, in his book on the cultural history of the Istanbul street dog, claims that because each mass eviction of the dogs coincided with natural disasters in the city, fires and storms in particular, many people looked upon the disasters as divine retribution for the brutal treatment of the animals. The people most inclined to these interpretations were those least invested in the Westernization process under way because they were not the ones directly profiting from it. They were the common people and the poor who historically shared the closest quarters with the street animals of the city. They were also the ones who clandestinely took food to the islands and refused to hunt dogs even when city officials offered 15 francs per head (Topçuoğlu). Frustrating the Sultanate's efforts to modernize Istanbul, local people insisted on maintaining their historical relationship with the dogs as neighbors and informal guardians of the city. When Cemil Topuzlu, twice the Mayor of Istanbul between the years 1912 and 1919, boasts in his memoirs of having killed 30,000 street dogs, he also notes that it was done quietly. The clandestine nature of the action suggests that by the early twentieth century, secrecy was necessary to avoid scandal because it was going against the will of the general population.

The physical war declared on the Istanbul street dog has thus been part and parcel of the Westernization process that began in earnest in the nineteenth century.[5] Though animals commonly lived on the streets of Western European and North American cities until the early twentieth century, reigning notions of progress, and the combustion engine that sent draft animals back to farms (or, in the case of some French horses, to the *Boucherie Chevaline* [horse butchers]), had led more and more to either the comprehensive domestication of urban animals or their systematic extermination. If a dog did not assimilate and become the property of humans, she was exiled to her original state in the wild, but a wilderness that could no longer sustain her in her degraded condition.[6] Urban life by the late nineteenth century meant living in mass society, far from wild things. Ecotheorists like Paul Shepard note that this culminating split between the urban and the wild led to increased psychological and social angst in the Victorian period: "As if to deny our poverty of wild things, we declare a cultural superiority over all that is deemed primitive ... Our schizoid alienation from the animals has led us to project the frightening confusion of our urban grayness upon them" (Shepard 103). This projection led to both the demonization and the sanctification of dogs in Western culture, a confusion that would play out in cultures like urban Istanbul where Western values were superimposed on an already-existent ambiguity over human–canine interaction. The conflation of Islamic and Western approaches, along with local attitudes that both borrowed from and rejected these influences, raises interesting questions in environmental ethics that continue to be relevant. In Istanbul, as in other metropolises in other parts of the world, the relationship between urban animals and urban people has not been thoroughly civilized and privatized. In other words, it has not been commodified.

The "reduction of the animal" to a manufactured commodity has a "theoretical and economic history," writes John Berger in his essay "Why Look at Animals?" referring to Cartesian dualism and industrial capitalism, respectively: this reduction is "part of the same process as that by which men have been reduced to isolated productive and consuming units" (Berger 13). The unresolved ambiguity and confusion that reflects postindustrial man's alienation from himself and nature remains public and visible on the streets of "developing economies." Unlike the domesticated dog in the West, the street dog is not "detached from what might be called the historical dynamics of a culture" (Burt 291). If the modern animal is often "associated with the archaic, the nostalgic rather than change, 'progress,' or even modernity," as Jonathon Burt argues in his discussion of the iconic or totemic role of the modern animal and her place in technology in "Illumination of the Animal Kingdom," the third world feral dog remains a stubborn physical hurdle to progressive Western conceptions of civic space. Against enormous odds, the animal has survived human bewilderment. In Istanbul, she continues to roam and scavenge, a site of a continued struggle of forces, both old and new, that would have men and women deny once and for all the "radical, plural otherness" of animals, and thus what is wild in our selves.

Humanism, Westernization, and the urban street dog

Ecotheory relies in general on the established argument that the urban/wild split has its most obvious roots in the humanist movement in its Early Modern guise. In the collective push to liberate early modern man's intellectual obligations to the church and usher him to the doors of experimental science, Renaissance scholars advocated an Aristotelian theory of human exceptionalism. What differentiated higher humans from the lower animals was their unique capacity for cognition. Placing thinking human over and above instinctive animal in a renewed enthusiasm for Classical Greek, rather than Christian medieval hierarchies, helped the movement in rationalism to establish an anthropomorphic, human-centered conception of life on earth. Speechless, soulless, void of self-consciousness, animals were defined by what they lacked when compared with humans. And as beings in body only, animals became particularly susceptible to dualistic excesses in mechanistic science.

Though Renaissance humanist hierarchies were meant to replace medieval ones, the ontological position of animals remained relatively unchanged. "Though mechanism may have been most succinctly defined by René Descartes in *Discourse de la Méthode* in 1637, his thought was anticipated by religious traditions of the soullessness and demonology of animals" (Shepard 279). The position of the animal, like the animal body it represented, had been differently, but equally, demonized by Christian Medievalism. Whatever the terms employed, "[P]hilosophy and religion all along insisted on the radical distinction between human and animal" (Shepard 279–280).

It is sometimes argued that Islam prevented the Ottomans from taking full advantage of the intellectual inheritance of the Renaissance, the Enlightenment. Called also the "Neo-Classical" movement, this "new" era of writers, thinkers, and experimental scientists, relying also on Greek and Roman sources, labored to popularize Early Modern enthusiasm for the human sciences. The eighteenth century was a period of frenetic scientific and technological change in Europe, change critics of the Ottomans say was neither embraced, nor properly applied in the Ottoman East. Though the Tanzimat era (1839–1876) was a period of reformation and modernization of the Ottoman Empire, which meant an opening to the West, some have maintained that it was too little too late. They suggest that Islamic tradition prevented technological advancement in the empire in the eighteenth and nineteenth centuries; others claim that it was not Islam per se, but an ineffectual Caliphate threatened and weakened by European colonialism and the rise of puritanical movements, that prevented it from responding creatively to discoveries in Enlightenment science.[7]

When we speak of Westernization in Turkey, it is useful to keep in mind the long story of humanism and its attendant anthropocentricism. When we speak of Westernization and its effect on the animal population of Istanbul, we should also keep in mind the ontological position of the animal and animal body in occidental philosophy and science. A Westernization program when applied to Istanbul street dogs brought with it the prejudices inherent in its discourse. If Islam considered the touch of the dog *haram*, the dog in an anthropomorphic model of being that historically vilified the animal had, in fact, a worse chance of survival. Because if Islam allowed that although polluted, the sanctity of life applied to her too, this meant that she would be allowed to live, perhaps even nourished, though not in the same physical space as humans. In an occidental humanist model, the dog would have to be rehabilitated; in other words, the street would have to be taken out of the dog if she was to survive human company. A sustained tension in the Islamic attitude toward dogs partly explains the survival of the Istanbul street dog long after she had disappeared from Paris, London, or New York.

An aggressive Westernization process dictated that the street dog could continue to exist according to his use-value to humans. Eastern conceptions of the practical value of dogs also reinforced this discrimination: the Prophet Mohammed, we will recall, allowed that dogs could be useful to humans in the form of shepherds, guardians, and hunting companions. To profit from the technological and social advances of the European Enlightenment, particularly in its English and French variety, meant the uneasy adoption of perspectives and attitudes that often clashed, and sometimes violently, with local Turkish ways of doing things. Local custom that nourished street life for its own intrinsic value, for example, countered both Western and Eastern utilitarian attitudes toward dogs. In a push to catch up and keep pace with the economic gains of the Industrial Revolution that threatened Ottoman and then Turkish independence, attempts were made to "normalize" the civic spaces of Istanbul so that they resembled civilized cities in the West. The result of the cleanup policy for the Istanbul street dog was that because she was ontologically and culturally unclear in Islam, and to Western powers in the city and the Ottoman elite who supported their influence, she was perceived as unclean on all sides of the power spectrum. The only options, in such a case, were exile and/or extermination.

A neo-Western crusade to "save" the Istanbul street dog

The attempts to exile the dog *en masse* to islands in the Sea of Marmara failed. They returned and continued to multiply as they had since they first arrived with Sultan Mehmet the Conqueror in the fifteenth century, as the legend goes. A society for the protection of animals in Istanbul (*İstanbul Himaye-i Hayvanat Cemiyeti*) was established in 1912 and helped to prevent deportations for a few years, though with the outbreak of the war in 1914 another group of dogs was sent to *Sivriada*, one of the Marmara Islands (Hür). The society addressed injustice and cruelty toward animals, focused on education, and lobbied for new legislation and regulations concerning the maintenance and welfare of street animals. Though an informal ethics had governed human–canine relations in the Istanbul streets for 400 years, Westernization coupled with hostile elements in the orthodox Muslim community required a formalized moral code. The society for the protection of animals would provide that blue print.

After the nineteenth century, overtly dramatic responses to the dog problem were not attempted again by those in authority. What persisted, however, was the mass poisoning of dogs, a covert cleanup policy that when and if found out and announced by animal rights activists and journalists continued to cause public scandal in Istanbul, particularly in the 1990s. In 2004, the "Animal Welfare Act, No. 5199" was passed, making the torture, abuse, and general mistreatment of all street animals a misdemeanor subject to fines ("Hayvanları"). Called the "Catch, Neuter and Return" plan (CNR), it required that animals be treated for diseases, neutered, and returned to the streets; this plan followed the guidelines of the only method for controlling street animal populations endorsed by the World Health Organization (Bodrumbulletin). Istanbul street marches in 2008 protested the continued mistreatment of street animals by municipalities and individuals alike and demanded stricter rules and the enforcement of them. Large protest marches in 2012 rallied to block plans to send street dogs to so-called forest sanctuaries, a promise nobody trusted. Many protesters marched with their domestic dogs on leashes. Thus, what has also persisted alongside the abuses of modernization and traditionalist interpretations of the Quran is the general defense and protection of dogs as free street dwellers. Yet while the marches defended a way of living side by side with animals that may appear to be liberal and new from the outside (and the marches themselves were certainly a positive, though fleeting contemporary result of modernization in that they exercised the right of universal free speech), the way of living defended was one that nevertheless predates the modernization period in Istanbul.[8]

The organized assaults on the street dog population in the form of mass poisonings and the general lack of enforcement for existing animal protection laws are the main target of contemporary animal rights activists. However, a general lack of human compassion for street dogs in Istanbul, and Turkey at large, is often noted by animal rights activists, Turkish and non-Turkish, in various online media, particularly in English. The Istanbul street dog and its social history is a long one, however, and one that requires scrutiny and deliberation if we wish to consider the animal in a context not solely dependent on definitions of human–animal relations grounded in Western ontology. To conclude that cruelty to animals in Turkey is an isolated, contemporary issue, one to be "fixed," is to misrepresent the case of the Istanbul street dog. Action against abuse requires an objective consideration of the historical, ideological, and philosophical background of the animal and the city in order to address more profoundly, and thus more honestly, what is too easily summarized on contemporary websites as a one-solution problem.

What is often presented in the print and nonprint media alike, as a universal, global attitude toward the street animal issue can be seen to be primarily a Western European and North American one. A common contemporary response, as far as organized action in Istanbul is concerned, is one that promotes the 2004 Animal Welfare Act, but downplays the "return" component of the "Catch, Neuter and Return" plan. It argues for animal adoption as the most humane alternative to poison and exile. The alternative to extermination in the case of the European street dog was, of course, domestication. The dogs that disappeared from the urban streets of twentieth-century Europe—along with the chickens, rabbits, and other small farm animals—reappeared on leashes and chains, behind fences and apartment windows. As Harriet Ritvo notes in "Animal Planet," "[I]n affluent cities … utilitarian animals have been replaced by burgeoning pet populations" (Ritvo 137). And although Ritvo is referring to affluent cities in the United States in her article, her observation is applicable to cities across the developing globe. The Iranian authority's observation of the rise of the domestic dog population is statistically true.

Considering the influential role of Westernization in the history of Turkey, it is not surprising that contemporary efforts to address the street dog problem in Istanbul often refer back, as it were, to Western solutions to urban animal problems. Contemporary animal rescue organizations offer information and links for people who wish to bring street dogs into their homes. Free adoption services are offered to foreigners who wish to take or import "homeless" animals abroad.[9] Though more often done with Turkish street cats (their size making them more viable air cargo than Istanbul street dogs that are not, on average, small animals), this program ensures the dogs a well-fed life, though fenced and/or indoors, and, perhaps, abroad. While this scenario cannot compare in kind to starvation and cannibalism on a deserted island, it could be argued, however, that both options concern enforced exile and stem from the same source. Whether the aim is to save or kill an animal, in both cases that animal is conceived of as a passive object whose destiny is to be controlled by an active human subject. Whether the result is to ban or embrace, the dogs are no longer at liberty to inhabit the territory they have freely roamed for 400 years.

Humanist anthropomorphism often leads to projection in the case of the animal rights movement: we tend to see animals living on the streets as living in danger—as humans might be, out of doors, in intemperate weather, at 3:00 in the morning. Our pity for street animals, the tourist's desire to take them home, or the contemporary liberal Turk's urge to bring them indoors may be partly accounted for by pathetic fallacy. This descriptive phrase coined by John Ruskin in *Modernist Painters, Vol. III* (1856) was invented in order to criticize the excesses of late-Romanticism, the tendency of fanciful, emotionally indulgent poets to graft human feelings onto things in the natural world, from sunsets to nightingales. In similar ways, we pity street animals because we project human needs and desires (preferably centrally heated ones) on a natural world we can conceive of only in human, often middle- or upper-middleclass, terms. It is true that domesticated dogs become as alien to the streets as they are to the wild. Like us, because of us, they are no longer able to survive without us. A pet dog left out overnight on the streets of Istanbul may very well not be there in the morning.

While ecofeminism has been influential in applied ecotheory in the form of animal rights activism, the move to extend human sympathy to nature in ecofeminism can become interventionist. A view of nature as a balanced organism, guided by a community ethics in which "competition only appears to be competition" but is really "cooperation, symbiosis, and interdependence" can become a form of reductive humanism that reinforces pity (Sideris 51). Unscientific data can lead to an outmoded romantic ecology, which, despite our best intentions, reinforces a model of humans as controllers rather than participants in the world around them (Gustafson in Sideris 43). Arguing for a return to scientific evolutionary theory in our social justice programs for animals, Sideris warns that "a general, positive reaction of love or affection may also be misapplied, as when we desire to treat a wild animal as though it were our pet dog or cat" (Sideris 246).

Post-humanist place consciousness and Istanbul

A defense of Darwinian evolutionary theory in a theocentric, Christian ecological argument concerning human responsibility to animals is an interesting testament to the idea that opposing sides of an argument eventually join at either end. Sideris and Gustafson both argue that a scientifically informed theocentric approach to nature is required if we intend to avoid imposing human conditions over a world we only partially comprehend, a fundamental intention in ecotheory across the board. "If we have a natural love for wild nature, it must be qualified by considerations of what is natural *for nature* as well as for man" (Sideris 251). The two may be part of a biological whole, but we must be ready to concede that "the two may not coincide" (Sideris 251). Sallie McFague, an ecotheorist respected on both sides of what is historically a theological, scientific divide, argues that to retrain the eye to see others as subjects, rather than objects of the human, objectifying gaze, we must learn to focus on "the distance, the difference, the particularity, the uniqueness; the 'in-itselfness', the indifference, the otherness of the other" (qtd. in Sideris 252) "'Our response to natural environments,' our desire to do good," argues Sideris on McFague, "should be constrained by natural processes themselves, and by a recognition that, as human beings, our moral reasoning is inherently fraught with ambiguity" (Sideris 250). To be "constrained by natural processes" means to study what is "natural for nature," not an easy task in the latest moment of a long history of human alienation from natural processes. Both Shepard and Sideris agree, however, that bioregionalism, the study of the history of individual species in the contexts of their particular native environments, may offer the best path to understanding the unique biological and social needs of animals in our present time. Through such understanding, human communities may learn to better promote animal welfare. Respect for the integrity of animals means limiting human intervention when that intervention is grounded in human, rather than animal, terms and realities.

The rise of interest in bioregionalism can be traced back to the 1970s in the United States with the growth in popularity of Aldo Leopold's *A Sand County Almanac*, published originally in 1949. Leopold's bioregional vision offers a holistic approach to environmental studies that includes humans, but not as the center of reference for biological relationships between species. Proposing a land ethics based on natural selection, Leopold's environmental policies had an important influence on philosophers, ecologists, and nature writers in the early stages of what would become the interdisciplinary field of ecotheory. Bioregions are particular geographical areas and bioregionalists advocate a "re-inhabitation" of these spaces that is scientifically and historically informed. Knowing about the natural history of a place can help us learn how to best live in a place without compromising its local character or the other inhabitants there. This is a land ethics that seeks to transcend human-centered attitudes toward the environment that often lead to the destruction of animals and their native habitats.[10]

If we contend that bioregionalism offers a sound revisionist approach to human–animal relations because it attempts to redistribute the balance of power within a post-humanist ethics, the model nonetheless runs into problems when we attempt to apply it to urban environments. It is difficult to speak of natural processes when most of them lie underneath concrete, when trees grow only where allotted by city planners and landscape architects, and when wild life consists primarily of rodents and pigeons. This difficulty is underscored by the fact that most discourse in bioregionalism draws a line between wild animals and domestic animals. It is a line many feel compelled to defend, however, because it is often an uneasy one. Shepard, who refers to domestic dogs as slaves and "perverse and dysfunctional wol[ves]," admits he has a dog himself (Shepard 267). "Nonwild animals make claims upon us that are founded in some sense upon their 'sameness' with us," Sideris concedes in one of her final chapters entitled "Love for Nonwild Nature" (Sideris 259).

Bioregional advocates, whether secular or theocentric, agree, for the most part, that human intervention into nature has left animals like dogs and cats in a position of vulnerability vis-à-vis the natural world, thus in a position of dependence on humans. This becomes an argument for an ethic of love that binds us to special obligations to these animals. This obligation often translates in practical terms to domestication. "To turn domestic animals loose, at this point, allow them to become wild (or more accurately feral), would probably only create more suffering and death," notes Sideris in her concluding remarks (Sideris 260). This division between wild and nonwild animals can be seen to be another human-centered construct, however, one that justifies a demarcation of social and biological limits that again refers to human rather than animal needs.

Because urban alienation from nature in the West, at least since the nineteenth century, has led to the proliferation of house pets and zoos, depositories for animals that are so common now that they are held to be nearly natural and certainly universal, animals that exist outside these familiar parameters are difficult to account for and categorize. Western visitors to foreign countries with active street animal life can often only qualify those animals that wander at will as "neglected." For some, it can be argued, this pity stems from displaced guilt toward animals whose natural roaming grounds, whatever they might have been, are no longer available to them. Animals, like us, have suffered the loss of empty wild spaces in their daily lives. We assume, though at unconscious levels for the most part, that they wish to hold on to us as the last vestiges of that "original" state as we do them. We focus on the vulnerability and dependence of animals as pets because it nourishes our own sense of security when it may in fact be we who feel insecure in an outside world, we who no longer know how to live without our homes and cars.

This is not a universal longing for, or attitude to animals and animal contact, as many people who do not live in the United States or Western Europe, know, however. Urban animals who wander the streets of Mumbai and Rio, Bucharest and Istanbul, are not always vulnerable or dependent on human protection. They are certainly dependent on humans as food sources, but their greatest adversaries, besides each other, are, in fact, the humans themselves.

The presence of the street dog has historically been seen as a testament to a city's underdeveloped status, particularly by Westerners or those influenced by Western ideology. Reigning notions of progress and development and animal ownership continue to go hand in hand. The street dog thus exerts pressure on Western conceptions of the primitive because she inhabits spaces that are not clearly accounted for in our discussions of human–canine relations. Defending domestication in the name of vulnerability and dependence can be seen to be a "first world" position when we take into consideration the wily inner-city street dog in other parts of the world. The case of the Istanbul street dog puts pressure, therefore, not only on our least self-conscious, because long naturalized, interactions with animals, but also on any approach to environmental ethics that attempts to improve on these same interactions.

The virtues of uncertainty

The Istanbul street dog has always sought the distant company of humans but has had no intention of living inside their houses. The oldest ancestors of modern dogs, themselves the descendants of wolves, lived on the outskirts of human communities, feeding on human debris and rubbish. This parallel proximity, rather than co-habitation, is what continues to characterize human–canine relationship in Istanbul as in other urban centers in other parts of the world. Arguing against traditional theories of the "ontology of companion species," and thus against a human-centered model of canine domestication, Donna Haraway suggests that ancient human–canine relationships reveal "an early co-evolution, human–canine accommodation at more than one point in the story, and lots of dog agency in the drama of genetics and co-habitation" (Haraway, "Cyborgs" 365). In other words, dogs domesticated themselves. Haraway goes on to suggest, with signature wryness, that dogs perhaps even trained humans to provision or "babysit" their pups. But in all cases, in her broadening of a definition of human–canine relations, she argues that "[C]ompanion species take shape in interaction, they more than change each other; they co-constitute each other, at least partly" (Haraway, "Cyborgs" 366).

Istanbul dogs, because they have maintained their historical place on the city streets, bear peculiar witness to such a notion of co-constitution. Travelers to Istanbul as far back as records reveal have commented on their ubiquitous presence. Descriptions of street dogs, like descriptions of the Grand Bazaar, Hagia Sofia, or the "slave" markets, have always been standard guide book fare. Street dogs are historically part of the cultural landscape of Istanbul in the cosmopolitan popular conscience. French travelers to Istanbul in the seventeenth century, for example, note how city dwellers cared for the street dogs from a distance, leaving out food and supplying shelter and straw. Jean de Thévenot, who visited Istanbul in 1665, writes that wealthy people sometimes provided for the street dogs in their wills by donating money to local butchers (Aşçi 10). Street dogs, he notes, would often adopt a neighborhood, or a house.

Sadri Sema in *Eski Istanbul Hatıraları* (*Old Istanbul Memories*) describes the symbiotic, if somewhat mythologized, relationship that existed between dogs and the streets in the nineteenth century:

> The dogs found a place at every house in every neighborhood. Never going near a house they were not bound to, they stuck close to the door that suited them. The house would feed them in the morning and night; if they had puppies they would be fed separately. They were given different names and would be known by them throughout the neighborhood. In their turn the dogs would help the garbage men clean the rubbish from the street in the absence of municipal services. They were also of great help to the city police, watching at night for neighborhood strangers, attacking and chasing them away if they were poorly dressed, barking fiercely to wake the policemen and watchmen up. They often assaulted burglars, wounded arsonists, and cornered trouble makers. ("*Dunya*" 1–2)

Folkloric anecdotes like this tell us perhaps more about canine–human relations by the way they are told then by what they tell. The act of naming the dogs, for example, is given its own sentence. The naming of things in nature—a hegemonic practice performing human authority over nature since Adam in a Judeo-Christian context—is not a silent, assumed right here, however. The dog chooses her territory or address and is depicted as receiving a name in return. The relationship between the local people and the dogs is offered as one of mutuality and reciprocity, though one that seems to take place outside of, or rather in place of formal jurisdiction. Though offered in terms of folklore, a genre that highlights the exceptional in the everyday, the relationship between the local dogs and the local population foreshadows Haraway's call for a view of history that sees a "much more radical accommodation between canids and hominids on the question of tameness, mutual trust, and trainability" (366).

Falling between definitions of the domestic and the wild in his social habits—he is both and neither—the street dog's ambiguous relationship to human communities thus urges us to assess him both apart from and in concert with them, yet with no clear boundaries indicating where the former leaves off and the latter begins. If post-structuralism taught us anything that modernism did not, it taught us to extend our attention to the gaps and paradoxes in constructed texts to all phenomena as text. The Istanbul street dog, as a quintessentially ambiguous, free-ranging sign, offers thus a fitting contemporary focus of scrutiny. She leads us to question existent theories that concern her. Haraway records her despair when confronted with the "fertile and usually diseased and starving" dog population of Puerto Rico (*Manifesto*, 90–91). A US-based foundation's measures to address the problem in the form of organized importation and domestication is action she calls both "inspiring and disturbing" (*Manifesto* 89). While she finds the action "racially-tinged, sexually infused, class-saturated" and notes its "colonial tones and structures," she nonetheless refuses to "disown" it "through Puritan critique" (*Manifesto* 89). Despite the truly revolutionary ideas proposed in *The Companion Species Manifesto* and elsewhere in Haraway's oeuvre, one notes a certain loss of momentum when the focus migrates from domestic to feral dogs, however. Although Haraway exposes her struggle with the problem of the foreign street dog, she nevertheless does not engage critically, at least here, with a notion of place consciousness when place is a feral space rather than a human home, an animal shelter, or the wild.[11]

Anne Milne, in her article "Fully Mobile and AWAITING FURTHER INSTRUCTIONS: Thinking the Feral into Bioregionalism," argues that although the feral is natural to nature, it is nonetheless most often conceived of as "disruptive" and "out of place" (Milne 329). However, "thinking the feral into bioregionalism results in a dynamic, lateral, and reflexive way of approaching the feral not as a problem but as a participant" (Milne 332). Given that most ecosystem theories accept the premise that human communities marginalize animal communities due to misguided notions of progress, and in marginalizing them, either drive them toward extinction or preserve them through domestication, an animal that survives or resists these two alternatives puts interesting pressure on the discussion. But the case of the Istanbul street dog also disturbs arguments in defense of marginalization as an environmental ethics in itself. The street dogs of Istanbul appear to survive because of their marginal status, not despite it.

Historically, the dog has had an unclear mix of enemies and friends as has been noted: while some Muslims have supported the organized rounding up of dogs due to their unclean status in a conservative reading of the Quran, just as many Muslims have called for their preservation due to a universalist, though not human-centered, reading of the sanctity of life. Most practicing Muslims, however, do not take dogs into their homes as pets. Some Turks, primarily upwardly mobile and upper-class, have called for the eradication of street dogs in their support for efforts by the authority to modernize Istanbul according to a Western civic model. In more recent times, these same people have begun taking dogs into their homes, though more often in the form of imported pure breeds, rather than species street dog. Toy dogs and Golden Retrievers are special favorites in the early twenty-first century. Such breeds are preferred partly because as Yi-Fu Tuan notes in "Animal Pets: Cruelty and Affection," dogs must be trained to be domestic: they "must not have too much vigor and initiative if in a house. They must learn to lie still for hours" (Tuan 148). Pet dogs as status symbols on leashes in Istanbul offer stark contrasts to their unfettered cousins hanging around unceremoniously on the streets. Like city dwellers and their sequestered pets in the West, it may be argued that the Istanbul bourgeoisie and their dogs have arrived at similar fates. John Berger notes that the "small family living unit lacks space, earth, other animals, seasons, [and] natural temperatures" (Berger 14). This, he says, is part of the "material process which lies behind the truism that pets come to resemble their masters or mistresses" (Berger 14). The contrast created by the presence of an alternative form of dog life in Istanbul adds acumen to Berger's further observation about human–canine relations: "the autonomy of both partners has been lost … the animal has become dependent on its owner for every physical need … the parallelism of their separate lives has been destroyed" (Berger 14).

Through Istanbul history, the man and woman on the street, as it were, have been the dogs' primary human cohorts. Less invested in the fixities dictated by both conservative Islamic and Western ideological frames of reference, due, in part, to the precarious experience of their own lives and livelihoods, these people have for centuries lived with the coming and going of unrestrained dogs. One should not romanticize this relationship in an anthropomorphic reading of friendship however: the man and woman on the street—though not usually the same ones—just as often throw a rock at the dogs as a piece of bread. One would not characterize them as the dog's friend, in a common reading of the term. And street dogs in Istanbul often avoid unknown humans when alone and ignore them when in groups. Their evasion and disinterest can be troubling, even disarming to a foreign visitor used to the obsequious attention of human-friendly domestic dogs. The human–canine relationship is thus part antagonism, part camaraderie, a relationship based on mutual fear and some respect that has perhaps best preserved the dog's nascent ambiguous nature in the case of Istanbul.

Bioregionalism, which is based in part on an evolutionary understanding of life and ecology, makes room in its theoretical base for strife and struggle in the animal world. To avoid death's role in the preservation of life is to avoid the reality of nature. Though Darwin resisted the application of his theory of evolution to human communities, the case of the Istanbul street dog reinforces the bioregional argument that human communities can and must learn something about their immediate animal world if they hope to participate in that world rather than merely control it. While foreigners often cite Turkish cruelty to dogs, they also record their amazement at the ubiquitous presence of an animal that hardly seems to notice the passing of the city around them. Mark Twain says the following of the Istanbul street dog in his travel narrative *Innocents Abroad*, his record, part fiction, part fact, of his 1867 visit to Istanbul:

> I find them everywhere, but not in strong force. The most I have found together has been about ten or twenty. And night or day a fair proportion of them were sound asleep. Those that were not asleep always looked as if they wanted to be. I never saw such utterly wretched, starving, sad-visaged, brokenhearted looking curs in my life. It seemed a grim satire to accuse such brutes as these of taking things by force of arms. They hardly seem to have strength enough or ambition enough to walk across the street—I do not know that I have seen one walk that far yet. ... In their faces is a settled expression of melancholy, and air of hopeless despondency ... In the Grand Rue the dogs have a sort of air born of being obliged to get out of the way of many carriages every day—and that expression one recognizes in a moment.

It does not exist upon the face of any dog without the confines of that street. All others sleep placidly and keep no watch. They would not move, though the Sultan himself passed by. (265–266)

Jeffery Mousaieff Masson and Susan McCarthy, in "Grief, Sadness, and the Bones of Elephants," write that "unpredictable, ambiguous abuse and suffering leads to a passivity in animals," something they call "a learned passivity" (Masson 97–98). This theory may account for the Istanbul street dog's historically abject attitude toward humans as noted in characteristically satirical terms here by Twain, but only partly. While she may not always engage actively in the human activity around him, the street dog nonetheless remains a vigorous survivor, despite human abuse. Many people living in Istanbul at present say they don't like the street dogs, and many admit that it is because they are afraid of them. Fear, however, is usually what motivates cruelty, and lack of understanding or ambiguity is most often the source of fear. Ambiguity is thus linked to cycles of fear and cruelty; a link that is relevant at all levels of human response to street dogs, from physical abuse, to the mental abuse that comes with locking an animal up. Twain's observation of the preservation but abuse of street dogs in 1910 still resonates today:

> The people are loath to kill them—do not kill them, in fact. The Turks have an innate antipathy to taking the life of a dumb animal, it is said. But they do worse. They hang and kick and stone and scald these wretched creatures to the very verge of death, and then leave them to live and suffer. (Twain 267)

It is precisely the ambiguity of the Istanbul street dog that has defined her for the past 400 years. It could therefore be argued that it is the contemporary Turk's own problem with this ambiguity that, in cases of cruelty, hinders his relationship with the animals. Because Westerners responded to their own ambiguous relationship to street animals by either exterminating or domesticating them long ago, contemporary Western, or Western-influenced commentary criticizing the state of the Istanbul dogs must be contextualized accordingly. Any theoretical approach to the animals must include the historical layers of demonization that have led to a lingering deep fear in the community.

There are many Istanbulers, however, who neither fear nor abuse the dogs. They are the people who honor the old unwritten rules of cohabitation. Many neighborhood shopkeepers continue to feed them on a regular basis and the dogs in turn settle in around the premises, sometimes informally guarding the territorial boundaries of their food source. As in the nineteenth-century accounts, they are often given names "in return." Freelance garbage collectors and itinerate people are often accompanied by a dog or small group of dogs as they go about their rounds sifting through the city's refuse for renewables and sustenance. Students and local women share what is left over. Feeding the dogs is considered more than casual charity by many people; it is considered a civic duty that is simultaneously a moral, even a spiritual, duty. And it may be argued that this notion of duty has roots that reach beyond both traditional Islam and Western notions of progress.[12]

The feeding of street dogs is a common subject in the literature of Sufism, a mystical branch of Islam whose influence, whether overtly acknowledged or not, continues to enjoy quiet, general appeal in many sectors of the Turkish population. In the stories, feral dogs are seen to represent virtues such as humility, fidelity, and gratitude, or are the recipients of kindness, often in the form of food, due to the presence of these virtues in humans. These humans are sometimes great Sufi masters as in the following example from the *Manāqeb al: ārefīn* in which a story is told of Rumi clandestinely securing fine food for a dog lying with her puppies in a 'derelict site': 'I watched, confounded by his kindness and his compassion, as he gave all the food to the dog. He then said to me, 'This poor creature has had nothing to eat for a whole week. She is unable to forage because of her puppies. God heard her appeal and commanded me to look after her" (qtd. in Nurbakhsh 16).[13] Another story from the *Nafahāt al-Uns* tells of another Sufi master who while on a Pilgrimage sees a thirsty dog in the desert: "He called out for anyone willing to buy the merit of seventy Pilgrimages with a drink of water. Finding a purchaser, he gave the water to the dog, saying, This is better than all my Pilgrimages for the Prophet has said, 'For every warm-blooded creature that one serves there is a reward' " (qtd. in Nurbakhsh 14).[14]

The ethos of humility and gratitude found in Sufism's interpretations of the teachings of the Quran, and represented in many anecdotes featuring feral dogs, reflects what Serra Tlili in *Animals in the Quran* notes is an ecotheological ethos found in many of the exegeses of the Quran, the *Hadith*, as well as the Quran itself when close attention is paid to the language of the texts concerning animal–human relations. In her study of *tadhlīl*, or the role of so-called subjugation in the status and function of nonhuman animals, Tlili argues that emphasis is consistently placed on a relationship based on grace rather than dominion, and that animal interests, particularly concerning pain, and the protection of animal rights, particularly in the form of kind treatment, are integral to the teachings of the Quran (Tlili 91). She argues that in a theocentric view based on the language of the Quran, humans will be punished for mistreating animals.

In some Sufi literature dogs are associated with nafs, or bodily urges and desires, "creating trouble ... ready to bite, whether one attacks it or leaves it alone" (Nurbakhsh 75). Tlili argues that despite textual evidence to the contrary, a description of animals as beings worthy of grace "conflicts with general ways humans experience non-human animals ... and with many of the perceptions that Muslims in general hold of other species" (Tlili 139). The situation is made particularly difficult by the fact that animals are presumed to lack rational faculties. Tlili makes an argument for the acknowledgment in the Quran of alternative ways of knowing, however; she quotes the exegete ibn Jarīr al-Tabarī (d 923) who, paraphrasing the Quran, writes: "He created them as various species. They have knowledge as you do, they manage that for which they have been created as you do" (qtd. in Tlili 143). Tlili suggests that this is an ecotheological view: the fact that human and nonhuman animals do not share the same type of knowledge does not imply that what other animals know does not qualify as knowledge. Similarly, the fact that nonhuman animals do not live or manage their lives the way humans do should not lead to assumptions that they have no system, as each species lives its life the way it is intended to (by God) (Tlili 143).

Islamic wisdom that teaches stewardship of the underdog, whether in mainstream or Sufistic readings of the Quran, is taken literally at face value in many quarters of Istanbul. One of the most frequently cited passages of the Quran concerning animals is from *Surah* 6, verse 38, which reads: "There is not an animal in the earth, nor a flying creature flying on two wings, but they are peoples like you. We have neglected nothing in the Book (of our decrees). Then unto their lord they will be gathered" (qtd. in Tlili 138).[15] The honoring of this Islamic animal ethics plays out in real time in the feeding of the dogs. People who feed them know they are taking part in a custom with deeper ethical and spiritual significance, even though the rite is casually enacted.

Running counter to this tradition of supporting the dogs is a new wave of modernization activity in the city, however. There has been a significant reduction in street dog populations in neighborhoods undergoing gentrification in recent years. Like urban gentrification processes worldwide, the areas began as historical, but dilapidated and poor. Artists, intellectuals, and bohemians moved in alongside the local population bringing new color and alternative lifestyles. Money followed, sometimes in the form of foreign investment. Many of the neighborhoods, for example, the old Galata district, have become popular tourist destinations. The streets are now cleaner; garbage is collected on a more regular basis. Because many newer residents of these old neighborhoods, often foreigners, are unaware or uninterested in the cultural history of their other neighbors, the street dogs, the centuries-old feeding rituals are often not honored. Improved sanitation and lack of hospitality are proving more effective at reducing the dog populations than exile on deserted islands or poison.

It is true that alpha males and females can become aggressive at times. Some are not familiar with joggers and can "chase them away." Rabies, despite active rumors to the contrary, is virtually nonexistent thanks to the Animal Welfare Act and the subsequent vaccination programs sponsored by the municipalities. The dogs can be thus feared and disliked for reasons not necessarily rooted in conservative Islamic prejudice or Westernization programs. It may be argued, however, that a certain amount of fear can be a good thing if it leads to respect for difference. When there is enough insecurity in peoples' minds to remind them that the dogs are not anthropomorphic extensions of humans, then uncertainty can function in favor of the dogs.

If the dogs are understood as a distinctive part of a region's historical, cultural, and natural heritage, then it is important to think critically about how to best live with the dogs on mutually agreeable terms. What, for example, might be the best way to ensure the safety of humans (who are also natural beings despite their belief to the contrary) against potentially dangerous members of the canine community, but without harming that community as a whole? History has taught us that one man, or a few men gone wrong, does not mean the entire race must be systematically punished or wiped out. While a certain amount of fear may be good, a disproportionate will to dominate warrants a defensive response from any animal, including humans. It is known that when there is enough food for everybody, levels of aggression go down on the streets. Living together in evolutionary terms means the maintenance of a sustained interconnectedness; but this interdependence which "is not a solution to strife but a *source* of it" must also be understood as mutually resistant (Sideris 222). Though it may be hard for Western-educated people to switch or dissolve categories that come too close to their own homes, it is necessary if we wish to apply our own tough terms to the reality of streets beyond our own.

An ecocritical consideration of the case of the Istanbul street dog can thus lead us down a number of interesting avenues. Neither wild, nor domesticated, a permanent fact of the city, the animal creates difficulties and defies categories on many fronts. A consideration of what is working in a city that at times manages, against great odds, to value the dog as a separate, partially indifferent being, can reinforce the post-humanist agendas of theoreticians and activists alike. Furthermore, the case of the street dog may help us identify the limitations that persist in fields focusing on environmental ethics, including animal ethics, limitations that prevent them from having more relevance beyond their traditional geographical borders. The fact that there are Turkish laws that have responded to the historical presence of the feral dogs and that acknowledge their right to remain in their traditional roaming grounds, the streets, is in itself a possible model for a post-humanist conception of the modern urban animal. Turning a domestic dog loose, allowing them to go feral once again, would certainly lead to chaos and despair, for animals and humans. Suffering and death would certainly rise, but in country like the United States that on the whole "advocates death control" and not enough "birth control," such a rise might be instructive (Shepard 320).

To allow dogs to wander in the grey areas where they live if given a choice means suspending the various forms of *intifada* against them in the case of Istanbul. An informed understanding of their environmental conditions, past and present, can reduce human misconceptions and subsequent fears about him. A true respect for the "radical, plural otherness" of the street dog would require a change of consciousness, one that would allow us to live with the animal on the edge of our categories for it, not just in theory, but in practice. This may demand an attitude toward ambiguity that pushes the limits of civilized behavior. And if all systems fail, a belief in the universal sanctity of all life, not just human life, may be what ensures his survival most effectively.

Ecopoetics, Dead Metaphors, and Bird Migration: The Bosporus Passage of the European White Stork

One often comes across the European White Stork (Ciconia ciconia) in the poetic geography of Istanbul. These long-distance migratory birds travel across the Dardanelles and along the Bosporus tracking the arrival of spring or anticipating the departure of autumn depending on the seasonal direction of the flight pattern. The reliable, yet remarkable, migration of these birds is a constant against which poets work through various themes of stasis and flux. Attila Ilhan, the modernist Turkish poet whom the late literary critic and writer Talat Halman admired for his "exploratory zeal" and "exhaustive metaphoric preoccupation" with the Turkish language, features the passage of the storks in his poem "One Three Five," a poem that contrasts movement in the natural world with the paralysis of the human speaker at the center of the poem:

> you who are that lonely cloud in the cold sky
> holding the familiar loneliness by the hand
> in the midst of a generous blue
> say that you are forgotten
>
> the seas roll forward with a great uproar
> you are coming up against time
> one three and five the storks are gone now
> now a haven in darkness calls you
> a haven where you are forgotten not forgotten where you are unknown
>
> (Halman 1)[1]

In another poem by Ilhan, "Maria Missakian," storks again mark the passage of the season, here the quickening of winter weather:

> if I could hide in her shadow at night
> the clouds growing in the sky
> if I could listen to the rain and tell
> lightning breaking
> if they left us in the streets
> if the storks left because of the cold
> never looking back once
> it's night again attila ilhan
> and you're alone a stranger of the autumn.
>
> (İlhan "one," 17)

Again, the poetic persona stands apart from the seasonal flux, seemingly trapped in a dislocated human consciousness whose conditional status (the "if" of the anaphoric "I") contrasts with the certainty of natural phenomena. As "a stranger of autumn" the speaker, unlike the migrating storks, does not know where or how to go.

Poetry has always relied on the natural world as compass, whether the geography be external or internal. While poetic engagement with nature has often been aestheticized and idealized, many twentieth-century poets have also relied on the natural world as immutable fact, a material given that often functions as the stabilizing referent in metaphoric constructions. In these two examples from Ilhan, the departure of the migratory birds signals a reality beyond the page, an avian truth that anchors the poems in biological constancy. The birds allow for the contrastive function of the human metaphors. The entanglement of poetry and the environments from which it emerges, or with which it engages, is nothing new. Postindustrial urban culture in the twentieth century, whether the United States or Turkey, has taken nature as a referent in new directions, however. As writers and readers have become increasingly aware of the depth and breadth of human manipulations of the environment, the place of nature in poetry has in many ways become further solidified in its role as a constant and in contrast to the vagaries of human activity. This new sense of emergency in the twenty-first century has led to a poetics and poesis now often categorized under the rubric Ecopoetics.

In an interview conducted at a 2011 literary conference that brought together authors, artists, farmers, and environmentalists in northern California, the American poet Brenda Hillman describes Ecopoetics as an approach to poetry and nature that "evokes a whole picture of the relationships between the human and the nonhuman" (Hume 754). Evelyn Reilly, another participating American poet, notes that there are multiple ways that Ecopoetics runs through poetry: it might be in poetry that engages the environmental sciences directly, or experiments with formal structures patterned after organic processes, or promotes activism (Hume 755). But what Reilly also notes is that "the ecopoetical predates us": "I often detect the ecopoetic in work that has no such intention, but which is colored by an ambient ethos of reframing the human within the ecological" (Hume 755).

It is this ambient ecopoetical ethos that will be the driving force of the ensuing argument. In it I will suggest that the scientific facts of nature that poetry historically protects and preserves may function as a check on modern environmental crises. To discuss twentieth-century Turkish poems in the context of current developments in North American ecopoetical theory runs the risk of weighing in on the problems of an "emerging economy" according to the hierarchical standards of a first world nation. As Elizabeth DeLoughrey and George B. Handley argue in the introduction to *Postcolonial Ecologies*, "[m]uch has been made of the irreconcilable differences between postcolonial concerns and the environmentalism of the privileged north in terms of their approaches to issues such as economy, development, conservation ... consumption, militarism, and (over) population" (DeLoughrey 21). But at the same time although environmental crises may stem from the economic and cultural conditions of particular nations, more often than not they are the result of activities by larger multinational projects. In all cases, the effects of these crises transcend national borders. All environmental problems are ultimately of global concern and postcolonial Ecocriticism, while it warns against the dangers of misrepresentation, also lays out important strategies for thinking about ways "to speak in ethical terms about the global and the local without reducing difference and without instituting old structural hierarchies" (DeLoughery 25).

The condition of one species of migratory bird is not the exclusive concern of one nation. An examination of the Istanbul passage of the European White Stork in its current poetic, scientific, and socioeconomic context offers a local window onto a global impasse. Current mega-projects in the environs of Istanbul that are either complete or in advanced stages of production pose serious hazards to migratory bird populations that rely on these construction sites for stopover and resting habitat during spring and winter migrations. The European White Stork is particularly vulnerable. A consideration of the recurrent figure of the stork in various twentieth-century Turkish poems suggests that the art and science tend to concur where the bird is concerned. The mega-projects that embody current twenty-first-century goals for economic progress and modernization in Turkey are rising in direct contradistinction to these alternative fields in the humanities.

The European White Stork migrates in large family flocks. The traditional route of migration takes them from spring breeding grounds in Central and Eastern Europe around the western end of the Black Sea, across Anatolia and around the eastern coast of the Mediterranean Sea to wintering habitats in East Africa (Cox 233). Storks, like cranes, migrate diurnally, or during daylight hours, meaning they use the energy of the sun. They depend upon rising columns of warm air or thermals that are the result of solar radiation or the heating of the earth's surface by the sun. "This kind of atmospheric structure, which the birds can use like an elevator to gain altitude with virtually no expenditure of their own energy, exists only in the daytime" and particularly during the warmer portions of the day (Cox 14). White Storks have broad but short breastbones and their bodies are small in comparison to their long wings, necks, and legs which makes them strong flyers even as they conserve energy by keeping their wings motionless as they let the thermals do their work for them (Van Grouw 174). Soaring birds like storks can fly higher than 22,000 feet (6,700 m), though altitude is affected by weather conditions such as tail and head winds and cloud conditions. Though large flocks of storks often pass silently above the city of Istanbul at great distances, it is also common to see and hear smaller flocks that descend, circling on thermals.

Gliding birds like storks prefer to cross narrow bodies of water rather than open seas and the European White Storks use Istanbul and the Bosporus Straits for their migration route. In his study of the migrating stork populations passing through Istanbul, Dr. Zeynel Arslangündoğdu, a Forest Industry Engineer at Istanbul University, notes in 2011 that approximately 400,000 Ciconia ciconia pass through Istanbul every year (Arslangündoğdu 78). Under normal conditions they can be seen on the hills and ridges of Üsküdar-Çamlıca and Beykoz-Toygatepe during fall migration south in

August, September, and October and after spending the winter in Africa migrating north in March, April, and May through the crests of Sarıyer to their spring grounds in Europe (Arslangündoğdu 77). European White Storks, like other migratory birds that pass through Turkey, have used this route for tens of thousands of years.

These scientific facts are observable phenomena in Istanbul. The cyclical movements of the storks function as living clocks and calendars for the urban inhabitants that witness this wild passage that the Bosporus affords. This traditionally predictable arrival and departure of the migratory European White Stork populations also function as a homing device for Turkish poets. The bird comes into being through migratory action. It is perhaps the only thing that is generally known of this resident migrant, the fact that she comes and then goes like circadian clockwork. The thermals on which she glides are the same winds that herald and dispatch the temperate seasons on the 41st parallel north that Istanbul occupies. In the "new logbook of old birds" that makes up Akgün Akova's poem "A Bird's-Eye View," storks play their anticipated migratory role along with an aviary of other Anatolian birds and their emblematic functions, and all in dedication to the look in a loved one's eyes (Akova 14):

> your look my love
> your look
> is that of a swallow flying cheek to cheek with the clouds
> an albatross who knows the meaning of the abyss
> a pigeon on rainy days, bringing on a revolution of the sun
> your look
> is that of a dove making love to my voice in the phone booth
> a crane soaring over the thunder
> an eagle lending a wing to the struggle of labour
> your look my love
> your look
> a stork that says "I must go so far away to find myself"
> a sparrow that says "You'll lose those that are near to you if you go away"
>
> (Akova 14)

In these lines each bird is assigned a role that is biologically accurate at the core of its metaphorical language. The swallow that feeds in mid-air at dusk flies "cheek to cheek with the clouds." The albatross that soars at great heights and also dives for its preferred deep-sea diet "knows the meaning of the abyss." The sparrow that prefers to stay close to human settlements rather than wild woodlands or grasslands is assigned the language of proximity: "You'll lose those that are near to you if you go away." The stork's actions are predictable, and the philosophical potential of the metaphor is contingent on the ornithological rhythms: the stork says, "I must go so far away to find myself." Again, movement is the constant. The long-distance travel of storks, unlike the domestic contiguity of sparrows, suggests another equally cogent message: survival depends on the continuous rhythm of intercontinental departure and return. Unacknowledged in this allusion is the reality that breeding numbers in Eastern Europe depend on food supplies in East Africa. Strong offspring wintering in Kenya depend on ample nesting habitat in Lithuania. For species human that might look to the bird as an existential sign, it says there is life in flux, death in stasis. In the poem, this is what the eyes of the lover say to the "sky" that is the speaker's face.

In another Turkish poem, "The Storks," by Ali Mümtaz Arolat, the autumn migration is introduced as a craving for winter, for night:

> How chill is the autumn this evening,
> Time itself is longing to see the night.
> Roll down the white curtains
> On which storks fly with yearning.
>
> (Arolat lines 1–4)

The voice covets a moment of suspended time. The only movement is a configuration of flying storks on white curtains. The domestic curtains are a screen across which a familiar, yet foreign, scene is projected by natural moonlight.

> Don't turn on the lamp thinking on my desk,
> Let our room stay dark;
> Let us see the moon rising on the horizon
> Of the night, let it fall on our curtain.
>
> (Arolat lines 5–8)

The speaker defers the intrusion of artificial lighting and the thinking it facilitates. This is a vision of instinctive flight and beauty. If all is still and suspended locally, the storks passing in autumn from north to south flood the scene with contrast and the color of foreign climates:

> The storks flying on our curtain
> Now by the light of the moon, will then appear to be
> Storks passing by, from a foreign,
> Far away, blue climate.
>
> (Arolat lines 9–12)

If home is dark with evening, the storks introduce blue daylight to the poem. Storks present time in motion, and with this motion comes a hint of the sensual:

> Then we will forget about love and longing
> And as our tired hearts beat with joy
> We will think this tumultuous sound in our breast to be
> That of wing beats.
>
> (Arolat lines 13–16)

Love has been added to the longing that begins and ends the short poem. The "tumultuous" "wing beats" of the migrating storks fuse with a physical joy that concludes the passage and the poem.

There is a brief reference to the seasonal passage of storks in Edip Cansever's longer poem "Friends." It is a reference that holds the poem in time and place as memory diffuses the poem's landscape. It is a reference that also announces a final leave-taking of the speaker toward an unspecified future. The present moment is sunset in autumn: the place, the juncture of the Golden Horn and the Bosporus at the Galata Bridge. The speaker has been traveling back in time to 1971 and from Istanbul to Izmir and back. He addresses an unidentified listener directly throughout the poem, musing on death and love as sources of his poems and those of fellow Turkish writers such as Ahmet Oktay. When a group of storks enter the poem, travel joins death, love and poetry as controlling leitmotifs: "Was it a vast love or what/Travelling across all the ages of the earth," he asks of the poetic drive (Cansever lines 85–86). With this reference to travel the speaker gives "a good cleaning to the lenses of my glasses" and observes with clarity the present moment:

> I look at the sky with squinted eyes
> A mustering of storks is travelling south

Above Yeni Cami
Flying for one last time
The pink gates of the city begin to melt
Sunset!

(Cansever lines 95–101)

A few lines later, the storks at sunset "spill melancholy" or *hüzün* (an agreeable sadness with no exact translation in English)[2] on the face of fellow writer Fethi Naci (Cansever line 109). It is the season for departure. The migrating storks present separate bodies traveling in formation, a union of particulars, "To be broken, but together/To be together, but unbroken" (Cansever lines 110–111). The figure corresponds to the condition of the congregation of poets whose hearts travel together "in an old and battered bus" (Cansever line 112). The poem will continue circling for several stanzas, but this introduction of storks migrating south for the winter announces a departure for the speaker, a letting go even as it seems to solidify a purpose for the poetic arts in a country where writers experience uneasy nights: "the sleeplessness of honor/Of being silenced":

A suitcase in my hand, I'm wandering around
It's as if I'm always about to go somewhere
Pigeons land on my hair on my wrists
They fly
A leaf from a plane tree falls next to my feet
Bone-dry
I take it in my hands, I draw my heart on it
My heart, I say
Even if it's tired, even if it's wounded, belongs to all of us.

(Cansever lines 106, 149–157)

The poems are the shared experiences of the country and its poets. The migratory birds are not a metaphor for hope necessarily, but they present to the poem the possibility, the inevitability of change.

In these three examples from modern Turkish poetry, stork migration functions as a score for variations on themes of departure and return, for movement and flux as life forces. These are not themes founded on fancy alone, but are rooted in empirical as well as theoretical nature. As in Nâzım Hikmet's poem, "On Ibrahim Balaban's Painting 'Spring,'" discussed in Chapter 2 in which the writer references a stork "just back from Egypt" in order to highlight not only the richness of Anatolian wildlife, but also the fluidity of movement not afforded the narrator confined in prison, these poems written later in the century rely on migratory movement as a biotic given.

Ornithological data corroborate the journey metaphors, particularly in terms of the deep-seated nature of the migratory impulse. The ancient seasonal journey of long-distance migratory birds appears to be the result of a combination of genetics and environment. Obligate migrants are those birds who migrate annually while some birds undergo irruptive migration, meaning some years they emigrate and some years they don't. Others undertake partial migration, meaning some remain sedentary while some migrate. Kenneth P. Able in *Gathering of Angels: Migratory Birds and Their Ecology* suggests that while these differences in migration behavior require more study, lab tests have shown that obligate migrants like storks display physiological changes that are strongly triggered by circadian rhythms connected to annual seasonal changes (Able 9). Migration has evolved within lineages of birds, and different species will respond to changes in the environment in various ways. While the behavior of some birds changes according to immediate outside conditions such as food availability, obligate migrants seem to display more rigid internal behavior controls. Migration has been seen to be triggered before any change in immediate environmental conditions is evident (Able 9). The conservative evolutionary nature of birds with more "rigidly programmed, internally controlled migratory habits" is less able to adapt to rapid change in an environment Able notes (Able 9). Genetics, therefore, can partially explain the consistent arrival and departure of the storks over the Bosporus for 10,000 or more years. The migration routes used by birds like the European White Stork appear to have much to do with deep evolutionary predispositions. Thus, in the case of the storks, their poetic function could be said to have genetic roots: their flight and what it affords the imagination are an ancient *koinos topos*, a "common place." The long-distance migratory bird is a deep given in the poetic lexicon. In the examples from twentieth-century Turkish poems offered here, the conservative evolutionary makeup of the bird is assumed. The poets may be less confident about the permanence of human conditions in the poems, isolation and love may alter a speaker's reality, but there is no doubt that the birds will come and go. This much is sure.

There are changes in the air due to changes on land, however. The terrain that has served as stopover habitat along the Bosporus for long-distance gliding birds like storks is under increased pressure due to climate change and direct human impact on the environment. The European White Storks are thus vulnerable on at least two fronts. First, change imposed on habitat means change imposed on the species that rely on it; second, genetics make this particular bird slow to change. Because these birds may be less able to biologically adjust to rapidly changing environmental conditions, it could be argued that it is no longer certain that the migratory stork will continue to function as a permanent common place in the poetic production of the local culture. Well-known ornithologist John Rappole argues in *The Avian Migrant: The Biology of Bird Migration* that it is difficult to determine precisely how "anthropogenic factors" cause bird mortality. He repeatedly brings to our attention "the complexity of the migrant life cycle and the incomplete state of our understanding of that complexity" (Rappole 295). He argues that because information about migratory bird populations only goes back a half century, there is a lack of the "long term data-sets" necessary for assessing population decline; thus much environmental science used in conservation is based on inference rather than hard science (Rappole 214, 225). He argues that more species-specific studies are necessary but allows that there are certain "density dependent factors" that are responsible for significant long-term decline in some migratory bird populations, significantly in our case, stopover habitat loss (Rappole 224).

With Rappole's cautionary approach to conservation in mind it is still possible to identify what threatens them in general terms. Habitat loss is the primary culprit, both the result of macro-level climate change and direct human impact on specific migratory bird habitats. George Cox in *Bird Migration and Global Change* notes that long-distance migrants between Eurasia and Sub-Saharan Africa, birds like storks, are particularly at risk because it is predicted that the Mediterranean region will be the area of Europe most vulnerable to global climate change: "Climatic warming and changes in rainfall patterns imply considerable modifications of seasonal patterns of food availability for both short-term and long-distance migratory birds" in this region (Cox 43). Cox sites various studies that show declines in migratory bird populations: the Pan-European Common Bird Monitory Project "covering all countries of

Western Europe, found that from 1990 to 2005, population trends for 80% of the forty long-distance migrants for which adequate data were available showed declines"; The Royal Society for the Protection of Birds also concluded that "27–37 species migrating to Sub-Saharan Africa have declined in numbers" (Cox 112).

Aggravating the larger problem of climate change are the site-specific problems of habitat loss. Migratory birds like storks rely on various habitats in different parts of the globe. They are particularly vulnerable to habitat change because of this reliance on a "range of seasonal environments" (Cox 251). The threat list includes habitat loss and habitat fragmentation in breeding, post-breeding, stopover, and winter environments. The destruction of any of these can create problems for the traveling bird. "Agriculture and urban development have transformed about 29% of the earth's natural ecosystems, particularly grasslands, savannas, and forests" (Cox 52). The fragmentation of any of these landscapes can create problems for long-distance gliding birds at all stages of migration. Weather conditions can change at the "edge zones" of fragmented ecosystems, meaning interior and exterior conditions differ leading to various problems from breeding conditions to vegetation supply (Cox 52). This is a global problem, a global condition that becomes a species-specific problem in the case of migratory birds. In *Their Fate Is Our Fate: How Birds Foretell Threat to Our Health and Our World*, Peter Doherty argues that migratory birds "serve as sentinels, sampling the health of the air, seas, forests and grasslands" (Doherty 8). Learning what distresses migratory birds can tell us much about the health of parts of the planet that are far from our own. Birds like migratory storks remind us that it is ultimately impossible to separate the local from the global.[3]

In *Storks, Ibises and Spoonbills of the World*, James A. Hancock, James A. Kushlan, and M. Philip Kahl report on the general decline of European White Stork populations in Western Europe. The list of reasons for the decline includes the destruction or alteration of feeding areas in breeding ranges; reduced food supply in winter range due to, for example, drought and insecticides; chemical pollution in summer and winter ranges (Hancock 102). The principal reason for these declines and reductions, however, is loss of habitat owing to "development, industrialization, and intense agriculture in Western Europe" (Hancock 102). They note that while European White

Stork populations have declined in Western Europe, they have increased in Eastern Europe, citing slower economic growth as the potential reason (Hancock 102).

The conflict between economic growth and the health of local wildlife puts an interesting twist on the story of the migrating storks in Turkey, a story that Gernant Magnin and Murat Yarar address in their introduction to *Important Bird Areas in Turkey*. In this valuable survey of regional avian life in Turkey the authors begin by addressing the topic of economic development in the nation. They begin their discussion with the 1947 Marshall Plan that led to large-scale investment in agricultural equipment (imported from the United States) and rapid agricultural development in Turkey. The DSI (State Water Works), founded in 1953, continued the project of the Marshall Plan, its primary tasks being "flood control, irrigation, reclamation of marshes, production of hydro-power, provision of drinking water and 'taming of rivers'" (Magnin 19). As production increased and the immediate living conditions of some sectors of the population improved, the land suffered, however: "conversion, flood protection, reclamation, damming, water diversion and forest clearing have caused extensive damage to Turkey's natural environment, in particular wetland-, steppe-, grassland-, and forest habitat" (Magnin 22). In their section on the site-specific area of the Bosporus (Boğaziçi), Magnin and Yarar note the various environmental issues that threaten European White Stork conservation in the area. The rapid post-1970 expansion of Istanbul has meant that migratory birds can no longer roost overnight before crossing the Bosporus. They are forced to search for areas "often several tens of kilometers away from the Strait" (Magnin 44). Storks in particular are affected by development because the meadows and large open areas they require for stopover food and habitat are disappearing to legal and illegal housing, "vast industrial complexes," mining, and road building (Magnin 44).

Zeynel Arslangündoğdu brings the story of the conflict between economic development and the European White Stork in the Bosporus closer to date in "The Effects of Future Projects in Istanbul on the Migration Routes of Birds." In this 2014 article from a collection written on the effects of Istanbul's "mega projects," namely, the third bridge, the third airport, and the Istanbul canal, Arslangündoğdu, an ornithologist at Istanbul University, points out that these projects will result in a considerable decline in the biodiversity of the region.

The bridge, the airport, and their access roads are all located on bird migration routes where according to local studies approximately 400,000 storks and 200,000 raptors and hundreds of thousands of songbird species, water birds, and coastal birds migrate during spring and fall (qtd. in Arslangündoğdu, 2011b). Ninety-four percent of the airport project site north of Istanbul is bird habitat: 81 percent consists of forest area, 9 percent lake, and 4 percent pasture, dry farmland, and heathland (qtd. in Arslangündoğdu, 2011b). Direct observation has revealed that migratory birds that fly over this area spend the night and feed in these sites. The clearing of forests and open land has destroyed these resting and stopover habitats of the migratory birds.

The current government and the construction firms they have engaged to build the mega-projects have both tried to deny and downplay the environmental damage that has been done to the region north of Istanbul. Arslangündoğdu argues that environmental impact assessment reports carried out by responsible parties have been inaccurate, insufficient, and misleading. The environment and social impact assessment report (ÇED) on the third airport issued by the Ministry of the Environment claims that there are seventeen bird species affected in the area when in fact the number is approximately 150–200 (Arslangündoğdu 4). The final ÇED for the third bridge claims that there are seventy-one species in the area when in fact there are closer to 200. No information is supplied in the report on how these species will be affected by the third bridge, and the threatened species list is incorrect (Arslangündoğdu 5). Like Rappole, Arslangündoğdu argues that more time is necessary to assess the environmental impact. The quick field surveys that were carried out by government agencies were conducted in November and December, a period when there is no migration of gliding migratory birds. Arslangündoğdu concludes that the environmental impact assessment reports of both mega-projects included only short-term ornithology studies. "In this respect, data offered are insufficient and misleading. For the aforementioned projects, it is imperative to observe the area regularly for a period of at least two years to be able to detect the seasonal distribution and density of bird migration. Results acquired through such survey will be more factual" (Arslangündoğdu 6). In all cases, Arslangündoğdu concludes, the annihilation of local migratory bird habitat caused by these latest waves of economic development will end in migratory birds no longer being able to rest and feed on one of "the most important migration routes in the Western Palearctic biogeograph[ies]" (Arslangündoğdu 1).

A 2015 story originally published in the Turkish daily newspaper *Birgün*, and re-circulated in the *North Woods Defense* website (Kuzey Ormanları Savunması) reports claims by the government and developers that bird migration routes can be altered using signal transmission technology. The local nature foundation "Doğa Derneği" has dismissed this as unscientific (kuzeyormanları). As George Cox has argued, "the migration routes used by some long-distance migrants appear to have an evolutionary basis" and because these migrants "tend to be conservative in their response to changes in breeding or non-breeding ranges," they may lack the evolutionary ability to adjust quickly enough to changes in the environment (Cox 76). In other words, birds that have been migrating along a route for 10,000 years or more will not be easily diverted by technology, no matter how advanced. Birds will continue to migrate despite the hazards. Damages incurred will be to humans as well as birds: because the migration patterns of these large-bodied birds will not adjust for aircraft, Arslangündoğdu and other scientific experts predict collisions and crashes in the future (Arslangündoğdu 4).[4]

The diminution of European White Stork habitat due to economic development in Western Europe and elsewhere has had another interesting effect. Storks have begun to look elsewhere for food: garbage dumps. One among a number of recent studies on this phenomenon is "The Foraging of White Storks Ciconia ciconia on Rubbish Dumps on Non-Breeding Grounds," by Michal Ciach and Robert Kruszyk from the University of Agriculture in Krakow, Poland. An "opportunist forager," the natural diet of Ciconia ciconia consists of earthworms, insects (mainly beetles and locusts), fish, amphibians, and small mammals (Ciach 101). Because "open habitats in large river valleys" are the main feeding places for White Storks, "human-induced habitat alternation has reduced the extent of suitable foraging areas and contributed to population declines. The species has been threatened with extinction in Western Europe" (Ciach 101). Some recent White Stork recovery has been noted, however, and increased numbers appear to be the direct result of changes in foraging behavior: "the phenomenon of regular foraging on rubbish dumps and slaughterhouse waste" (Ciach 101). The use of rubbish dumps also appears to be "common behavior" along "traditional migration routes across the Mediterranean Sea" (Ciach 102). Ciach and Kruzzyk go on to note that this behavior could have repercussions on White Stork biology and create potential threats to humans and livestock through the transmission of disease when storks nest near water sources (Ciach 103). "Anthropogenic modifications of the environment can impact the biology of species, and the distribution and breeding ecology of the White Stork is a well-known example" (Ciach 103).

The Yavuz Sultan Selim Bridge, connecting Europe and Asia by rail and road north of Istanbul, opened in August of 2016. The Istanbul Airport due to open in 2019 is expected to be one of the world's largest airports, or the largest according to the ruling party. These potential threats to bird habitat are thus *faits accomplis*. The physical landscape has been changed for many human generations to come. It is reasonably clear what these results of economic progress will have on local migratory bird habitat and thus bird populations. It is less clear how it will matter to the human beings who have taken dominion over what has been until quite recently, a shared geography. What will the reduction of a bird population really mean, especially one that only passes by and stops to rest, feed, and sometimes nest, before it takes off again for warmer or cooler climates?

If it is relatively clear what will happen to European White Storks once economic progress has claimed dominion in the region north of Istanbul, the poetic arts will help indicate what this means along the migration routes. There will be changes in the lexicon of the poems that have taken the presence of the birds for granted for hundreds of years. Twentieth-century poems featuring white storks are of course only the latest in a long Turkish poetic tradition. Folk traditions have long included the migratory stork in their zoological menageries. For ages, storks have functioned as vessels of memory and wisdom for the communities who share their geography. Mahfuz Zariç in "From Cranes to Storks: Migratory Birds in Folk Poetry" surveys the various anthropocentric functions of migratory birds in Turkish folk verse, identifying these roles in general groupings such as symbols of mindfulness of the natural world, as guides for human behavior and as testimonials to the human need for aesthetic beauty. Writing of migratory storks Zariç notes their cultural associations with hope, and good luck. In this fragment of a poem by the nineteenth-century poet-musician, Aşık Ruhsati, the stork is both "a listening ear and reminder" of the presence of God.

My troubles are enough for me
Day by day my sorrow increases
A stork comes squawking
It also speaks of God.

(Zariç 9)

But mostly storks have been historically associated with travel in the Turkish folk tradition, in some cases with the wandering poet who plays the *saz*, a type of lute. Like the migratory bird the poet "tell of the passage of time, the changes of fate and fortune" (Zariç 2). In an example from the sixteenth-century *aşik* or folk poet-musician Karacaoğlu, storks punctuate the various terrains through which the speaker has traveled:

From Aden quay, from the Arab mountain
Sick with being separated from its master
From Acem quay from the Arab mountain
Storks fly far away
...
Until they get to Kuh-i Kaf mountain
There they offer sacrifices
They visit Sultan Süleyman
There the storks shed their tears.[5]

(Zariç 4)

The fifteenth-century poet Kaygusuz Abdal, lamenting the graceless quality of his verse, compares his art to a stork wandering in an alien environment:

My words are jarring and uneven
Each one of them an unripe melon
I wander without a purpose
Like a stork in the desert.

(Zariç 9)

Zariç also notes the mythical quality of the "eternal return" of migratory birds in much of the poetry (Zariç 13). The promise of return the birds represent is a trope that solidifies communities by mythologizing the connection of generations.

The migratory birds of folk poetry appear and disappear in these poems according to the seasons. The poet who observes the crane by a lake, the stork nesting on top of a minaret or a swallow sheltering under the eaves of a roof is repeating what his ancestors did before him, re-experiencing feelings and excitements similar to those they felt in their time.

(Zariç 13)

European White Storks, like other migratory birds that pass through Turkey, do not play fleeting roles in cultural memory: they are integral to it. As mnemonic devices, the storks in their passage embody the presence of time.[6]

Turkish folk poetry, like Turkish twentieth-century poetry, complements the scientific data we have on migratory birds. The European White Stork has traveled through the lines of poems for a long as humans have witnessed their passage over land. A threat to or loss in one will be registered as a threat to or loss in the other. What touches an ecosystem touches a culture. When natural facts disappear due to human impact on an environment, poetic traditions live the repercussions. When the material referent from which a metaphor gains its meaning disappears, the metaphor itself dissolves. The poet Brenda Hillman remarks in the interview cited earlier that "in addition to endangered species, there are endangered forms of thought" (Hume 762). In the case of the figural migratory stork, the notion of eternal return that it embodies is at risk of losing an ancient ally.

Laurence Buell in *The Future of Environmental Criticism: Environmental Crisis and Literary Imagination* reminds us that direct associations between art and the natural material world like the one presented here can be considered a "retrogression to a pretheoretical [sic] trust in art's capacity to mirror the factual world" because it relies on a "reductive model of mimesis" (Buell 32). However, in the case of migratory storks the scientific and the figurative have maintained a consistent mirror relationship that predates post-structuralist constructivism: what is true in observable, "objective" nature reflects historical human thinking about existential contiguity. Arguments that rely on a contingent relationship between the representational and the biological should, of course, remain aware of the hazards of oversimplification. To suggest that the stork will disappear from the poetic lexicon is disingenuous. But something will change, and poetry will mark the change as it unfolds. Those that pay attention to the relationship between art and nature will mark this change in their turn. If Buell advocates a "spirit of skepticism" when it comes to environmental rhetoric, especially its "propensity for distortion and overreach," he also notes that we should be open to the "potentialities" of environmental rhetoric: "descriptive and visionary as well as polemical" (Buell 46).

"Poets keep track of the radical and intimate encounter with the nonhuman," continues Brenda Hillman (Hume 762). When asked how Ecopoetics might track this encounter more precisely, Hillman offers a notion of place often echoed in ecopoetical discourse. Place is seen as a composite of the physical, the abstract, and the scripted: "For me, place is three-fold. The local bioregion is one kind of place that is very specific ... Another has to do with the symbolic realms, the world of spirit, myth, and dream ... A third aspect of place for me is the site of material syllable, the composition" (Hume 764). This threefold description of place maps out the descriptive, visionary, and polemical potential that poetics has to offer the social and the scientific according to Buell. Poetry that has until now maintained a conservative relationship to an animal with conservative habits will inevitably begin to record the changes in the air and on the ground. As changes on the biological level are registered by poets and artists, abstract symbolic values will realign with these new realities. Writing will readjust; composition practices will shift.

For example, general environmental changes due to climate change are affecting migratory birds in the Palearctic-African system. White storks throughout Europe have advanced their spring migration schedules while some have even begun to overwinter in southern Europe rather than migrate at all (Cox 178). Those birds that continue to migrate under increasingly difficult climate conditions may exchange old diminished stopover habitat for new more bountiful sites. As recent studies on the changing foraging habits of European White Storks indicate, migratory storks may soon be found in greater numbers in rubbish dumps than in open pastures, freshwater marshes, and coastal lagoons, the kind of traditional habitat found on the Bosporus route. A 2004 study of White Storks in Montpellier, France, suggests that the increase in overwintering migratory stork populations is directly connected to the location of a garbage dump near the Lattes Reserve. The birds are responding to a "strong selective pressure not to migrate to Africa and/or stay close to their (potential) breeding grounds" (Archaux 443). Thus, in time, and for the various environmental reasons mapped out here, the traditional passage of storks in spring and autumn along the Bosporus route may become a thing of the past, on both the biological level and, *en suite*, the figurative.

Nature poetry or poetry grounded referentially in nature constantly adjusts as it tracks the changing relationship of the world and the word. Poetry has always found ways to respond figuratively and formally to anthropogenic modifications of the environment. At the present historical moment, the disappearance of habitat will lead to modifications in poetic practices. Forrest Gander and John Kinsella attempt to describe what Ecopoetics as a poetic practice might look like on the page in their book *Redstart: An Ecological Poetics*.

> Many of the descriptions of the relationship between poetry and ecology are metaphorical, and the metaphors have been thoroughly mixed. A poetry expressing a concern for ecology might be structured as compost, it might be developed rhizomatically, it might be described as a nest, a collectively. Its structure might be cyclical, indeterminate, or strictly patterned. The formal possibilities are as infinite as ever since there isn't any formal structure for representing ecology or nature. And writing is a constructed system.
>
> (Gander 13)

Turkish poetics will adjust to the shifts in bird migration. The metaphorical potential of garbage dumps or migrant populations staying put in the north over winter is clearly rich.

These may give rise to new ways to think about and inscribe change and flux, new signs of the passage of time. Perhaps storks as living embodiments of eternal return will become the material of memory, exploited only by writers nourished by the past, those who feed on nostalgia, the caste away refuse of a dying cultural idiom. Grounded flight, rather than global travel, may give rise to a poetics of stasis because, biologically speaking, white storks will become dead metaphors.

There have never been simple, non-polemical ways to respond to the environmental conditions that give rise to the kind of hermeneutic crisis suggested here. The current historical moment presents interesting twists to the problem of nature as "natural." In "Politics of Nature: East and West Perspectives," Bruno Latour argues that science alone is no longer a stable option for conservationists. Scientists and experts cannot be counted on to prevent interest groups and the politicians who support them from hiding behind the hard facts of science "to disguise their arbitrary decisions" (Latour 72). "It is no longer possible to appeal outside this political arena, to nature and its laws as if it were a higher court and a higher transcendent authority, in order to stop political disputes and religious conflicts" (Latour 73). In economies and cultures of consumption, ecological crisis is considered an "obstacle" to growth and development, a threat to progress (Latour 74). It could be argued that ecological crisis matters either too little or too much in the global marketplace. Latour suggests a shift in the way we approach environmental conservation.

> I take the politics of nature, cosmopolitics, to be simultaneously a new phenomenon that forces every one of us to reinvent politics and science in a new combination so as to absorb controversies about natural issues, and a very old fact of civilization that can be experienced through the many different traditions that have always rejected the idea of a human totally detached from her conditions of existence, from her life support, and from fragile artificial spheres. (Latour 74)[7]

Those interested in the conservation of places like stopover habitat should include in their scientific evidence the sociopolitical complexities that lead to the propagation of scientific controversies and also the cultural traditions that present inclusive visions of the biosphere. In all cases, non-human subjects such as white storks, cannot be treated as mere objects: "matters of concern should not be degraded into matters of fact" (Latour 79).

Migratory birds remind us that ecological crisis is simultaneously of local and global concern, demanding cosmopolitical action. George Cox suggests strategies for migratory bird conservation such as the long-term monitoring of ecological and evolutionary responses to climate change. He also joins hundreds of nature conservancy groups, local and international, who are working to devise and enforce international plans for habitat protection. For Cox these plans must also incorporate "the flexibility necessary to keep pace with environmental change" (Cox 249). He recommends a number of directions for migratory bird management, including expanding monitory networks; enhancing corridor and stopover networks; employing "anticipatory" approaches to preserve design, meaning learning to anticipate where habitat problems are bound to rise due to development; developing systems of "assisted range adjustment" that will address habitat encroachment and the protection of nesting and roosting areas (Cox 259).

Garnant Magnin and Murat Yarar note the number of international treatises on nature conservation that Turkey has signed, including the Bern Convention of 1979, and list the many important bird areas (IBAs) that are legally protected in Turkey but most with no long-term guarantee (Magnin 25–26). They also note that conservation efforts at the governmental level in Turkey have been greatly hampered, citing "chronic lack of trained staff and equipment," "lack of dialogue and the equivocal situation of responsibilities on an inter-ministerial level, the lack of scientific data from (long-term) monitoring schemes, the lack of long-term conservation strategies (including schemes to alter prevailing public attitudes), and insufficient funds to implement even small components of existing conservation programmes" (Magnin 28).

In a "cosmopolitics" suggested by Latour, recommendations for global conservation measures and factors that restrict local action must be addressed simultaneously. This is asking a lot of the world. In order to change public policies, hearts and minds must first engage. The threat to the biosphere must take on the urgency that is inspired by threats to religious creeds or temples (Latour 75). The literary arts may seem to have little pragmatic place in the lives of European White Storks at a time when national pride rides on the success of mega-projects rather than participation in the preservation of stable, healthy migratory corridors and stopover habitat. It may seem to have even less when the modern politics of nature, both in the West and in the East, is crippled by controversy over the very existence of scientific objectivity. But it is now that we might stop and take stock of how cultural memory might provide an impetus to conservation. The Turkish poet Turgut Uyar shares recollections of boyhood in the poem "Reminiscence." In it a sedentary stork figures centrally in the glow of domestic imagery:

> The gas lamp burning in the middle of the room,
> And nights sometimes lit by lightning.
> The stork nest on our chimney flue,
> How beautiful were the fairy tales, the riddles.
> The gas lamp burning in the middle of the room.
>
> (Uyar lines 16–20)

Rather than participating in a metaphor of flight and flux, the stork seems to hold sentinel over the house and stories that protect the boy. Here

Uyar anticipates the future role of the migratory bird. She will be frozen in air, grounded in time, a thing of fiction. If and when we begin to forget her former passage in our urge for progress, the poems, however, will not. They will continue to supply the world with the data that tells us how we are connected to other creatures, even those in air, and how their rhythms, like our own, cannot be checked or altered by what passes for material progress, at least for now.

6

The Benefits of Doubt: A Sea Turtle and the Ecological Sublime

The encounter

A few years back I had an experience while swimming out in the Mediterranean Sea on the southwestern coast of Turkey. I was about a quarter of a mile out and alone, or so I thought. The sea was warm and slightly agitated due to wind, but calm enough to allow for an easy crawl. The sun was high, about 2:00 and the water around and below was lapis lazuli blue and clear as if backlit. The further from shore I swam the more my mind emptied. I was a head with arms and feet in a blue bowl. I was aware of my immediate material reality only: my breathing, the water moving over my skin, the taste of salt. It was on an inhale that she surfaced. I saw her perpendicularly. She was about fifteen feet to my right, vivid enough to be tactile, far enough to be wild. Immediately my body short-circuited. My systems surged and something cracked and flashed in my mind or my body I didn't know which. I stopped short. I knew two things at once: I was afraid/I was fascinated. These responses occurred simultaneously, as if wires had crossed in the recesses of my occipital and temporal lobes. And then almost as suddenly I understood who she was. A sea turtle. Her shell was the size of my trunk, her head a large fist. Once I recognized her the first thing I did was whisper toward her in Turkish, *Çok korktum, ama çok güzelsin* ("I was really frighted, but you're so beautiful,"). I could see her left eye. It was the size of my own and dark. She hung on the surface, passing slowing for fifteen seconds, no more. And then she lithely sounded. And there I remained, treading water, overwhelmed, laughing. I felt I had received a gift I could never have anticipated.

Later, upon reflection, I noted the textbook nature of my response. Physiologically I had experienced, apparently, a simple flight or fight instinct. This accounted for the fear that resulted from the sudden changes in my physical body that were, in turn, responses to a perceived physical threat. Intellectually or aesthetically, my experience suggested another formula, one associated with the physical, but one that in the historical narrative of the formula told me that I had, in an instant, transcended the material encounter. The encounter, it seemed, was not actually between a sea turtle and me, but between me and my higher faculties prompted by a visitation from the sea creature. I had had, it appeared, a sublime experience in nature.

I then began to wonder how the sea turtle and I would fare under a sustained reading of the sublime. I was curious where the sea turtle, or more specifically what I know now to be the loggerhead or *Carreta carreta*, might fit into this investigation. In other words, I wanted to explore the juncture of the abstract and the material, the idea of the animal and the animal herself. Christopher Hitt's theory of the ecological sublime offers a narrative that serves this quest. In the following pages I will engage Hitt's argument put forth in a 1999 article entitled "Toward an Ecological Sublime." My initial goal will be to test my own experience against the canon. I will therefore begin where most discussions of the sublime tend to begin, with the first-century text "On the Sublime" ascribed to Longinus and "The Analytic of the Sublime" by eighteenth-century Immanuel Kant. I will then move toward more contemporary schools of thought until I take a cross-disciplinary turn toward the marine sciences. Herpetology, the branch of zoology concerned with amphibians and reptiles, the latter of which include turtles, will allow me to put abstract ideas in aesthetics and philosophy to a physical test. I will note how the science adds to or detracts from notions of the sublime put forth. It is then a short distance to the ecological sublime, which will carry the chapter toward approaches to conservation and the place of the sublime in this worldly effort.

The sublime tradition: Longinus and Kant

The sublime, although an intrinsically elusive and paradoxical concept, is perhaps one of the more overexposed in intellectual and aesthetic history. From

Homer and Hesiod and on into the present continuous, writers, both creative and other, devotedly revisit the sublime in an effort to refine, refute, or reinvent yet another manifestation of the ancient noun/adjective with uncertain Latin roots. In popular usage the sublime is associated with the exalted, the elevated, the awe-inspiring, the majestic, often in nature. The following passage from Immanuel Kant's second book of the "Analytic of the Sublime" in *Critique of Judgement* (1790) is often cited as a quintessential description of sublime magnitude in nature:

> Bold, overhanging, and as it were threatening, rocks; clouds piled up in the sky, moving with lightning flashes and thunder peals; volcanoes in all their violence of destruction; hurricanes with their track of devastation; the boundless ocean in a state of tumult; the lofty waterfall of a mighty river, and such like. (Kant 125)

A catalogue of synonyms for "sublime" emphasizes the fearsome in Kant's description, ones more in keeping with the murky connotations of the "oblique" or the "threshold" of the original *limus* or *limen*. These synonyms also tend to steer the sublime away from direct correspondence with the external, natural world toward interior frames of reference. James Porter in "The Sublime without Longinus," for example, suggests the following "rough typology": "extremes, contrasts, intensities, and incommensurabilities ... transgressed limits, excesses, collisions, and collapses of structures, whether of physical objects or of meanings" (Porter 120).

While Longinus' "On the Sublime" is often the starting point for academic discussions of the sublime, direct reference to the relationship between the sublime and nature is limited in his reflections because he principally writes of the sublime in terms of rhetoric and stylistics. The sublime in Longinus is a literary or language experience rather than an experience of natural phenomena. It is the experience of the record of the sublime. When he does directly reference the natural world as he does in section XXXVI, it is in terms of a model for aesthetic precision and restraint. While he notes that the human response to art and nature have differing orientations, "in art we admire exactness, in the works of nature magnificence," and rather obliquely acknowledges the material source of language, "it is from nature that man derives the faculty of speech," he ultimately argues that it is under the yoke of art that nature achieves sublime grandeur (Longinus XXXVI). And just as nature who "in her loftier and more passionate moods, while detesting all appearance of restraint, is not wont to show herself utterly wayward and reckless," art with the aid of right "ballast" can achieve sublimity (Longinus II.4). Ultimately nature must be made to negotiate with art in Longinus' formulae for the rhetorical sublime: "it is proper on all occasions to call in art as an ally to nature. By the combined resources of these two we may hope to achieve perfection" (Longinus XXXVI).

Up to this point there is little in Longinus that helps position my personal encounter with the *Carreta carreta* as a sublime experience. There is not enough material nature to work with. Longinus does admit mid-sentence, as if in passing, that "the vital informing principle is derived from her," nature being feminine here (Longinus I-4). This does suggest that the physical encounter might be seen as something that precedes any idea I might have had of it, as if there were indeed a cause–effect relationship to consider in other than abstract terms. He also offers what might be seen as a very contemporary reading of nature's ecocentric function, but only in what amounts to a comparative aside in a discussion of artfulness: "How much more do these principles [of, for example 'right degree and right movement'] apply to the Sublime in literature, where grandeur is never, as it sometimes is in nature, dissociated from utility and advantage" (Longinus XXXVI). This suggests that there may be a non-anthropomorphic way to think about my encounter, a way that does not require that I be the center of it. Perhaps the very lack of utility and human advantage was what made it a sublime experience.

These two references to material nature that seem to exist outside the assimilation of human mind offer a window of opportunity in this seminal text on the sublime. Porter argues for a more historically contextualized reading of Longinus, one that allows him to exist in a continuum of chronicles of the sublime, one "prepared by long traditions in poetry and philosophy starting with Homer and Hesiod" (Porter 100). In his bid to realign Longinus with "unfashionable" rhetoric, Porter reminds the reader that wherever theories of the sublime may lead us, they all begin on land, or water, as it were:

> All forms of the sublime involve contact, initially, with the material world and with the frictions that come with matter and materiality; some bear greater signs of a struggle to gain release from such contact than others. Perhaps that is why one and the same object can be taken to be a source

of either material or immaterial sublimity depending on the perspective of the beholder. (Porter 122)

Though his main object has been to point out ways in which rhetoric and stylistics have been pushed to the wayside by the various abstractions that dominate most discourse on the sublime since the Roman period, Porter's inclusion of "the frictions that come with matter and materiality" in the concluding comments of his monograph invites the turtle's body, as well as my own, into the list of exclusions. In the final analysis, however, Longinus has not given me much to work with unless my aim is to write a poem about my encounter. In this he is rich.

After Longinus, narratives of the sublime tend to turn in succession to Immanuel Kant. Kant will also allow for our physical presence in his theory of the sublime in nature, but only to a point. But before anything can begin I am told, and then reminded many times over, whatever I think I may have experienced was precisely that, thinking only: "in general we express ourselves incorrectly if we call any *object of nature* sublime, although we can quite correctly call many objects of nature beautiful ... the object is fit for the presentation of a sublimity which can be found in the mind; no sensible form can contain the sublime properly so-called" (Kant II.52) Justification for this exclusion is given in what Kant calls the division of the mathematically sublime. Microscopes and telescopes have helped humans see that size is relational: "nothing can be given in nature, however great it is judged by us to be, which could not if considered in another relation to be reduced to the infinitely small, and conversely there is nothing so small, which does not admit of extension by our Imagination to the greatness of a world, if compared with still smaller standards" (Kant II-109). The Imagination, according to Kant, tends to venture toward the infinite, be it infinitely small or infinitely large. The Reason, by contrast, strives for full comprehension, or "absolute totality" of phenomena. The Reason fails in the face of the scales offered up by the Imagination, however. Paradoxically, it is this "inadequateness ... for estimating the magnitude of things of sense" that "excites in us the feeling of a supersensible faculty." In other words, we seem to push our rational faculties beyond their human limits. Following this, "it is not the object of sense, but the use which the judgement naturally makes of certain objects on behalf of this latter feeling, that is absolutely great ... Consequently," and finally, "it is the state of mind produced by a certain representation with which the reflective Judgement is occupied, and not the Object, that is to be called sublime" (Kant II-109). According to Kant, because I registered the sea turtle in sublime terms she is now effectively out of the picture, or, in the language of chemistry, which uses the noun/adjective sublime as a verb, she has sublimed from a solid substance into vapor via the heating action of my mind. In the end she is all about me.

Kant has helpful things to say about my initial response to the loggerhead out in the open water—the feeling of short-circuiting, the sensation of fear and fascination impacting my aesthetic response, "*çok güzelsin.*" He contrasts the beautiful with the sublime in a number of ways. The contrast that concerns me here identifies the difference between what he calls "positive pleasure" and "negative pleasure" (Kant II-42). The Beautiful, he claims,

> directly brings with it a feeling of the furtherance of life, and thus is compatible with charms and with the play of the imagination. But the other [the feeling of the Sublime] is a pleasure that arises only indirectly; viz. it is produced by a feeling of a momentary check of the vital powers and a consequent stronger outflow of them, so that it seems to be regarded as emotion ... and as the mind is not merely attracted by the object but is ever being alternately repelled, the satisfaction in the sublime does not so much involve a positive pleasure as admiration or respect, which rather deserves to be called negative pleasure. (Kant II-42)

Confronted as I was with something relatively large that I did not initially understand within an environment in which I was somewhat vulnerable, I had mixed feelings. In the context of the mathematically sublime, the unidentifiable object pushed my rational faculties beyond their limits. It blew, as it were, my mind. But if I was afraid, I was also fascinated because as Kant notes further along, negative pleasure is the result of an "inner perception of the inadequacy of all sensible standards for rational estimation of magnitude," a perception which "arouses in us the feeling of supersensible destination, according to which it is purposive and therefore pleasurable to find in every standard Sensibility inadequate to the Ideas of Understanding" (Kant II-122). While each term in this convoluted phrasing has its own genealogy in the "Analytic of the Sublime," the basic message is this: if my reason had failed, so had my imagination. And it was at this point that my mind, stimulated to a supernatural degree, like a mother lifting a vehicle off her injured child, came to the rescue of my stressed imagination and released it. This rescue, a countering of repulsion with attraction, is central to Kant's theory of the sublime. In that split instant I had discovered "the consciousness of an unlimited faculty" that allowed me to take aesthetic pleasure in the natural object. The object was no longer a monstrous predator, but an object of desire.

With safety comes reason, although Kant suggests that it is Reason that creates the safe distance that transcends danger, at least in the abstract. I had judged that the turtle and I were on equal footing concerning size. In retrospect I understood that if I had been smaller and resembled a mollusk, crustacean or an echinoderm (i.e., a starfish) she would have eaten me, probably before I was aware of her approach. But at that moment the turtle was very large, but no larger than myself. I had a fighting chance. And this realization, this rationalization meant that even as my vital powers ruptured then surged, I experienced something akin to pleasure, a pleasure Kant further explains through the concept of the "dynamically sublime." Thanks to the distance my rationalizing mind had already begun to establish between the mighty object and myself, I experienced a "dominion" over that object (Kant II-123). And in this moment of ruling control, the unsuspecting emissary was transformed into a sublime object because she had given me the opportunity to transcend my own limitations: "we readily call these objects sublime, because they raise the energies of the soul above their accustomed height, and discover in us a faculty of resistance of a quite different kind, which gives us courage to measure ourselves against the apparent almightiness of nature" (Kant II-125). In this sublime encounter with nature I had discovered, at least in my mind, "a superiority to nature even in its immensity" (Kant II-125).

Needless to say, I have remained unconvinced. It is true I spoke to the sea turtle in the traditional oxymoronic phraseology of the sublime, *çok korktum ama çok güzelsin*, and this ability to verbalize the contradictory emotions of fear and allure suggests in Kantian terms that I was already re-empowered by the dissociation from a perceived physical threat. And the fact that I spoke to her in human language, and in the past tense, would suggest, in more contemporary theories of the relation between language and power, that I was already assimilating the amphibious reptile into my own sign system, thus colonizing or establishing dominion over her. But I did not believe for an instant that my whisper was heeded. I had simply greeted her, as I would have anybody I came across, alone, a quarter of a mile out to sea. Though it is true I would not have taken the liberty immediately of telling a human stranger they were beautiful. And could the mere identification of a general species (I did not understand that she was a loggerhead or female until later on land) and a vague sense that I was not going to be challenged or attacked, created, perhaps, by her calm regard and consistent distance, could either of these really be considered knowledge? When she sounded I began laughing, perhaps as a release of tension, though it felt more like a wordless expression of awe and joy. But what leaves me the least convinced by Kant's delineation of my experience is that, as with Longinus, the material world, the non-human species that was the other half of this encounter is sublimated and ultimately erased in this theory of the sublime. All I am left with is my assimilated sublime judgment of her, a judgment so weak in biologically relevant detail that it can hardly qualify as *logos*. By resisting this final transcendence of my co-conspirator the turtle, I am insisting that she remain in the picture, at least until I can claim to know her well enough to let her go.

Sublime alternatives

Peter Heyman in *Animality in British Romanticism: The Aesthetics of Species* also agrees that there is something important missing in Kant's analysis of the sublime in nature. Nature. Kant's "solipsistic denial of the real" has as much "ecological benefits," he argues, as postmodernism's "nihilistic deflation of subjectivity" (Heyman 26). Referring as most commentaries on the postmodern sublime do to Jean-François Lyotard's reflections on Kant's aesthetic of the sublime in *The Postmodern Condition: A Report on Knowledge*, Heyman argues that in the case of both postmodernism and Kant "a reconciliation between matter and consciousness seems impossible, because in the former there no longer exists a subject capable of admiring nature and in the latter there is no longer an objective world to be admired" (Heyman 26). Lyotard's early portrayal of the postmodern sublime, derived from the aesthetics of painting, not nature itself, certainly "beheads" Kant's sublime in its denial of mastery, or the "climactic return of reason": the postmodern sublime, according to Lyotard, would be that which, in the modern, puts forward the unpresentable in presentation itself; that which denies itself the solace of good forms, the consensus of a taste which would make it possible to share collectively the nostalgia for the unattainable; that which searches for new presentations, not in order to enjoy them but to impart a stronger sense of the unpresentable. (Heyman 25, Lyotard 81)

Because Lyotard's focus here is ultimately aesthetics rather than materiality, which in any case can be no more than a network of unstable signs, he might satisfy my own skepticism vis-à-vis the vaporizing action of Kant's sublime, but he cannot address my desire or instinct to retain material nature in a conception of sublime nature.

Louise Economides, in *The Ecology of Wonder in Romantic and Postmodern Literature*, tells me I must forswear the sublime if I insist on involving the loggerhead in my reality of her. The reason for the persistent dominance of sublimity, at least in literary theory, she argues, is its emphasis on mastery. As an aesthetic it "supports a distinctly masculinist and humanist agenda that is critical to the project of modernity" (Economides 19). Economides cites the position of those working in Gender Studies who promote a "female" or "feminine" sublime that has been withheld or curbed in traditional metaphysical theories of the sublime. Scholars of the feminine sublime "avoid an aesthetic that 'master[s] its objects of rapture'" and promote a "valorization of non-violent awe" (Economides 18). Wonder, she argues, has historically fared better as a concept than sublimity. Economides reiterates Gordon C. F. Bearn's claims in *Waking to Wonder*, a study itself of the "ethical implications" of wonder in the philosophy of Nietzsche and Wittgenstein, that "[W]aking to wonder is saying "yes" to the groundless surfaces of our lives ... Again and again it vanishes before the tendency to sublime the logic of our language and life" (Bearn qtd. in Economides 24). "Accepting the wonder of a groundless existence," writes Economides, "entails loving the other *as other*, not seeking to use the other as a foundation for transcendental 'truth' or reducing the other to a reliable means whereby subjectivity defines itself in opposition to what it is not" (Ecomomides 24). Wonder, like the feminine sublime, allows the object, the other, or, in the case at hand, the sea turtle, to remain in the *tableau vivant*.

In offering wonder as an alternative to sublimity Economides downplays the role of fear, however. While wonder, like sublimity, is a "state of radical indeterminacy," "fear is not primary to the experience of wonder" as it "clearly is for the sublime" (Economides 22). Because fear is so intertwined with the rhetoric of violence that runs through theories of sublime nature, it is understandable that an alternative would be required to neutralize the fear factor in nature in the name of non-violent awe. But this creates a problem for me. I cannot deny that one thing I felt when I first perceived the magnificent turtle was fear: heart stopping, adrenalin pulsing fear. I am, it seems, back to where I began. As ethically sound as discussions of wonder strike me, I must be honest and admit that despite what I also see as masculinist and overt human-centeredness in the theories of sublime nature discussed above, they still come closer to describing my own experience due to the inclusion of fear at the center of their systems.

Luckily I am reminded often that the sublime is an infinitely variability concept. In antiquity, Porter notes, the sublime can be "either broad and expansive or pointillistic and intense, the result of sundering and scattering or collision and compression, terrifying or uplifting, humiliating or exalting, disorienting or supremely pleasure-affording, a source of shock or of wonderment, or even of utter serenity" (Porter 121). Joseph Addison in what might now be considered a sinfully bourgeois commentary represents the sublime as entertainment in a 1712 article in *The Spectator* (No 412):

> Every thing that is new or uncommon raises a Pleasure in the Imagination, because it fills the Soul with an agreeable Surprize, gratifies its Curiosity, and gives it an Idea of which it was not before possest. We are indeed so often conversant with one Set of Objects, and tired out with so many repeated Shows of the same Things, that whatever is new or uncommon contributes a little to vary human Life, and to divert our Minds, for a while, with the Strangeness of its Appearance: It serves us for a kind of Refreshment, and takes off from that Satiety we are apt to complain of in our usual and ordinary Entertainments.

Heyman brings us closer to date on "scholarly consensus": "the sublime constitutes an extremely protean discourse that covers the entire political spectrum and whose meaning depends on its interaction with a number of subjective parameters" (Heyman 24). In other words, I have choices.

I am also not alone in my discomfort with what I feel to be a hegemonic discourse. Christopher Hitt in "Toward an Ecological Sublime" argues that "it has been the overwhelming tendency of literary criticism over the past few decades to evaluate the aesthetic of the sublime primarily as an expression of asymmetrical power relationships: between human and nature, self and other, reader and text, male and female, conqueror and oppressed" (Hitt 603). The asymmetrical power relationship that concerns me is that between species human and a non-human species. In the service of what I hope to be a realignment of this asymmetry, my next goal is to think about what role logos might play in a theory of sublime nature that does not exclude nature. Just because I have rejected Kant's vaporizing form of reason along with my contemporaries does not mean I have not been interested in knowing all I can about the Sea Turtle. The more I have learned, and it is very little, the more my awe and respect have grown. Knowledge in my case has served to increase the stature of the turtle in my mind rather than diminish her effect on me. Reading cannot be compared with direct experience of course, although theories of sublime nature consistently elide the two. I have yet to experience the physical form of fear in a narrative or poem that I experienced in the water, though some texts have come ominously close. Perhaps it is the embodied materiality of my response that has led me to Herpetology.

Sublime science: Homing and earth's magnetic field

Longinus had suggested in his letters on the sublime that nature, though lofty and passionate, nevertheless displayed something resembling feminine *sprezzatura*: she, we will recall, "is not wont to show herself utterly wayward and reckless" (Longinus II-4). The field where humans "determine" or define her "right degree" and "movement" and "contribute the precision of practice and experience" to these definitions is, he tells us, "the peculiar province of scientific method." This alliance of nature and science is offered, of course, in the service of an analogy of the language arts and rhetoric, the science of language: art is to council what nature is to the scientific method. In both cases frames are required so that humans have access to raw materials in ways that are meaningful to them or move them. It can be argued that access is not necessarily the same thing as full control, however. Access is temporary, non-binding. The frame of science can only approximate "the vital informing principle" that "in all cases" is derived from nature and is therefore dynamic and, we might add, ultimately unknowable (Longinus II-4). Thus, while Longinus admits science into his cursory reference to nature, it is limited to an extended, albeit anthropocentric and masculinist, metaphor concerning the art of rhetoric: "The great passions, when left to their own blind and rash impulses without the control of reason, are in the same danger as a ship let drive at random without ballast. Often they need the spur, but sometimes also the curb" (Longinus II-4). Here the passions, like all things in nature, require the control of reason so that we can ride them.

Kant is less generous toward the role of the sciences in the passages from "The Analytic of the Sublime" discussed above. Knowledge about nature garnered from the sciences should not be confused with Reason's higher knowledge, which transcends the material world:

> If then we call the sight of the starry heaven *sublime,* we must not place at the basis of our judgement concepts of worlds inhabited by rational beings, and regard bright points, with which we see the space above is filled, as their suns moving in circles purposively fixed with reference to them; but we must regard it, just as we see it, as a distant, all-embracing vault. Only under such a representation can we range that sublimity which a pure aesthetical judgement ascribes to this object. (Kant 137)

The language of astronomy concedes to the language of poetry when nature, thanks to the alchemy of the human mind, attains sublime status. The case is true for marine biology, meteorology, and oceanography:

> And in the same way, if we are to call the sight of the ocean sublime, we must not *think* of it as we [ordinarily] do, endowed as we are with all kinds of knowledge (not contained, however in the immediate intuition). For example, we sometimes think of the ocean as a vast kingdom of aquatic creatures; or as the great source of those vapors that fill the air with clouds for the benefit of the land; or again as an element which, though dividing continents from each other, yet promotes the greatest communication between them. (Kant 137–138)

Scientific knowledge is "teleological judgement"; it is determined by concepts and is therefore not a free act of judgment (Kant 138). Kant contrasts this to "aesthetic purposiveness," which is "the conformity to law of the Judgement in its *freedom*." The reason "paradoxically" stimulated by the confusion that nature presents pushes beyond the material world and reconciles itself in an aestheticized version of the stars or an aquatic creature. As in Longinus' theory of sublime nature, science in Kant takes a subordinate back seat to art.

Many commentaries on the sublime in Romantic poetry hearken back to this final transcending stage of the reason in the mind's confrontation with nature. If a youthful relationship had been physical, instinctual, and joyful because raw, a mature relationship, while elegiac, is enriched by the understanding which brings with it access to the mystical, a necessary component of the Romantic sublime experience. William Wordsworth's "Tintern Abbey," *Ode: Intimations of Immortality* and "Prelude" to the *Lyrical Ballads* are most often cited as examples. This reading performs a similar purging action on material nature as that of Kant. Critical attention has turned more recently, however, to alternative ways of reading Romantic poems that reinstate the natural world and scientifically informed readings of it at the center of the Romantic sublime. Speaking of animals, Peter Heyman, for example, wonders in *Animality in British Romanticism* if in Romantic writing we might find a "consciously rather than surreptitiously rational ecological sublime, in which our insight into the animal's independent existence results not from a failure of our logical thought experiment or a profane illumination but from a very rational thought experiment enabled by these patterns" (Heyman 32). Heyman quotes an illustration of this enabling process from Wordsworth's fragmentary piece "The Sublime and the Beautiful": "it is certain that [our] conceptions of the sublime, far from being dulled or narrowed by common frequency, will be rendered more lively & comprehensive by more accurate observation and by increasing knowledge" (Wordsworth qtd. in Heyman 32). "The sensation of the sublime," argues Heyman paraphrasing Wordsworth, "results from the complex interplay between an immediate sensory response and a more reflective reaction, which relates one's spontaneous aesthetic feeling to one's rational memory and scientific knowledge" (Heyman 32). According to Heyman, Wordsworth believed that "rational abstraction heightens rather than diminishes the sensation of the sublime" (Heyman 33).

In this spirit, and thus in indirect defiance of Kant, I would like to turn now, finally, to the animal herself. As stated earlier, the knowledge I have gained of loggerhead sea turtles since the direct "friction" of my surprise encounter with one has done little to tame or control her in my mind. Quite the contrary has occurred: the more "facts" I have gathered, and thanks to the professional integrity of herpetologists these proposed facts rarely come without caveats attesting to the ongoing, ever-unfolding nature of zoological research, the deeper my amazement has grown. Testing and retesting the hypothesis of fellow researchers, experimental biologists offer up verifiable data the way a good literary critic offers another layer of meaning to a poem they did not create yet have devoted their lives to honoring through close analysis, and due respect.

I'd like to share some things I know about the turtle. In general terms sea turtles are part of an ancient group of reptiles that have adapted to life in seas and oceans. Although they have adapted to water, paddle like flippers have replaced clawed feet, they still retain landlubber characteristics: they breathe air and nest on dry land. The fact that they nest on land determines the life cycle of the species. Females lay "clutches" of 100 to 150 eggs and bury them in sand on nesting beaches. One area of active research focuses on the understanding that the temperature of sand, not chromosomes, will determine the sex of the embryo: hotter temperatures lead to higher female embryos. After approximately two months the baby turtles hatch and dig themselves out of the sand and make for open water. Juvenile sea turtles tend to stay close to the area where they were hatched, though they can also migrate great distances relatively soon to feeding sites. Most species of sea turtle, in the same way ocean-going Chinook salmon return to the streams where they were spawned, appear to exhibit natal beach homing, meaning they return to the beach or same general geographic area where they were hatched to lay their own eggs. After mating in waters near shore, the females crawl to land, dig their nests, and lay their clutches before returning to the water and setting off for distant feeding grounds.

One of the more awe-inspiring aspects of the humble sea turtles' routine existence is their ability, on any given day, to detect the earth's magnetic field. Hatchlings use cues to find the sea once they dig themselves free from the sand-womb: they move toward the horizon of open water, which is usually lower and brighter than the dunes and vegetation of an unadulterated nesting beach. The ocean or sea reflects more starlight and moonlight than land does and, in any case, the infant turtles' visual "core of acceptance" appears to be 180 degrees horizontal by 30 degrees vertical (Lohmann, Orientation 46). Thus, reflective moonlight, not the moon itself, guides them initially. Once the bite-size turtles are in the water, however, visual clues no longer appear to work. Instead they begin to orient themselves toward the wave surge. And when they reach deeper water they use other sources of information to guide them, sources that from a human perspective might seem rather extraordinary: the earth's magnetic field.

It is still unknown precisely how hatchling sea turtles develop a magnetic directional preference: "The physiological mechanisms that underlie magnetic field detection in sea turtles and other animals remain to be determined" (Lohmann, Orientation 50). Some laboratory experiments have shown that as hatchlings distance themselves from shore, "magnetic compass orientation supplants wave orientation" (Lohmann, Orientation 49). There still seems to be much uncertainty whether this orientation ability is inherited or whether it is learned while hatchlings are crawling across the beach toward a light source or initially swimming toward the light source, or by swimming into waves (Lohmann, Orientation 51). It may be both and all three of the latter.

What follows is as fantastic. The migrations of *Caretta caretta* are the longest on record for a marine animal, so to discuss the sea turtle I encountered in the context of migration and magnetic fields is particularly poignant. Young loggerheads that migrate through oceans enter gyres. They appear to use the earth's magnetic field to help position themselves and to remain inside a gyre system because to drift out means to enter hostile conditions, which are often temperature differences. Because each oceanic region has a unique magnetic field turtles use them as maps to help them navigate toward specific regions (Lohmann, Sea R786). Features of the earth's magnetic field that are predictable could "in principle" be used by long-distance migratory sea turtles like loggerheads in position finding: these would include geomagnetic inclination angles and magnetic field intensity (Lohmann, Oriention 52). "[G]eomagnetic field lines intersect the earth's surface at specific angles of inclination" and three kinds of magnetic intensity or strength, including total field, horizontal field, and vertical field intensity also provide other potential magnetic features that young loggerheads use as navigational markers (Lohmann, Orientation 52–53). Again, this navigational ability is probably both inherited and learned, though K. J. Lohmann and C. M. Lohmann suggest that it may be inherited because turtles who have never been in an ocean display the same behavior (Lohmann, Sea R786).

Different regions have different magnetic fields and populations of sea turtles have evolved in response to them. Loggerheads in coastal feeding grounds like the Mediterranean "learn the magnetic topography of the geographical areas in which they feed. The turtles can then use magnetic cues to help them navigate back to particular areas" (Lohmann, Sea R786). Things become even less clear when we begin to consider the migration of adult turtles to nesting beaches. It is still uncertain what initiates the journey home. More is known about the chemistry of bird migration: "In birds, prolactin and corticosterone work in conjunction to prompt the vernal and fall migration" (Patel 31). Various hormones drive the behavior of adult loggerheads, but it is still unclear which cues initiate the journey home. Loggerhead turtles in the Mediterranean travel between 220 and 2,500 kilometers when migrating to nesting beaches (Patel 12). It is still unknown if they use magnetic information in natal beach homing. "A plausible scenario is that the turtles imprint on the magnetic signatures of their natal region, allowing them to navigate back when it is time to reproduce" (Lohmann, Sea R786). This could be used along with visual and chemical cues. Lohmann offers the following tentative hypothesis on the hormonal or chemical impetus of homing:

> No one knows for certain how any animal detects the earth's magnetic field. One idea is that crystals of the magnetic mineral magnetite are coupled to the nervous system and function as receptors for the magnetic sense. Magnetic particles have been detected in sea turtles, migratory birds and some other magnetically sensitive animals. A different hypothesis, however, is that magnetic field detection might be accomplished through a complex series of chemical reactions associated with the visual system. How sea turtles detect magnetism remains a mystery.
>
> (Lohmann, Sea R786)

Mystery. Most articles and books on *Caretta caretta* either include or conclude on this note of suspended uncertainty. Verifiable knowledge and the unverifiable enigmatic share space in the field and in the paragraphs that describe them. And wonder of the unknown always hovers at the end of the line. Economides reminds us that Aristotle linked wonder with "a state of ignorance that is overcome with the acquisition of knowledge": Francis Bacon echoed this view when he claimed in "Of the Advancement of Learning" that wonder was "a symptom of 'broken knowledge'" (Economides 27–28). But this display of chauvinistic trust in science does not reflect the rhetoric of wonder we encounter in the writing of contemporary field scientists, especially where *Caretta caretta* is concerned. In their texts there are honest confessions at thresholds of knowledge, thresholds that are forever shifting, forever in flux: thus, just where Kant's teleological judgment turns to free judgment, one important difference he claims for the human location in sublime nature, is far from certain or clear.

John Urry refers to this doubt driven state of knowledge in science as "complexity." Systems in complexity practices, and this includes intersections in the physical and social sciences as well as the humanities, are seen as existing "on the edge of chaos" as the "orderly disorder" of chaos (Urry 113). "Complexity science," for example, "investigates systems that can adapt and evolve as they self-organize through time" (Urry 114). This is a way to view science that expands, rather than restricts, the capacity of the sciences to augment, rather than extinguish, a sense of wonder that may occur in the face of the uncertainties nature presents us. We both know and don't know what we are faced with. *Caretta caretta* migrates from the coast of Turkey to the coast of Africa and back via earth's magnetic field. We know they come and we know they go but we are uncertain how they know. The facts of homing known to humans are limited; the reality is limitless. There is no way to overcome this gap in understanding and therein lies the rush. Complexity science "investigates emergent, dynamic and self-organizing systems that co-evolve and adapt in ways that heavily influence the probabilities of later events" (Urry 114). We can rest assured that the gap in knowledge will maintain itself. The loggerhead I met a quarter mile off the beach had maybe just laid her clutch and was returning to feeding grounds five hundred miles to the east. Or maybe she was still displaying hormonal migratory behavior that sometimes lingers even after turtles have reached their sites of residency: when I saw her she was perhaps diving frequently and remaining relatively shallow in the water (Patel 32). This knowledge has given me no aesthetic dominion over her, however. Nor has it done anything toward offering me comforting thoughts I may have begun to develop concerning a personal interaction with a marine animal. What I encountered was a three-foot mystery. If I saw her again, and with all I now know about her, my heart would stop and my fascination would be fivefold. She, however, would remain an ordinary *Caretta caretta*.

The ecological sublime

With his provocative 1996 article "The Trouble with Wilderness: Or, Getting Back to the Wrong Nature," William Cronon helped launch contemporary ecocritical debate on the place of the sublime in sublime nature. In it he warns that focusing, somewhat enraptured, on the edge of mystery, means falling into an old, predictable trap. If in the early days of my own North American heritage I would have perhaps seen a form of satanic temptation in my encounter with a wild being, now I was more inclined to view it as a sacred temple. His New Historicist reading of my reading of my sublime encounter in the wild would tell me that there is nothing natural about my concept of the wilderness. It is only that, a conception, and one with history. My excited response indeed might serve as the "unexamined foundation on which so many of the quasi-religious values of modern environmentalism rest" (Cronon, Trouble 16). Was and is my fascination really a misdirected longing for a higher reality? "The sacred, after all," admits Cronon in his "apology" to the retractors in the environmental movement whom he made uncomfortable with his provocation,

> is the place where we imagine that phenomena from another, more eternal world enters and ruptures the flow of time in our own. Historians can document and situate such ruptures, but in some ultimate sense we cannot explain them ... This is one reason why we need poets and priests, and not just historians if we hope to discover the many meanings of the world in which we make our home. (Cronon, Response 54)

He might have included marine biologists in this catalogue.

It seems that however grounded my fascination continues to be I cannot give much credit to science. According to Cronon, the moment I begin to travel mentally in realms I have no real firm judgment of, that is, earth's magnetic field; and the more stimulated I am by the mystery of how the loggerhead herself travels physically by way of these fields, I surrender, albeit actively, both our mortal bodies (hers and mine) to a more eternal world than our own on earth.

I do this much in the same way I experience a logos-driven aesthetic leap in the face of my awe and trembling in Kant's reading of the sublime. In both cases I am no longer in the water, but above the deep. Cronon admits that he is after practical results in his theoretical argument. A true lover of nature, he wants environmentalists to rethink the kinds of anti-anthropomorphic positioning that alienate those whose partnership is necessary in any sustainable effort to protect the environment. Look carefully in the mirror, he warns, before you throw stones. Our Romantic attachment to the ideology of the sublime must go he concludes.

Christopher Hitt in his influential 1999 article "Toward an Ecological Sublime," defends Cronon's ends, though respectfully disagrees with his means. "I am far from convinced that this ideology is *fundamentally* or *intrinsically* maleficent. On the contrary, I believe the concept of the sublime offers a unique opportunity for the realization of a new, more responsible perspective on our relationship with the natural environment" (Hitt 605). Hitt contends that the fundamental contradiction between humbling fear and "ennobling validation for the perceiving subject" inherent in traditional theories of the sublime has been the source of problems (Hitt 606). Ever since the eighteenth century, he argues, more emphasis has been placed on the latter, which in Kant's formulation means the imagination re-masters nature once a direct threat is surmounted (Hitt 604). Like other late twentieth-century and early twenty-first-century commentators on the sublime, Hill suggests that we forgo this latter emphasis and focus our efforts of assimilation on the ecological potential of "humbling fear": "Part of the sublime experience … is the realization that we are mortal creatures, 'beings of nature' whose lives are entirely dependent on forces greater than we are" (Hitt 607). Hitt thus argues that ecological principles can indeed be salvaged from the traditional sublime in a reconfigured version in the form of an "ecological sublime."

Hitt cites a number of critics who support such a reconfiguration of the sublime in the discourse of nature. Neil Evernden in *The Social Creation of Nature* (1992) ultimately argues for the decentering of the subject and the liberation of nature: "leaving it outside the domain of mind—neither as an object nor as a 'wider self' but as a mysterious, alien 'divine chaos'" (Hitt 613). Peter Reed in "Man Apart: An Alternative to the Self-Realization Approach" (1989) argues for "preserving the radical alterity of nature while resisting its objectification or reification" (Hitt 613). In his re-historicizing of the Longinian sublime in "The Sublime without Longinus," James Porter more recently goes as far as to conclude that because Longinus' ideas on the sublime were absorbed into the realms of the moral, spiritual, and the abstract and away from the rhetorical, this "chrystaline" form of the sublime was also cut off from the material nature that Longinus and his classical predecessors relied so heavily upon in their discourse of sublime nature (Porter 105).[1] In other words, the dissociation of phenomenal nature from the sublime was problematic from the very start.

Contemporary ecocritical theories of sublime nature tend to offer an ecological ethics grounded in deep ecology, or the humbling understanding that humans are not masters of ecological systems, but part and parcel of them only. Christopher Hitt offers the following warning, however, to those like myself interested in ecocritical readings of the sublime. The cautionary advice is worth quoting at length:

> We must be careful, however, before embracing a sense of humility, mortality, and dependence as either a panacea for our environmental predicament or as the defining element of an ecological sublime. The difficulty is that the consistent response of Western civilization (especially since the scientific revolution of the seventeenth century) to this recognition of vulnerability has *not* been eventual acceptance, but dogged resistance. The unfathomable otherness of nature unnerves us, and the idea that we are somehow part of this alien entity shocks us. Hence we devise ways to circumvent, deny, escape, or overcome it. Such efforts, indeed, constitute the story of the conventional sublime—a story which describes the validation of the individual through an act of transcendence in which the external world is domesticated, conquered, or erased. (Hitt 611)

It is with this warning in mind that I move toward the denouement of the anecdote and subsequent exegesis of my acquaintance with one *Caretta caretta*.

The ecological sublime and conservation

Hitt's warning is particularly relevant when we turn to present threats to loggerhead nesting beaches along the south and southwest coast of Turkey.

But before I enter this territory that is well chartered in circles concerned with environmental issues in Turkey, I need to acknowledge another warning by Cronon that compounds that of Hitt. Cronon counsels me that as a North American concerned with ecology in Turkey, I am at risk of error. It may be that it is easy for me to express opinions about what is right for an ecosystem that is remote from my native "first world" country. When I argue that the conservation of nature must take precedence over local commercial concerns, as I will, am I not assuming that people and their livelihoods are expendable in this "second world" country? Although Cronon cites the Amazonian rainforest in the 1970s as a case in point, might I not be "exporting a notion of American wilderness" to the southern coast of Turkey that may very well be a form of cultural imperialism (Cronon, Trouble 18)? I have asked this question a number of times in various contexts in the course of this book, evidence of unresolved ethical disease. But here my answer to Cronon (and myself) is that in this instance I am not alone. I am in fact an interloper and latecomer to an established, though challenged, local and international effort to protect loggerheads on their visits to and from Turkish territorial waters and the Turkish coast.

But first the ecological facts. There are plenty of threats to sea turtle populations in and along the Mediterranean. Many become the victims of incidental bycatch, especially by gill nets and bottom longlines. Boat strikes account for many deaths a year: a 2013 study by a group of Turkish marine biologists notes "high frequency head trauma" in sea turtles, including loggerheads, the result, most likely, of boating and fishing activities (Türkozan 14). While marine pollution is a problem in most part of the Mediterranean, crude oil in particular, a 1998 study in Turkey and Cyprus showed that few turtles were affected (Margaritoulis 189). Rapid coastal development since in Turkey may well have increased this threat to marine health, however. Natural factors such as predators like fox and feral dogs and sand erosion due to wave action and some say global warming also impact turtle populations. The threat factor that I will address in this section, however, is the direct anthropogenic damage done to nesting beaches.

The Turkish Mediterranean coast from Ekincik in the west to Samandağı in the east is about 1,577 kilometers (about 980 miles). About 481 km (299 miles) is sand, a necessary component for sea turtle nesting, and about 173.9

km (108 miles) is used by *Caretta caretta* for nesting (Canbolat 86). After Greece, the Turkish coast is one of the most important sites for sea turtle nesting in the Mediterranean. It may be the second most important site for loggerhead nesting, after Libya, though numbers are inconclusive (Canbolat 88). Considering that female loggerheads nest on average three times a year and that the number of female loggerheads that nest annually in Turkey is estimated to be approximately 668 according to a 2004 study by Ali Fuat Canbolat (though he notes that this figure still needs corroboration), this is potentially a lot of activity. These numbers are declining, however, as are all sea turtle populations worldwide. But because information on loggerheads is limited to the past thirty-five years or so worldwide, and even less in Turkey, the long history of loggerhead numbers is still a mystery, though recent decline is certain (Witherington 302). This "shifting baseline syndrome" can present problems for conservation and is yet another argument for increased funding in areas such as genetic research (Witherington 304). Loggerheads are now categorized as endangered on the IUCN (International Union for the Conservation of Nature) Red List and the species is protected by Turkish law.

Loggerheads require certain conditions for nesting: they prefer clean sandy beaches with no vegetation, a certain beach width which they evaluate according to the length of background silhouettes like dunes, trees, and, increasingly, houses and hotels (Kaska 48). Importantly, they require darkness and peace. Needless to say, all these factors—clean sand, appropriate space, darkness, and silence—are becoming increasingly harder to come by on the Turkish coast, which like coastlines all over the world is also coveted by humans. The list of anthropogenic threats affecting these beaches is long: "vehicular and pedestrian traffic, human presence at night, beachfront lighting and noise, uncontrolled development and construction, beach furniture, sand extraction, sand erosion, beach pollution ... planting of vegetation ... nearshore fishing and underwater explosives" (Margaritoulis 188). Light pollution from structures behind nesting beaches disturbs turtles and causes them to abandon these beaches (Kaska 48). It also confuses emerging hatchlings. In Turkey many of these pressures on loggerheads are generated by the tourism industry.

According to a 2015 press release by MEDASSET (Mediterranean Association to Save the Sea Turtles), two recommendations were adopted that year by the Bern Convention on the Conservation of Wildlife and Natural Habitats urging Turkey "to prevent habitat destruction and improve management of SPAs (Specially Protected Areas)" (MEDASSET). The SPAs singled out in the Bern Convention were the beaches of the popular tourist destinations Fethiye and Patara, beaches the press release ranks among the most important *Caretta caretta* nesting sites in Turkey. Local conservation groups in Turkey often cite the Bern Convention. Recommendations included all the threats listed above plus bans in Fethiye on beachside building, road and shipyard construction, and the removal of fixed structures from nesting zones; in Patara the prevention of vehicle access and the regulation of light pollution and beach furniture were emphasized (MEDASSET). Vehicles are not only a direct hazard to nests but cause the compaction of sand-creating inundations that are not only a problem for turtles (Erdoğan 34). In 2016, the following year, MEDASSET announced in a report that there had been no improvement in site protection or managements in Fethiye and that in Patara 255 new buildings were under construction directly behind the nesting beach with many more planned (MEDASSET). Wealthy Turks with second summer homes, retired Europeans, investment-savvy Russians, and tourists, both local and international, desire panoramic views of the sea and nesting beaches. Contractors, in this case a Northern Cyprus firm, Özyalçın Construction, are only happy to profit from this love of nature. Humans are drawn to the sea, especially from the safe and sand-free distance provided by the balcony of a condominium. From there we feel less vulnerable to the elements because we are more in control of their power over us. Our admiration is comfortable and abstract. We will pay good money to safely view the "unfathomable otherness of nature" (Hitt 611). And so continues the concurrence, domestication, and, ultimately, the erasure of the natural world.

While biologists and conservation groups in Turkey are at present relatively powerless against government-sanctioned domestic development projects such as the construction of luxury villas near or on SPAs, micro-management recommendations are still offered in efforts to circumvent the destruction of nesting beaches. Both international and local groups highlight the necessity of increased public awareness. "Educational programs should be prepared for both local and international tourists," suggests Canbolat: "more stringent control of lights and beach usage should be enforced on nesting beaches with high amounts of tourist activity" (Canbolat 90). Herpetologist Blair E. Witherington goes so far as to recommend the exploitation of loggerhead "charisma" in the service of education. "Sea turtles as a group seem to fit the set of characteristics that people consider to be either cute (in hatchlings: large heads and eyes relative to body size, rounded features, hyperactivity) or otherwise charismatic (in older turtles: large size, a nonthreatening nature, mysterious, ancient)" (Witherington 302). While he admits that conservation strategies based on charisma do not rely on sound science, like Cronon above, he resorts to a utilitarian ecological strategy, one that potentially sacrifices animal ethics along the way in order to preserve the animal in the long run. Witherington proposes turtle watches "in which visitors to a nesting beach sit behind a turtle at night to watch her nest" as a way to inspire emotional commitment to turtle conservation (Witherington 303).

He also offers a number of other pragmatic "opportunities" in the form of coalitions that are not necessarily directly concerned with loggerhead conservation, that is, with government agencies responsible for coastal tourism, thus beach erosion and marine debris (Witherington 307). *Caretta caretta*, in all cases, cannot thrive where human activity and development on "critical" nesting beaches are not controlled, and conservation efforts aimed at nest protection alone cannot accomplish this without help from parties interested in mutual means, even if ultimate aims diverge (Patel 126–127). In a similar, somewhat cynical, approach to conservation, William Cronon notes that if we don't pay enough attention to human-centered needs, desires, and interests, conservation efforts are doomed. Furthermore, if the behavior of environmentalists leads to "political behavior" that alienates "the very people whose support is crucial if the environment is to be protected in a sustainable way," it defeats itself (Cronon, Response 52). In other words, he says, conservation must compromise: it must promote a "wise-use" rather than a hands-off approach to, in our case, nesting beaches (Cronon, Response 53).

If one way to protect environments is to address issues that alienate those in power, we turn again to knowledge or the war against it. Dinesh Wadiwell in *The War Against Animals* argues there are three levels of violence we must address if we hope to begin to make fundamental changes in attitudes toward, among other things, the protection of wildlife: direct individual violence on the intersubjective level; institutional or structural and systemic forms of violence; and epistemic or hierarchical and inegalitarian ways of thinking and understanding. Power that is averse to environmental protection whether in the United States or in Turkey must be addressed at all levels within a particular society. It also requires efforts that function cohesively at the local and global levels. Surveying the various waves, or as Lawrence Buell prefers "palimpsest" of ecocriticism since the founding of the first professional association ASLE (Association for the Study of Literature and the Environment) in 1992, Pippa Marland notes that by 2009 a third wave of eco-cosmopolitics began to emerge. Ursula Heise, for example, argued for an ecocritical model more "globally nuanced and embracing" yet "sensitive to environmental justice issues at the local level" (Marland 1516). When we talk about long-distance migrating species, be they bird or marine reptile, we have no choice but to address the global and local simultaneously. This includes the kinds of pressure we put on power. Multinational holdings with construction interests and the local and national agencies that too often work for them would seem to exist in parallel or alternative realities to those of academicians and conservationists. It can be argued that before engagement can occur at the institutional level, it must transpire at the epistemic. And confrontations and crossings often begin with the intersubjective.

Conclusion

I learned a number of things thanks to my encounter and subsequent research. I learned that I had to give up some of the more off-road kinds of adventures I had enjoyed as a young traveler and was still partial to as an adult. No more midnight bonfires on nesting beaches or sunset tractor rides offered by local farmers across the sand to the base of local Mount Chimaera that we would hike up to experience the phenomenon of gas seeping and burning like answering flames to the stars. One kind of sublime experience gave way to another. One that acknowledged what was not immediately apparent to my imagination. The turtle reminded me that I was not alone. She also told me that no matter how much knowledge of her I might glean from science, she would always exist somewhere beyond the capacity of my human reason. In a very Kantian way, as Peter Heyman notes of Thomas Nagel in "What Is It like to Be a Bat," I seemed to have associated this humbling insight into my cognitive limitations with a "re-empowering view" that emphasized my "ability to know that the unknowable exists" and that its experience is as "complex and multidimensional" as my own (Heyman 34).

I may have rejected Kant's form of re-empowerment granted to me by the sublime: I do not believe that my supersensible, cognitive human abilities render me "superior to nature within, and therefore also to nature without" (Kant 127). My consciousness of sublime nature influences me; my destination does not transcend it: it is completely dependent on it. I will agree with Kant, however, that this position is the result of education. What I view as sublime in nature I may have regarded as simply terrible if I had not developed a respect for the "might" displayed in nature and been somehow prepared for the manner in which the "energies" of my "soul" seemed to raise above its "accustomed height" when I encountered her (Kant 125). Perhaps, as Kant suggests, sublime judgment, even when defanged, requires culture and "moral feeling" (Kant 131).

For years I have been using my story of *Caretta caretta* in the university classroom in Istanbul. I will confess this now that I have hopefully justified my intentions. I offer the story usually to incoming freshmen, students who have either never really thought about the word "sublime" as more than a heady adjective, somewhere in the lexical vicinity of "awesome" or who because they are for the most part intensely urban people have a very hard time connecting to the poetry of Wordsworth, Shelley, or even any Turkish poet writing feverishly about nature. It is true that our students because they are young adults in the first half of the twenty-first century are more receptive to non-sentient, postmodern forms of the sublime, for example "the technological sublime," that is, human-created phenomena like cyber warfare. Due to our geopolitical location and many factors leading to instability in the country and region at present, the students live directly and recurrently with the "aesthetics of terror," a term adopted in academic discourse on the sublime after 9/11. Bombs have exploded in their lifetimes, and the explosions have been replayed over and over on television and YouTube until viewers know them by heart and can distinguish their geometries and pigments.

It is therefore a challenge to talk about sublime nature now and here. But when I start my story, "a few years back I was swimming out in the sea at Çıralı.

I was about a half a kilometer out and alone, or so I thought," they listen. When I tell them "the sun was high, about 14:00 and the water around and below was lapis lazuli blue," they're still listening. By the time I get to the part where I see her and my body "short-circuits," they're with me. They understand the paradoxical implosion of fear and fascination; they are young and happy it exists. They do not know yet that we, me and unknowingly the turtle, are introducing them one by one to the ecological sublime, an introduction that I hope, for her sake and theirs, they will take with them out the door when the story is over. "There will always be limits to our knowledge, and nature will always be, finally, impenetrable," concludes Hitt:

> An ecological sublime would remind us of this lesson by restoring the wonder, the inaccessibility of wild nature. In an age of exploitation, commodification, and domination we need awe, envelopment, and transcendence. We need, at least occasionally, to be confronted with the wild otherness of nature and to be astonished, enchanted, humbled by it. (Hitt 620)

When I finish by telling them what I told her, "*Çok korktum, ama çok güzelsin,*" they nod because they understand.

Afterword

In a 2013 survey of the trajectory of Ecocriticism as an academic field, Pippa Marland describes four waves of ecocritical discourse beginning with the formal organizing of an informal group of writers and academics in 1992. As mentioned, this group would establish the first association for professionals interested in crossings between nature and literature. At least initially. The Association for the Study of Literature and the Environment (ASLE), while originally a North American project made up primarily of English professors focusing on nature writing, and with Thoreau as their guide and guru, would adjust and swell, in sync with the undulating movements of English departments. Strict focus on literary studies would open up to cultural studies and all the variations of what constitutes text that this shift made possible. While Lawrence Buell may have preferred "palimpsest" to "wave" to describe the evolution of the field through time, the word "wave" is metaphorically, if not nominally, accurate: as ecocritical discourse gathered, broke, and retreated, what came next was a mixture of beached flotsam and new water. Elements mixed. The organic metaphor is perfectly appropriate.

As suggested in the introduction, the present book is an accumulation of at least the first three waves of ecocritical inquiry. As a first wave "primitive" ecocritic, I most definitely "admire the environmental imagination" of Thoreau, Edward Abbey, and Annie Dillard (Marland 1508). *Walden*, *Desert Solitaire* and *Pilgrim at Tinker Creek* were personal companions before I introduced myself to Ecocriticism as a field of academic study. The aesthetic engagement with the natural world in these assemblages of creative non-fiction fused two realms central to my own well-being: literature and nature. This fusion was also central to the ethos of the early critical movement. I admit my approach to nature is "celebratory" and due to a youth spent rooting around the natural world my instincts vis-à-vis my field of study can reflect a "relatively uncritical understanding of nature" (Marland 1510). Any critical distance achieved in this text is hard earned.

I have also "reject[ed] certain conventions of critical discourse," at least in the introduction, in Chapter 6, and in these conclusive remarks, and have reverted to a "narrative scholarship" that "brings autobiographical accounts of interaction with the natural world into responses to literature" or, in the case of Chapter 6, into a response to a non-human being (Marland 1510, endnote 10). This is a rhetorical mode, Marland notes, common in first-wave ecocritical discourse. The book also holds assumptions endemic to second-wave Ecocriticism. "Deep ecology," a holistic ecological philosophy that endorses the equality of species, informs the post-humanist narrative that runs through these chapters. I repeatedly take umbrage with the "anthropomorphism at the heart of modern society and the kind of 'shallow ecological' standpoints that see the natural world as merely a resource for humanity" (Marland 1512).

As a third-wave ecocritic I have adjusted the circumference of my comments to include cross-cultural, transnational perspectives. It is a development that Scott Slovic and Ursula Heisse have advocated for, one that "recognizes ethnic and national particularities and yet transcends ethnic and national boundaries" (qtd. in Marland 1516). Heisse's transnational positioning in *Sense of Place and Sense of Planet: The Environmental Imagination of the Global* is in many ways a critique of third-wave Ecocriticism and the environmental movement in general in the later twentieth and early twenty-first centuries. She adheres to constructivist readings of nature that "dismantle appeals to 'the natural' or the 'biological' by showing their groundedness in cultural practices rather than facts of nature," and thereby runs counter to my more essentialist conception of nature as a biological a priori (Heisse 46). However, Heisse's arguments for reorienting ecocritical discourse "toward a more nuanced understanding of how both local cultural and ecological systems are imbricated in global ones" reinforce my own advocacy in these chapters for transnational studies of literature, culture, and nature (Heisse 59). The lands, waters, and animals examined in this book are treated as situated and local: they are rural Anatolian, Mediterranean, of urban Istanbul. They are also deterritorialized in that they are approached as cosmopolitan spaces and life forms. American voices mingle with Turkish voices in cross-cultural conversations concerning the state and fate of a world whose bits and pieces belong to separate nations in theory only. Through the close reading of poems and prose generated by these selected Turkish and North American writers, the chapters explore "the ecological imagination of the global" (Heisse 210). But rather than seeing these transnational and global reaches as "supplements" to local bioregions or local-based identities, a problem Heisse sees in much North American nature writing, the chapters attempt to approach the literature and culture in ways that suggest why local inhabitation, whether Turkish or North American, in reality "*needs ... encounter with cultures one does not inhabit*" (Heisse 43).

In many ways the ambitions of the book stop at this transnational turn in third-wave Ecocriticism. While a focus on "trans-corporeality" that has emerged in more recent fourth-wave Ecocriticism is evident in discussions of biotic and cross-species interconnectivity, the present text does not venture into the realm of technology or man-made things and therefore does not pursue some current directions in the field. It adheres to a relatively conventional vertical hierarchy of being rather than a radically horizontal one and thus reinforces somewhat traditional distinctions between organic and inorganic matter (Marland 1519). This adherence is also a form of resistance to what I see as a move to re-center human cultural production in current trends in environmental critical discourse. *Animals and the Environment in Turkish Culture: Ecocriticism and Transnational Literature* confronts the problem of human exceptionalism that Thom van Dooren also counters in *Flight Ways: Life and Loss at the Edge of Extinction*. Like van Doreen I continue to pick away at the problem of human failure to grasp or at least imagine the "multiple connections and dependencies" between ourselves and sentient non-human species as well as the environments we are born to share. While van Dooren focuses on various bird species either extinct or close to extinction, his fundamental criticism of the dysfunctional and detrimental consequences of human exceptionalism is relevant to the ambitions of the present text. I concur with his conclusion that "the affective separation of human exceptionalism holds the more-than-human world at arm's length: human exceptionalism plays a central role in the active process of our learning *not* to be affected by nonhuman others" (van Dooren 141).

I also agree with van Dooren's call for the multilateral cooperation between all branches of the natural sciences and the humanities in all efforts to readjust miscalculations that have led to current environmental crises. If the natural sciences can give us information on the experiential worlds of non-human species, their evolution, and the ways ecosystems function, the humanities by joining forces with "hard science" can facilitate the cultural appropriation of knowledge and thus work toward the material application of measures that honor the environmental integrity of the planet. "This is the domain of the 'environmental humanities', of a thinking that inhabits complex multi-species worlds without the aid (and impediment) of simplistic divisions between the human and the nonhuman, the cultural and the natural. The world is far messier and more interesting than that" (van Doreen 147).

Marland recaps a projection of future avenues for Ecocriticism and literature that Lawrence Buell offered in 2005 and that appeals to the ambitions of the current text: "As literary ecodiscourse becomes more widely practiced, more globally net-worked, more interdisciplinary and thus even more pluriform, the participant must become more aware of speaking from some position within or around the movement rather than for it" (qtd. in Marland 1508). In many ways this book offers a series of exercises in applied theory. Each chapter speaks from very particular positions within the movement and attempts only modest forays toward larger meta-theoretical hypotheses. This tapering or grounding of goals accepts Plato's thrice-removed reality as interesting in itself and attempts to inform, perhaps move the reader from within the productive limitations of that other reality forth removed, writing.

Notes

Introduction

1. Donna Haraway, among others, has been writing about the question of language and poetics within critical discourse since the 1980s. The language we use, the stories we tell are important determinants, not mere reflections, of being in the world. See, for example, Haraway's "Cyborg Manifesto" and *Primate Visions*.
2. My use of the term "post-humanism" here and later elides current critical debates over what is assumed by both the "post" and the "humanism" in this noun phrase. My usage adheres to an amalgam of "second-wave" and "third-wave" ecocritical discourse in that it expresses a resistance to the global exploitation of land and animals that human exceptionalism continues to foster. Holding the Humanist tradition responsible for all the sins of the Anthropocene is reductionist, of course. Haraway advocates the term "compost" over post-humanism (the human being etymologically rooted in *humus*, as well as, *homo*) even as she admits an "alliance and disalliance" with the term "post-humanism" (see "Companions in Conversation (With Cary Wolfe)." *Manifestly Haraway*, 261–2). And while I agree completely with this more recent biopolitical alternative, I am continuing to employ the "old-fashioned" term "post-humanism," for the time being.
3. The simultaneous engagement of arts and sciences in this book is a gesture toward what Haraway calls a "'new new synthesis' in transdisciplinary biologies and arts" ("Preface." *Cosmopolitan Animals*. Ed. Kaori Nagai et al. (London: Palgrave McMillan, 2015): ix.

Chapter 1

1. Basem L. Ra'ad in *Hidden Stories: Palestine and the Eastern Mediterranean* emphasizes the Christian nature of this trend, arguing that "the advent of sacred geography," whether clerical or laic, was primarily a fundamentalist Protestant and Anglican enterprise, one that "transformed earlier imagings about the 'Holy

Land' from theoretical typologies into literal, physically oriented applications of biblical accounts" (79).

2   For a response to Said's assessment of American Orientalism (but one that focuses primarily on the case of Indian Sanskrit), see Mishka Sina, "Orienting America: Sanskrit and Modern Scholarship in the United States, 1836-94." *Debating Orientalism* (London: Palgrave Macmillan, 2013): 73-93.

3   All further reference to the journals will be indicated by J.

4   The majority of the quotations from Ahmet Hamdi Tanpınar's *Five Cities* are from an unpublished English translation by Ruth Christie, 2007. These will be indicated by *FC* in the citations. Two quotations are from "Three Sections from 'Istanbul' in *Beş Şehir (Five Cities)*." Trans. Ruth Christie. *Texas Studies in Literature and Language*. 54.4 (2012): 456-67. These will be indicated by *TSLL*.

5   After the War of Independence and the founding of the modern Turkish Republic in 1923, Ataturk instigated a script reform program that replaced Ottoman script with a Latin alphabet. He would go on to found the Turkish Language Association (TDK) in 1932 and promote the replacement of words of Arabic and Persian origin with contemporary Turkish words used by average people or older Turkish equivalents. Part of the rationale behind the reforms was to align the new republic with the West.

6   There is a rich literature on the severing of the Ottoman past, Turkish language reform, and questions of culture and identity. See, for example, Geoffrey Lewis' definitive *The Turkish Language Reform: A Catastrophic Success* (Oxford: Oxford University Press, 2002). See also Mahmut Mutman, "The Nation-Form." *Third Text* 22.1 (January 2008): 5-20 and Hale Yılmaz, *Becoming Turkish: Nationalist Reforms and Cultural Negotiations in Early Republican Turkey 1923-1945* (Syracuse: Syracuse University Press, 2013).

7   For discussion on a related ambiguity in the poetics of Abdülhak Hâmid Tarhan (1852-1937), another, though older, Turkish writer (poet and playwright) whose life spanned the transition from empire to nation state, see Arif Camoğlu, "Inter-imperial Dimensions of Turkish Literary Modernity." *MFS Modern Fiction Studies*. 64.3 (Fall 2018): 432-57. Camoğlu illustrates how Hâmid, like other nineteenth-century writers who were once "agents of empire," became "engineers of the nation state" (449). The article questions "the neatness of the divides between empire and state, and hence between the past and present" and in turn the "truism" that Republican Turkey did not allow for Ottoman literary modes in its canon. The article investigates ways in which "national aesthetics and politics contain the epistemological residues of the antagonized empire" (449).

8   All title translations are mine unless otherwise noted.
9   Ra'ad includes a discussion of Melville's epic poem *Clarel* in this discussion of "unlearning," saying the protagonist "graduates into experiences whereby he grows out of all the old notions, and is constantly learning, unlearning, word by word" (Ra'ad 85). See William Potter for further discussion on Melville's own exercise in comparative religious studies in the long poem and the spiritual power afforded to Islam in the character of Djalea, the Druize guide (*Melville's Clarel and the Intersympathy of Creeds* [Kent OH: The Kent State University Press, 2004]).
10 For more recent studies on the central influence of the Bible on *Moby-Dick*, see Richard Forrer, *Theodicies in Conflict: A Dilemma in Puritan Ethics and Nineteenth-Century American Literature* (Westport, CT: Greenwood Press, 1986) and Jonathon A. Cook, *Inscrutable Malice: Theodicy, Eschatology and the Biblical Sources of Moby-Dick* (DeKalb, IL: Northern Illinois University Press, 2012). See also T. Walter Herbert who suggests that the theocentric crisis in *Moby-Dick* leads to a pluralistic and provisional representation of reality in the novel (*Moby-Dick and Calvinism* [New Jersey: Rutgers University Press, 1977]).
11 See Wai Chee Dimock. *Empire for Liberty: Melville and the Poetics of Individualism*; Donald Pease. "*Moby-Dick* and the Cold War." *The American Renaissance Reconsidered*; and William Spanos. *The Errant Art of "Moby-Dick": The Canon, the Cold War, and the Struggle for American Studies*.
12 For another more recent book on the influence of Islamic Mysticism on nineteenth-century American writers, including a brief examination of Melville's engagement with various Sufi poets, see *Sufism and American Literary Masters*. Ed. Mehdi Aminrazavi (Albany: State University of New York Press, 2014).
13 An interesting example of what Einboden calls the "refracting" of Islamic "implications latent within" Melville's text is the discussion of the translation challenges posed by vocabulary in chapter 35, "The Mast-Head" (*Nineteenth-Century* 2). With no clear Arabic word for "Pantheist," "Abbas" chooses an expression common in Sufism: Pantheist becomes "believer in the Oneness of Being" (Einboden, *Nineteenth-Century* 108). In this rendering the contrast between the world and all that is in it as a "self-manifestation of God" with "Descartian vortices," "ontic reality" with material plurality is reinforced. Coloring Ishmael's speech with the phrasing of mystical Islam opens the philosophical range of the chapter. It is also a reminder that translation is interpretation.

14 See again *Sufism and American Literary Masters*. Ed. Mehdi Aminrazavi for a recent book-length study of Emerson's engagement with Mediaeval Islamic mystical poetry.
15 See Kim Fortuny, "Herman Melville in Istanbul: Ishmael, Urban Naturalist." In *American Writers in Istanbul* (Syracuse: Syracuse University Press, 2009): 1–29.

Chapter 2

1 *Vatan* stems etymologically from *al-watan*, Arabic for homeland, home country.
2 Recent examples of such protests have been organized against hydroelectric power plants (HEPP) in the east of Turkey and on the Black Sea coast. In 2010 protestors from over fifty regions in Turkey protested in front of the Ministry of Environment in Ankara. Over 1,700 HEPP and dam projects in Turkey have had devastating effects on the environment. See Hayriye Özen's "Overcoming Environmental Challenge by Antagonizing Environmental Protestors: The Turkish Government Discourse Against the Anti-Hydroelectric Power Plants Movement." *Environmental Communication*. 8.4 (2014): 433–51. Similar protests took place in March of 2015 in Zile, north-central Turkey.
3 The open library offered an eclectic choice of books, local and foreign. While Hikmet's poetry collections figured prominently, there were also many other Turkish poets represented, especially "İkinci Yeni" (Second New) writers such as Edip Cansever and Turgut Uyar. Lines from these poets also graced the makeshift banners and posters.
4 In 1995 the Islamist Welfare party led by Necmettin Erbakan was shut down by the military. The current president, former prime minister Recep Tayyip Erdoğan, and former member of the Islamist Welfare party, has countered numerous attempts at what his ruling Justice and Development party (AKP) perceives to be threats to national security. A 2016 coup d'états attempt was unsuccessful.
5 Recent studies that consider the interrelationship between Romantic poetry and science help to dispel the validity of this polarity. See Richard Holmes, *The Age of Wonder: How the Romantic Generation Discovered the Beauty and Terror of Nature* (New York: Pantheon, 2008); Robert Logan, *The Poetry of Physics and the Physics of Poetry* (Singapore: World Scientific, 2010); Mary Midgely, *Science and Poetry* (London: Routledge, 2001); Ashton Nichols, "The Loves of Plants and Animals: Romantic Science and the Pleasures of Nature." *Romantic*

Ecology. November, 2001, http://www.rc.umd.edu. Timothy Morton's *Ecology Without Nature: Rethinking Environmental Aesthetics* (Cambridge, MA: Harvard University Press, 2007) and *The Ecological Thought* (Cambridge, MA: Harvard University Press, 2009) also argue for the interdependence of nature and culture with reference to Romantic poetry.

6   I have used two English translations of selected poems by Hikmet: *Poems of Nâzım Hikmet*, by Randy Blasing and Mutlu Konuk Blasing which appears as *"Poems"* in the citations; and *Beyond the Walls*, by Ruth Christie, Richard McKane and Talât Halman which appears as *"Beyond."* I have chosen the versions of particular poems that I feel most successfully convey the original Turkish both in terms of sound and sense.

7   Mutlu Konuk-Blasing's biography, *Nâzım Hikmet: The Life and Times of Turkey's World Poet*, to which my own study of Hikmet's poetry is strongly indebted, will be indicated as "KB" throughout the remainder of the text.

8   For a discussion of ways in which Hikmet observes Divan and Turkish Folk traditions even as he revises and transforms them in his modernist poetics, see Özge Öztekin "A Poet Revising Tradition in Modern Turkish Poetry: Nâzım Hikmet and Intertextuality (*'Modern Türk Şiirinde Geleneği Yeniden Üreten Bir Şair: Nâzım Hikmet ve Metinlerarasılık')*." *JFL* (Journal of Faculty of Letters). Hacettepe University Faculty of Letters. 25.1 (2008): 129–50. In Turkish. See also Mutlu Konuk-Blasing, "Nâzım Hikmet and Ezra Pound: 'To Confess Wrong Without Losing Rightness.'" *Journal of Modern Literature*. 33.2 (Winter 2010): 1–23. Here, Konuk-Blasing notes that the preexisting forms of Ottoman poetry—the quantitative meters of court poetry and the oral folk poetry composed in syllabics—offered no precedent for Hikmet's modernist idiom. Hikmet challenged the "two kinds of poetry [divan and folk] of two different socio-economic classes—a privileged class and a dispossessed class at a great remove from the center of Ottoman court power," both of whom "conspired to protect a poetic domain, if a domain strictly divided within itself" (8). Hikmet's free verse revolution "broke down those borders, crossing formal and political borders without a passport" (8).

9   As a "young" language, at least in its Latin script form, Turkish has not undergone the changes that time brings to the relationship between script and sound. Unlike English, Turkish is still a phonetic language.

10 This study is limited to the poems presently available in good English translations for the convenience of international readers. These translations include the more frequently anthologized poems in Hikmet's oeuvre.

11 For further reading on nation building and representations of Anatolia in early Republican Turkish literature, see Nüket Esen, "The Turkish Novel: From Model of Modernity to Puzzle of Postmodernity." In *Turkey's Engagement With Modernity: Conflict and Change in the Twentieth Century.* Ed. Celia Kerslake, Kerem Öktem and Philip Robbins (London: Palgrave MacMillan, St. Anthony's Series, 2010): 323–35; Chapter three of Azade Seyhan, *Tales of Crossed Destinies: The Modern Turkish Novel in a Comparative Context* (New York: The Modern Language Association of America, 2008); Frank Tachau, "The Search for National Identity Among the Turks." *Die Welt des Islams.* VIII.1–2 (1962): 165–76; Murat Belge. "Genç Kalemler and Turkish Nationalism." In *Turkey's Engagement With Modernity: Conflict and Change in the Twentieth Century.* Ed. Celia Kerslake, Kerem Öktem and Philip Robbins (London: Palgrave MacMillan, St. Anthony's Series, 2010): 27–37.

12 Köksal argues that because Hikmet created problems early on for the official authority by looking beyond the nationalist paradigm in Turkish literature his socialist modernism was considered "doubly dangerous" (44). It "challenged not only aesthetic and literary conventions, but also the politics of nation-building in early republican Turkey" (44). Hikmet responded to the need for new forms and language that attended to local economic and political concerns in Turkey: "Nâzım's literary enterprise was found threatening because he challenged the nationalist paradigm and vocabulary through a 'leftist internationalism'" (44). Köksal underscores the transnational character of Hikmet's poetics arguing that his literary modernism should not be considered a belated imitation of Western modernist trends but rather a re-contextualized cultural translation of an "international wave of decolonization and modernity" (31, 37). See also Duygu Köksal, "Art and Power in Turkey: Culture, Aesthetics and Nationalism during the Single Party Era." *New Perspectives on Turkey.* 31 (Fall 2004): 91–119 for a discussion of the project of Turkish modernism in the plastic arts.

13 Contemporary studies that include Hikmet in discussions of the literary representation of Anatolia in the context of nation building in the 1920s and 1930s include Hercules Millas, "The 'Other' and Nation Building: The Testimony of Greek and Turkish Novel," first published in *Representations of the "Other/s" in the Mediterranean* World *and Their Impact on the Region.* Ed. Nedret Kuran-Burçoğlu and Susan Gilson Miller (Istanbul: The Issis Press, 2005) and, more recently, Erik J. Zürcher, *The Young Turk Legacy and Nation Building: From the Ottoman Empire to Atatürk's Turkey* (New York: Palgrave Macmillan, 2010).

14 Free verse is considered one of Hikmet's most important contributions to Turkish poetics. He acknowledged his familiarity with French *vers libre*, and, though critics compare his work to that of the Russian poet Vladimir Mayakowsky, Hikmet claimed to have been interested only in its appearance on the page because he did not learn Russian until later in life (Halman 17). Studies have also been done on the influence and relation of Whitman's free verse on Hikmet's aesthetic. See Neslihan Günaydın, "Forerunners of Modern Poetry: Nâzım Hikmet and Walt Whitman." *ASOS: The Journal of Academic Social Science*. 2.1 (June 2014): 225–33.

15 It should be noted, however, that contrary to my reading here, these lines, as well as this poem, have often been read and continue to be read in paternalistic terms in public discourse serving a nationalist agenda.

16 For a discussion of how environmental policy became the focus of political dissent at Gezi Park and the place of the poem "The Walnut Tree" as its anthem, see Ayşem Mert, "The Trees in Gezi Park: Environmental Policy as the Focus of Democratic Protests." *Journal of Environmental Policy and Planning*, 2016. https://www.tandfonline.com/doi/full/ 10.1080/1523908X.2016.1202106.

17 References to Hikmet and his poems, and especially the last two poems discussed here, abounded on social media both during and shortly after the Gezi protests. Nilüfer Göle offers Hikmet's lines "To live like at tree alone and free and like a forest in brotherhood" as the epigram for her article "Anatomy of a Public Movement, Istanbul, Turkey." *Insight Turkey*. 15.3 (Summer 2013): 7–14. In it she illustrates how the Gezi Park Movement "opened up a new arena of creative experience and provided a home for democratic imaginaires growing and resonating from Istanbul, Turkey." The opposition leader Kemal Kılıçdaroğlu (CHP) was cited on several news sources quoting from "Galloping Full-tilt ... " and suggesting that Hikmet whose grave is in Moscow should be buried in Gülhane Park. Kaya Genç reporting in June 2013 on the anniversary of Hikmet's death relates how protestors chanted verses from the poem "The Walnut Tree" together (http:www.englishpen.org/pen-atlas/the-walnut-tree- of-gezi-park/). Hikmet's poems were often quoted in tweets and Facebook posts, particularly in connection with the young victims of police brutality. The hashtag #siirsokakta (poetry on the streets) documents street graffiti in Istanbul and around Turkey, much of which includes lines from Hikmet poems. The rich public and critical response to Gezi since 2013 has manifested in various forms of collective memory, including interviews, stories, photograph collections, historical research, and political commentary.

18 A university library copy of Nâzım Hikmet's poems used in the writing of this chapter was confiscated from an airmail envelope in September 2015. This says much about Hikmet's continued relevance. Boğaziçi University, in Istanbul, Turkey, where I teach, opened the Nâzım Hikmet Cultural and Artistic Research Center in December of 2014.

Chapter 3

1 For a study of the railway as a vehicle for modernist formal innovation in Hikmet's poetics, see Marian Aguiar, "Nâzım Hikmet's Modernization of Development." *Journal of Modern Literature*. 30.4. (Summer 2007); 105–121. According to Aguiar, Hikmet's epic poem *Human Landscapes from My Country* provides a vision of a modern space in the 1940s where social hierarchies are simultaneously transgressed and maintained. The railway as a "haunted object of modernity" represents the disjuncture of Mustapha Kemal's European modernization program and Turkey's Ottoman past.

Chapter 4

1 This chapter began as a collaborative project with the Istanbul film producer Gülen Güler. In the end, I wrote an essay and she made a documentary film, *Taşkafa: Stories of the Street*. John Berger provided the frame narrative with readings from his novel *King: A Street Story*. *Taşkafa* premiered April 12, 2013, in the Istanbul International Film Festival.
2 My dilemma concerning the application of the personal pronoun "she" to a dog throughout this essay can perhaps be best expressed by Robin Wall Kimmerer in "Learning the Grammar of Animacy": "English doesn't give us many tools for incorporating respect for animacy. In English, you're either human or a thing. Our grammar boxes us in by the choice of reducing a non-human being to an 'it,' or if it must be gendered, inappropriately a 'he' or a 'she'" (Kimmerer 175).
3 I am referring here to Jacques Derrida's "The Animal That Therefore I Am (More to Follow)." *Critical Inquiry*. 28.2 (2002): 369–418.

Commenting on Derrida's essay in her book *When Species Meet*, Haraway herself notes that while Derrida "came right to the edge of respect" in his assessment of his morning encounter with his cat, he was "sidetracked by his textual canon of Western philosophy and literature and by his own linked worries about being naked in front of his cat" (*Species* 33). The implication for the present argument here is that the alterity of animals, here a domestic pet specifically, is not adequately accounted for. Derrida, Haraway argues, is ultimately more concerned with his own philosophical tradition, which is of "no consequence" to the cat, and, I would add, even less so to an urban street dog in the developing world.

4   There were smaller-scale movements to remove street dogs to less populated areas as early as the seventeenth century. In her investigation of Ottoman human–animal relations, particularly equine relations, Donna Landry in "English Brutes, Eastern Enlightenment" writes that the English Clergyman Thomas Smith reports during the 1670s that dogs were removed to Üksüdar during an outbreak of plague by order of the Grand Mufti, because he would not hear of their being killed or culled, though they were potential carriers of infection (Landry 22). Smith notes that "the Mufti … would by no means give way to so bloody and cruel a sentence, maintaining that it was unlawful" and furthermore that because "Dogs had Souls," they were to be "exempt from this universal and horrid carnage" (qtd. in Landry 22).

5   For a discussion of "the violence of modernity" and the street dog population of Istanbul, see Colin Dayan's discussion of the feature length documentary essay, *Taşkafa: Stories of the Street* in *With Dogs on the Edge of Life* (New York: Columbia University Press, 2015): 123–36 (Zimmerman qtd. in Dalan 124, 123).

6   For a survey and discussion of "dogs as workers" in the United States, see Haraway's subchapter, "Valuing Dogs: Technologies, Workers, Knowledge" (pages 68–75), in *When Species Meet*.

7   This notion of belated modernism was promoted in the post-Republican era and taught in schools in Turkey until quite recently. For a good source on the Tanzimat period, see *The Cambridge History of Turkey: Turkey in the Modern World*. *Vol. 4*. Ed. Reşat Kasaba (Cambridge: Cambridge University Press, 2008).

8   For a discussion of large-scale culling of street dogs in modern Bangalore, neoliberal hierarchies and alternatives offered by "entangled [interspecies] associations," see Anuradha Ramanujan, "'Stray' Dogs in Indian Cities." In *Cosmopolitan Animals*. Ed. Kaori Nagai et al. (London: Palgrave Macmillan, 2016): 216–32. Ramanujan presented a version of this chapter at *Cosmopolitan Animals*, a conference held at the Institute of English Studies, University of London, in October 2012, jointly organized by the Schools of English and

History at the University of Kent. This paper helped me think early on about my own work on feral urban dogs.

The right to assemble and protest is presently curbed at the time of this writing due to measures taken under the state of emergency after the 2016 coup attempt.

9. I've used the word "adoption" here, but the term "rescue" is also often used by these organizations. Haraway reflects on the problematic replacement of adoption discourse for rescue discourse in "Companions in Conversation (With Cary Wolfe)" in *Manifestly Haraway* (199–298).

10. The activist and writer, Brian Tokar continues the work of Leopold in formulating bioregionalism. See *The Green Alternative: Creating an Ecological Future* (San Pedro, California: R.& E. Miles, 1987, 1992) onward.

11. Haraway's self-confessed struggle with the health conditions of the Puerto Rican street dogs in *The Companion Species Manifesto* is a brief moment in a long discursive history of caring for canines, wild and domestic, wolves and dogs, wolf-dog hybrids. For an extended study of her "entanglement" with canines, see *When Species Meet*.

12. For a divergent but allied discussion of the dog as a "figure for defying politics while existing on the periphery of the polis" in the context of Diogenes Cynicism and animal cosmopolitanism, see Andrea Haslanger, "The Cynic as Cosmopolitan Animal." In *Cosmopolitan Animals*. Ed. Kaori Nagai et al. (London: Palgrave Macmillan, 2016): 29–42.

13. The *Manāqeb al ʿārefīn*, (*The Feats of the Knowers of God*) is a fourteenth-century biography of the Sufi mystic poet Jalal al-Din-e Rumi by Shams al-Din Ahmad-e Aflākī.

14. The *Nafahāt al-ʿUns* (*The Lives of Notable Figures of the Spiritual Path*) is a ninth-century Persian Sufi mystical text by Abdul al-Rahman Jami.

15. An alternative English translation of these lines in Ibrahim Özdemir's "Environmental Ethics from a Qur'anic Perspective" reads: "There is not an animal [that lives] on the earth, nor a being that flies on its wings, but [forms part of] communities like you" (Özdemir 28).

Chapter 5

1. All translations of poems from Turkish to English in this chapter are by İpek Kotan.
2. See discussion of *hüzün* in Chapter 1.

3   For more discussion on migratory birds and the relationship between the local and the global that they oblige us to consider in a shared world, see Thom van Dooren, *Flightways: Life and Loss at the Edge of Extinction* (New York: Columbia University Press, 2016). Van Dooren, an environmental philosopher and anthropologist at the University of New South Wales, is an important pioneer in the emerging field of "extinction studies."

4   For a study of migrating birds, collisions, and the unaccommodating materiality of cities in North America, see Nadia Berenstein's "Deathtraps in the Fly Ways." *Cosmopolitan Animals*, 79–92.

5   Acem is originally a derogatory term for non-Arab or Persian meaning one who is illiterate or mute; Kuh-i-kaf is a mythical mountain; Sultan Suleyman: King Solomon.

6   There are a number of folkloric anecdotes that continue to circulate in Turkey. The most common is that storks are a sign one will travel soon. Another observation common in Anatolian villages is that storks are "Hajji storks," whose migration route closely follows the route of the Haj (pilgrimage) to Mecca. It is considered good luck to have a stork nest on one's roof. Lady Mary Montague, the early eighteenth-century epistler and wife of the English Ambassador to the Ottoman Capital, writes the following of her experience of storks in Turkey, from Adrianople, modern Edirne, in April 1717:

> Here are some birds held in a sort of religious Reverence and for that reason Multiply prodigiously: Turtles on the Account of their Innocency, and Storks because they are suppos'd to make every Winter a Pilgrimage to Mecha. To say the truth, they are the happiest Subjects under the Turkish Government, and are so sensible of their previleges they walk the streets without fear and generally build in the low parts of Houses. Happy are those that are so distinguish'd: the vulgar Turks are perfectly perswaded that they will not be that year either attack'd by Fire or Pestilence. I have the happiness of one of their Sacred nests just under my chamber Window. (Montague 341)

7   Latour's adoption of Isabelle Stengers' cosmopolitical terminology here underscores Stengers' own call for an "opening out of the cosmopolitan beyond the human" (Haraway qtd. In Landry, "Introduction: Cosmopolitics," *Cosmopolitan Animals* 9). Kaori Nagai in the general introduction to *Cosmopolitan Animals*, follows the lead of Stengers and Haraway stating that "to think of the possibility of cosmopolitan animals, we have to start by redefining 'a cosmos' as a tangled-up 'knot of species coshaping one another,'" rather than as "an orderly 'good world'" as put forth in

Kantian terms (Nagai 2). See Isabelle Stengers, "The Cosmopolitical Proposal."
In *Making Things Public: Atmospheres of Democracy*. Ed. B. Latour and P. Weibel
(Cambridge, MA; London: MIT Press, 2005): 994–1003.

Chapter 6

1   This is a practice Porter blames principally on seventeenth-century Nicolas
    Boileau, who is thought to have introduced Longinus to the European West with
    his translation and commentary *Traité du sublime* 1674 (Porter 105).

Bibliography

Able, Kenneth P. *Gathering of Angels: Migrating Birds and Their Ecology*. Ed. Kenneth Able. Ithaca: Cornell University Press, 1999.

Addison, Joseph. *The Spectator*. London: George Routledge and Sons Limited, 1891. Vol. 2, No. 412, Monday, June 23, 1712. *The Project Gutenberg*. April, 2004. https://www.gutenberg.org/files/12030/12030-h/SV2/Spectator.2.html.

Akova, Akgün. "'Kuş Bakışı' ('A Bird's-Eye View')." In *Aşk ve Kuyruklu Yıldız*. Istanbul: Çınar Yayınları, 1997: 14.

Anayurt. http://www.anayurtgazetesi.com/haber/Hidroelektrik-santrali-protesto-edildi/576655.

Archaux, Frédéric, Gilles Balanca, Pierre-Yves Henry, and Gérard Zapata. "Wintering of White Storks in Mediterranean France." *Waterbirds: The International Journal of Waterbird Biology* 27.4 (Dec, 2004): 441–45.

Arolat, Ali Mümtaz. "'Leylekler' ('The Storks')." *Bir Gemi Yelken Açtı*. Dünya Aktüel, 2006. https://www.antoloji.com/leylekler-siiri/.

Arslangündoğdu, Zeynel. "İstanbul'da Yapılması Planlanan Projelerin Kuş Göç Yolları Üzerindeki Etkileri" ("The Effects of Future Projects in Istanbul on the Migration Routes of Birds"). Istanbul: Tema Vakfı, 2014: 76–84.

Aşçı, Arif. *İstanbul'un Sokak Köpekleri (The Street Dogs of Istanbul)*. Istanbul: Türkiye İş Bankası Kültür Yayınları, 2009.

Barthes, Roland. *Mythologies*. London: Paladin Books, 1984.

Berenstein, Nadia. "Deathtraps in the Fly Ways." In *Cosmopolitan Animals*. Ed. Kaoir Nagai et al. London: Palgrave Macmillan, 2015: 79–92.

Berger, John. *About Looking*. New York: Vintage International, 1991.

Birlik, Nurten. "Tanpınar's Attempts to Go Beyond Temporal Reality: 'The Dance', A Bergsonian Analysis." *Middle Eastern Literatures* 10.2 (2007): 175–83.

Burt, Jonathon. "Illumination of the Animal Kingdom: The Role of Light and Electricity in Animal Representation." In *The Animals Reader: The Essential Classic and Contemporary Writings*. Ed. Kalof Linda and Fitzgerald Amy. New York: Berg, 2007: 289–301.

Camoğlu, Arif. "Inter-imperial Dimensions of Turkish Literary Modernity." *MFS Modern Fiction Studies* 64.3 (Fall, 2018): 432–57.

Can, Okan. "Süzülen Kuşların Göç Rotaları." *Bilim ve Teknik Dergisi*, Mayıs, 2004: 5. http://www.bilimteknik.tubitak.gov.tr/system/files/gokyuzundeki_yollar.pdf.

Canbolat, Ali Fuat. "A Review of Sea Turtle Nesting Activity Along the Mediterranean Coast of Turkey." *Biological Conservation* 116 (2004): 81–91.

Cansever, Edip. "'Dostlar' ('Friends')." In *Yerçekimli Karanfil: Toplu Şiirleri 1*. Istanbul: Adam Yayınları, 1997: 390.

Ciach, Michal and Robert Kruszyk. "The Foraging of White Storks Ciconia ciconia on Rubbish Dumps on Non-Breeding Grounds." *Waterbirds: The International Journal of Waterbird Biology* 33.1 (March, 2010): 101–4.

Cook, Jonathon A. *Inscrutable Malice: Theodicy, Eschatology and the Biblical Sources of Moby-Dick*. Dekalb, IL: Northern Illinois University Press, 2012.

Coren, Stanley. "Dogs and Islam: The Devil and the Seeing-Eye Dog." Mar 23, 2010. http:www.psychologytoday.com/blog/canine.

Cox, George W. *Bird Migration and Global Change*. Washington: Island Press, 2010.

Cronon, William. "The Trouble with Wilderness: Response." *Environmental History* 1.1 (1996): 47–55.

Cronon, William. "The Trouble with Wilderness: Or, Getting Back to the Wrong Nature." *Environmental History* 1.1 (1996): 7–28.

Dayan, Colin. *With Dogs on the Edge of Life*. New York: Columbia University Press, 2015.

DeLoughrey, Elizabeth and George B. Handley. *Postcolonial Ecologies: Literatures of the Environment*. New York: Oxford University Press, 2011.

Dimock, Chee Wai. *Empire for Liberty: Melville and the Poetics of Individualism*. Princeton: Princeton University Press, 1989.

Dimock, Chee Wai. "Deep Time: American Literature and World History." *American Literary History* 13.4 (2001): 755–75.

Dimock, Chee Wai. "Hemispheric Islam: Continents and Centuries for American Literature." *American Literary History* 21.1 (2009): 28–52.

DOEN. https://web.archive.org/web/20160125143917/http://www.doen.com.tr:80/kurumsal.aspx.

Doherty, Peter. *Their Fate Is Our Fate: How Birds Foretell Threat to Our Health and Our World*. New York: The Experiment, 2012.

Economides, Louise. *The Ecology of Wonder in Romantic and Postmodern Literature*. New York: Palgrave Macmillan, 2016.

Einboden, Jeffrey. "The Early American Qur'an: Islamic Scripture and US Canon." *The Journal of Qur'anic Studies* 11.2 (2009): 1–19.

Einboden, Jeffrey. *Nineteenth-Century US Literature in Middle Eastern Languages*. Edinburgh: Edinburgh University Press, 2013.

Elliott, Emory. "'Wandering to-and-fro': Melville and Religion." In *A Historical Guide to Herman Mellville*. Ed. Giles Gunn. New York: Oxford University Press, 2005: 167–204.

Elmarsafy, Ziad, Anna Bernard, and David Attwell. Eds. *Debating Orientalism*. London: Palgrave Macmillan, 2013.

Erdoğan, Ali, Mehmet Öz, Yakup Kaska, Serdar Düşen, Aziz Aslan, Mustafa Yavuz, M. Rızvan Tunç, and Hakan Sert. "Marine turtle nesting at Patara, Turkey, in 2000." *Zoology in the Middle East* 24 (2001): 31–34.

Erzincan. http://www.radikal.com.tr/cevre/erzincan-da-hes-protestosu-1528517/.

Finkelstein, Dorothee Metlitsky. *Melville's Orienda*. New York: Octagon Books, 1961.

Forrer, Richard. *Theodicies in Conflict: A Dilemma in Puritan Ethics and Nineteenth-Century American Literature*. Westport, CT: Greenwood Press, 1986.

Fortuny, Kim. "Herman Melville in Istanbul: Ishmael, Urban Naturalist." In *American Writers in Istanbul*. Syracuse: Syracuse University Press, 2009: 1–29.

Franchot, Jenny. "Melville's Traveling God." In *The Cambridge Companion to Herman Melville*. Ed. Robert S. Levine. Cambridge: Cambridge University Press, 1998: 157–85.

Gander, Forrest, John Kinsella. *Redstart: And Ecological Poetics*. Iowa City: University of Iowa Press, 2012.

Göknar, Erdağ. "Ottoman Past and Turkish Future: Ambivalence in A. H. Tanpınar's *Those Outside the Scene*." *The South Atlantic Quarterly* 102.2/3 (2003): 647–61.

Gündüz, Olgun. "Ahmet Hamdi Tanpınar: A Unique Figure in Turkey's Westernization Quest." *U.U. Fen-Edebiyat Fakültesi Sosyal Bilimler Dergisi* 3 (2002): 13–28.

Haberler. https://www.haberler.com/bakanlik-hes-icin-ced-uygundur-raporu-verdi-7848740-haberi/.

Halman, Talât Sait. "Atilla Ilhan and the Promise of Turkish Poetry." *Books Abroad*. Oklahoma: Board of Regents of the University of Oklahoma. 37.4 (1963): 403–05. http://www.jstor.org/stable/40118098 (accessed February 17, 2017).

Halman, Talat Sait. "Modern Turkish Literature: Disorientation and Reorientation." *Books Abroad* 46.2 (1972): 226–31.

Halman, Talat Sait. "Introduction: Hikmet: Turkey's Romantic Revolutionary." In *Hikmet: Beyond the Walls: Selected Poems*. Trans. Christie, McKane, Halman. London: Anvil Press Poetry Ltd., 2002: 9–18.

Haraway, Donna. *The Companion Species Manifesto: Dogs, People, and Significant Otherness*. Chicago: Prickly Paradigm Press, 2003.

Haraway, Donna. "Cyborgs to Companion Species: Reconfiguring Kinship in Technoscience." In *The Animals Reader: The Essential Classic and Contemporary Writings*. Ed. Kalof and Amy Fitzgerald. New York: Berg, 2007: 362–74.

Haraway, Donna. *When Species Meet*. Minneapolis: University of Minneapolis Press, 2008.

Haraway, Donna. *Manifestly Haraway*. Minneapolis: University of Minneapolis Press, 2016.
Hawthorne, Nathaniel. *The English Notebooks*. Ed. Randal Stewart. New York: Pierpont Morgan, 1941.
Hayvanları Koruma Kanunu. http://www.resmigazete.gov.tr/eskiler/2004/07/20040701.htm.
Heide, Markus. "Herman Melville's 'Benito Cereno,' Inter-American Relations, and Literary Pan-Americanism." *Amerikastudien/American Studies* 53.1 (2008): 37–56.
Heisse, Ursula. *Sense of Place and Sense of Planet: The Environmental Imagination of the Global*. Oxford: Oxford University Press, 2008.
Herbert T., Walter. *Moby-Dick and Calvinism*. New Jersey: Rutgers University Press, 1977.
Heyman, Peter. *Animality in British Romanticism: The Aesthetics of Species*. New York: Routledge, 2012.
Hickman, Jared. "The Theology of Democracy Author." *The New England Quarterly* 81.2 (2008): 177–217.
Hikmet, Nâzım. *Poems of Nâzım Hikmet*. Trans. Randy Blasing and Mutlu Konuk. New York: Persea Books, 2002a.
Hikmet, Nâzım. *Beyond the Walls: Selected Poems*. Trans. Ruth Christie, Richard McKane and Talât Sait Halman. London: Anvil Press Poetry Ltd., 2002b.
Hikmet, Nâzım. *The Poems of Nâzım Hikmet*. Trans. Randy Blasing and Mutlu Konuk. New York: Persea Books, 2002c.
Hitt, Christopher. "Toward an Ecological Sublime." *New Literary History* 30.3 (1999): 604–620.
Huggan, Graham and Helen Tiffin. *Post-Colonial Ecocriticism: Literature, Animals, Environment*. London: Routledge, 2010.
Hume, Angela. "Imagining Ecopoetics: An Interview with Robert Hass, Brenda Hillman, Evelyn Reilly, and Jonathan Skinner." *ISLE* 19.4 (2012): 751–66.
Hür, Ayşe. "İstanbul'un Kıdemli Sakinleri: Sokak Köpekleri ('The Old Inhabitants of Istanbul: Street Dogs')." *Birgün*. June 28, 2008. http://durustavci.com/forum/index.php?topic=3869.0.
İlhan, Attila. "maria misakian." In *Yağmur Kaçağı*. Ankara: Ok Yayınları, 1971: 53.
İlhan, Attila. "'bir, üç ve beş' ('one three five')." In *Bütün Şiirleri 2: Sisler Bulvarı*. Ankara: Bilgi Yayınları, 1997: 17.
Jeffery, Moussaieff Masson and Susan McCarthy. "Grief, Sadness, and the Bones of Elephants." In *The Animals Reader: The Essential Classic and Contemporary Writings*. Ed. Linda Kalof and Amy Fitzgerald. Oxford: Berg, 2007: 91–103.

Kahraman, Hasan Bülent. "'Yitirilmemis, Zamanın Ardında: Ahmet Hamdi Tanpınar ve Muhafazakar Modernliğin Estetik Düzlemi'. ['In Pursuit of Time Not Lost: Ahmet Hamdi Tanpınar and the Aesthetic Dimension of Conservative Modernism']." In *Bir Gül Bu Karanlıklarda. [A Rose in This Darkness]*. Ed. Abdullah Uçman and Handan Inci. Istanbul: Kitabevi, 2002: 612–45.

Kalof, Linda and Amy Fitzgerald. Eds. *The Animals Reader: The Essential Classic and Contemporary Writings*. Oxford: Berg, 2007.

Kant, Immanuel. *Kant's Critique of Judgement*. Trans. J. H. Bernard. St Martin's Street, London: Macmillian and Co., Limited, 1914. *The Project Gutenberg*. March 2015, https://www.gutenberg.org/files/48433/48433-h/48433-h.htm.

Kaska, Yakup, Eyüp Başkale, Raşit Urhan, Yusuf Katılmış, Müge Gidiş, Fikret Sarı, Doğan Sözbilen, A. Fuat Canbolat, Fevzi Yılmaz, Murat Barlas, Nedim Özdemir, and Mehmet Özkul. "Natural and Anthropogenic Factors Affecting the Nest-Site Selection of Loggerhead Turtles, Caretta Caretta, on Dalaman-Sarıgerme Beach in South-West Turkey." *Zoology in the Middle East* 50.1 (2010): 47–58.

Kimmerer, Robin Wall. "Learning the Grammar of Animacy." In *The Colors of Nature: Culture, Identity, and the Natural World*. Ed. Alison Hawthorne Deming and Lauret E. Savoy. Minneapolis, MN: Milkweed Editions, 2002: 167–77.

Kimmerer, Robin Wall. "Learning the Grammar of Animacy." In *Colors of Nature: Culture, Identity, and the Natural World*. Ed. Alison H. Deming and Lauret E. Savoy. Minneapolis: Milkweed Editions, 2011: 167–77.

Knickerbocker, Scott. *Ecopoetics: The Language of Nature, the Nature of Language*. Boston: University of Massachusetts Press, 2012.

Konuk-Blasing, Mutlu. *Nâzım Hikmet: The Life and Times of Turkey's World Poet*. New York: Persea Books, 2013.

Köksal, Duygu. "Domesticating the Avant-Garde in a Nationalist Era: Aesthetic Modernism in 1930s Turkey." *New Perspectives on Turkey* 50 (2015): 29–53.

Köroğlu, Erol. *Ottoman Propaganda and Turkish Identity During World War I*. New York: Tauris Academic Studies, 2007.

Kuzeyormanları. http://www.kuzeyormanlari.org/2015/05/10/kuslari-egitiriz-iddiasina-yanit-goc-yollari-degistirilemez/.

Landry, Donna. "English Brutes, Eastern Enlightenment." *The Eighteenth Century: Theory and Interpretation* 52.1 (2011): 11–30.

Latour, Bruno. "Politics of Nature: East and West Perspectives." *Ethics & Global Politics* (Routledge) 4.1 (2011): 71–80.

Leopold, Aldo. *A Sand County Almanac*. Oxford: Oxford University Press, 1949.

Leroux, Jean-François. "Wars for Oil: Moby-Dick, Orientalism, and Cold-War Criticism." *Canadian Review of American Studies* 39.4 (2009): 423–42.

Llewellyn, Othman Abd-ar-Rhaman. "The Basis for a Discipline of Islamic Environmental Law." In *Islam and Ecology*. Cambridge: Harvard University Press, 2003: 185–247.

Lohmann, Catherine M. F. and Kenneth J. Lohmann. "Orientation Mechanisms of Hatchling Loggerheads." In *Loggerhead Sea Turtles*. Ed. Alan B. Bolten and Blair E. Witherington. Washington: Smithsonian Books, 2003: 44–62.

Lohmann, Catherine M. F. and Kenneth J. Lohmann. "Sea Turtles." *Current Biology*. 16.18 (2006): R784–R786.

Longinus. *Longinus On the Sublime*. Trans. H. L. Havell. New York: Macmillan and Co., 1890. *The Project Gutenberg*. March, 2006.

Lyotard, Jean-François. *The Postmodern Condition: A Report on Knowledge*. Minneapolis: University of Minnesota Press, 1989.

Magnin, Gernant and Murat Yarar. *Important Bird Areas in Turkey*. Istanbul: Doğal Hayatı Koruma Derneği, 1997.

Makdisi, Ussama. *Artillery of Heaven: American Missionaries and the Failed Conversion of the Middle East*. Ithaca: Cornel University Press, 2008.

Manes, Christopher. "Nature and Silence." In *The Ecocriticism Reader: Landmarks in Literary Ecology*. Ed. Cheryll Glotfelty and Harold Fromm. London: The University of Georgia Press, 1996.

Margaritoulis, Dimitris, Roberto Argano, Ibrahim Baran, Flegra Bentivegna, Mohamed N. Bradai, Juan Antonio Camiñas, Paulo Casale, Gregorio De Metrio, Andreas Demetropoulos, Guido Gerosa, Brendan J. Godley, Daw A. Haddoud, Jonathon Houghton, Luc Laurent, and Bojan Lazar. "Loggerhead Turtles in the Mediterranean Sea: Present Knowledge and Conservation Perspectives." In *Loggerhead Sea Turtles*. Ed. Alan Bolten and Blair E. Witherington. Washington: Smithsonian Books, 2003: 175–98.

Marland, Pippa. "Ecocriticism." In *Literary Theory: An Anthology*. Ed. Julie Rivkin and Michael Ryan. London: Wiley Blackwell, 2017: 1506–28.

Marr, Timothy. "Without the Pale: Melville and Ethnic Cosmopolitanism." In *A Historical Guide to Herman Mellville*. Ed. Giles Gunn. New York: Oxford University Press, 2005: 133–65.

Marr, Timothy. "'Out of This World.' Islamic Irruptions in the Literary Americas." *American Literary History* 18.3 (2006): 521–49.

MEDASSET. "Press Release: Council of Europe's Bern Convention Urges Turkey to Improve Management of Protected Sea Turtle Habitats." January 4, 2015. www.medasset.org.

MEDASSET. "Turkey's Fethiye and Patara Sea Turtle Nesting Beaches Still Need Better Protection." September 22, 2016. www.medasset.org.

Melville, Herman. *The Portable Melville*. Ed. Jay Leda. New York: Viking Press, 1952.

Melville, Herman. *Journal of a Visit to Europe and the Levant*. Ed. Howard C. Horsford. Princeton: Princeton University Press, 1955.

Moavenii, Azadeh. "The Latest Enemies of Iran: Dogs and Their Owners." *Time World* April 19, 2011. http://www.time.com/time/world/article/0,8599,2065873,00.html.

Montagu, Lady Mary Wortley. *The Complete Letters of Montagu, Lady Mary Wortley: Volume I*. Ed. Robert Halsband. Oxford: The Clarendon Press, 1965.

Moore, Marianne. *The Complete Poems of Marianne Moore*. New York: Macmillan Publishing Co., Inc., 1967.

Moran, Berna. "'Bir Huzursuzluğun Romanı Huzur'. ['*Peace*, A Novel of Anxiety']." In *Bir Gül Bu Karanlıklarda. [A Rose in This Darkness]*. Ed. Abdullah Uçman and Handan Inci. Istanbul: Kitabevi, 2002: 291–308.

Munzur. http://www.radikal.com.tr/cevre/mecidiyekoyde-munzur-eylemi-1528504/.

Nagai, Kaoiri et al. Eds. *Cosmopolitan Animals*. London: Palgrave Macmillan, 2015.

Nurbakhsh, Javad. *Dogs from a Sufi Point of View*. London: Khaniqahi- Nimatullahi Publications, 1989.

Orwell, George. "Politics and the English Language." In *Why I Write*. New York: Penguin Books, 1884: 102–120.

Özdemir, İbrahim. "Environmental Ethics from a Qur'anic Perspective." In *Islam and Ecology*. Ed. Richard C. Foltz, Frederick M. Denny, Azizan Baharuddin, and Kaveh L. Afrasiabi. Cambridge: Harvard University Press, 2003: 3–38.

Pamuk, Orhan. *Istanbul: Memories and the City*. New York: Vintage International, 2006.

Patel, Samir Harshad. *Movement, Behaviour and Threats to Loggerhead Turtles (Caretta caretta) in the Mediterranean Sea*. Diss. Drexel University, 2013. UMI 3605481 (2013).

Pease, Donald. "*Moby-Dick* and the Cold War." In *The American Renaissance Reconsidered*. Ed. Walter Benn Michaels and Donald Pease. Baltimore: Johns Hopkins University Press, 1985: 113–55.

Porter, James I. "The Sublime without Longinus." *boundary 2*, 43.2 (2016): 74–124.

Potter, William. *Melville's Clarel and the Intersympathy of Creeds*. Kent, OH: The Kent State University Press, 2004.

Ra'ad, Basem L. *Hidden Stories: Palestine and the Eastern Mediterranean*. New York: Pluto Press, 2010.

Rappole, John H. *The Avian Migrant: The Biology of Bird Migration*. New York: Columbia University Press, 2013.

Ritvo, Harriet. "Animal Planet." In *The Animals Reader: The Essential Classic and Contemporary Writings*. Ed. Linda Kalof and Amy Fitzgerald. Oxford: Berg, 2007: 129–40.

Said, Edward. *Orientalism*. New York: Vintage Books, 1979.

Scott, David. "Rewalking Thoreau and Asia: 'Light from the East' for 'A Very Yankee Sort of Oriental'" *Philosophy East and West* 57.1 (2007): 14–39.

Shepard, Paul. *The Others: How Animals Made Us Human*. Washington, DC: Island Press, 1997.

Sideris, Lisa. *Environmental Ethics, Ecological Theology and Natural Selection*. New York: Columbia University Press, 2003.

Spanos, William. *The Errant Art of "Moby-Dick": The Canon, the Cold War, and the Struggle for American Studies*. Durham: Duke University Press, 1995.

Spanos, William. *The Exceptionalist State and the State of Exception: Herman Mellville's Billy Budd, Sailor*. Baltimore: The Johns Hopkins Press, 2011.

Tanpınar, Ahmet Hamdi. "Istanbul." In *Beş Şehir*. [*Five Cities*]. Ankara: Ülkü, 1946.

Tanpınar, Ahmet Hamdi. *Yaşadığım Gibi*. [*As I Lived*]. Istanbul: Dergah Yayınları, 2000.

Tanpınar, Ahmet Hamdi. *Five Cities*. Unpublished English translation by Ruth Christie, 2007.

Tanpınar, Ahmet Hamdi. "Three Sections from 'Istanbul' in *Beş Şehir* (*Five Cities*)." Trans. Ruth Christie. *Texas Studies in Literature and Language* 54.4 (2012): 456–67.

"The Animal Protection Law, Temporary Shelters and Stray Animals on The Bodrum Peninsula." http://www.bodrumbulletin.com/Turkish-Animal-Protection-Law.pdf.

Tlili, Serra. *Animals in the Quran*. New York: Cambridge University Press, 2012.

Topçuoğlu, Sinan Ümit. *İstanbul ve Sokak Köpekleri (Istanbul and Street Dogs)*. Istanbul: Sepya Yayıncılık, 2010.

Tuan, Yi-Fu. "Animal Pets: Cruelty and Affection." Kalof: 141–53.

Türkozan, Oğuz, Şükran Yalçın, Özdilek, Serap Ergene, Aşkın Hasan Uçar, Bektaş Sönmez, Can Yılmaz, Yasemin Kaçar, and Cemil Aymak. "Strandings of Loggerhead (Caretta Caretta) and Green (Chelonia Mydas) Sea Turtles Along the Eastern Mediterranean Coast of Turkey." *Herpetological Journal* 23 (2013): 11–15.

Twain, Mark. *The Innocents Abroad or, the New Pilgrims' Progress*. New York: The New American Library, 1966.

Urry, John. "Complexity." *Theory, Culture and Society* 23.2–3 (2006): 111–17.

Uyar, Turgut. "'Yad' ('Reminiscence')." In *Büyük Saat-Bütün Şiirleri*. Istanbul: Yapı Kredi Yayınları, 2003: 17.

Van Doreen, Thom. *Flight Ways: Life and Loss at the Edge of Extinction*. New York: Columbia University Press, 2014.

Van Grouw, Katrina. *The Unfeathered Bird*. Princeton: Princeton University Press, 2013.

Verslius, Arthur. "American Transcendentalism and Asian Religions." *American Oriental Society* 115.1 (1995): 160–61.

Wadiwell, Dinesh. *The War Against Animals*. Leiden: Brill, 2015.

Watson, David. "Melville, Interrupted." *ESQ: A Journal of the American Renaissance* 57.4 (2011): 355–89.

Witherington, Blair E. "Biological Conservation of Loggerheads: Challenges and Opportunities." In *Loggerhead Sea Turtles*. Ed. Alan Bolten and Blair E. Witherington. Washington: Smithsonian Books, 2003: 295–312.

Wordsworth, William. "Preface." In *Lyrical Ballads. Norton Anthology of English Literature, Eighth Edition*. New York: W.W. Norton & Company, 2006.

Zariç, Mahfuz. "'Turnadan Leyleğe Türk Şiirinde Göçmen Kuşlar'. ('From Cranes to Storks: Migratory Birds in Folk Poetry')." *Hece Gezi Özel Sayısı* 22 (2011): 102–117.

Zimmerman, Andrea. *Taşkafa: Stories of the Street*. Text and voice John Berger. Yalan Dünya Film LTD, 2013. Documentary 2.

Index

Abdal, Kaygusuz 120
Able, Kenneth P.
  Gathering of Angels: Migratory Birds and Their Ecology 113
Addison, Joseph 136
Akova, Akgün
  "A Bird's-Eye View" 109
Anatolia 108
  mega-projects in 6, 62–3
  in poetry 44–9, 59, 109, 112
  religions in 30, 48, 81
  rural 41, 44, 46, 48, 155
animacy 65, 70, 165 n.2
Animal Studies 3, 7–8
animals. *See also* European White Stork; Istanbul street dogs; sea turtles
  abuse of 83–4, 88–9, 99, 101
  anthropocentricism and humanism 87, 90–2, 119
  bioregionalism 92–3, 96, 98
  commodification of 85, 87, 89, 94
  conservation and protection efforts 63, 88–92, 101–2, 122, 150–1
  cosmopolitan 155, 168 n.7
  domesticated 78, 80, 84–5, 88–90, 92–4, 96–9, 103, 166 n.3
  feral and street 1, 84–5, 88–93, 96–7, 103, 166 n.4
  human-centralism 79–80, 85–6, 89, 92–3, 98, 101, 156, 158 n.2
  marginal 77–8, 96, 103
  poetic conceits 47
  in the Quran 79, 81–3, 88, 97, 100–1, 167 n.15
  speciesism 80, 82
  and the sublime 128, 139
Animal Welfare Act (2004) 88–9, 102
animism 47, 57, 65–6
anthropocentricism 5, 79, 87, 119, 138
Arolat, Ali Mümtaz
  "The Storks" 110–11

Arslangündoğdu, Zeynel 108–9
  "The Effects of Future Projects in Istanbul on the Migration Routes of Birds" 116–18
Atatürk, Mustafa Kemal 16, 22, 31, 43, 159 n.5

Bacon, Francis
  "Of the Advancement of Learning" 142–3
Barthes, Roland
  Mythologies 61
Berger, John 4, 165 n.1
  "Why Look at Animals" 85, 97
bioregionalism 92–3, 96, 98, 156
  poetic 69, 121
Black Sea 108
  environmental damage to 5–6, 62–3, 161 n.2
  literary accounts of 45, 52
Blasing, Mutlu Konuk 42–3
Bosporus
  literary accounts of 3, 14, 27, 33–4, 53, 111
  stork migration along 7, 105, 108–9, 111, 113, 116, 122
Buell, Laurence 151, 154, 157
  The Future of Environmental Criticism 121–2
Burt, Jonathon
  "Illumination of the Animal Kingdom" 85
Byatt, A. S.
  "Feeling Thought: Donne and the Embodied Mind" 66–7

Canbolat, Ali Fuat 148–50
Cansever, Edip
  "Friends" 111–12
Caretta caretta. *See* sea turtles
Christianity 13, 158 n.1
  disillusionment with 14, 19–20, 24

human-centralism in nature 64, 79,
    81–2, 86, 91, 95
literary representations of 21, 25, 28–9,
    57
Ciach, Michel
  "The Foraging of White Storks" 118
climate change 113–14, 122, 124
colonialism
  American exceptionalism 18–21, 96
  environmentalism 107
  European 86
  Islamic 81
Cox, George
  Bird Migration and Global Change
    114–15, 117–18, 124
Cronon, William 150
  "The Trouble with Wilderness" 144–5,
    147

Darwinism 78–9
  human responsibility to animals 91, 98
Dede, Ismail 33
DeLoughrey, Elizabeth
  Postcolonial Ecologies 107
dervishes 28, 30–1, 41
Dimock, Wai Chee
  "Hemispheric Islam" 26–7, 29
dogs 165 n.2, 167 n.11. *See also* Istanbul
    street dogs
  anthropomorphism of 90–1
  domestication of 85, 87, 89–90, 92–4,
    97, 103, 166 n.3
  feral 78, 80, 83, 85, 93, 96, 100, 147,
    167 n.8
  in Islam 80–3, 87–8, 97, 100–2, 103,
    166 n.4
  as literary conceit 80–2, 85, 100
  use-value of 78, 80, 82, 85, 92
Doğuş Group 62
Doherty, Peter
  Their Fate Is Our Fate 115
Donne, John 66–7
Dooren, Thom van
  *Flight Ways: Life and Loss at the Edge of
    Extinction* 156

Ecocriticism 6, 8–9, 103, 107, 151, 154–7,
    160 n.13
  and the sublime 144, 146
ecofeminism 90–1

Economides, Louise
  *The Ecology of Wonder in Romantic
    and Postmodern Literature* 135–6,
    142–3
Ecopoetics 6, 8, 106–7, 121–3
  and environmental movements 7, 73
ecotheology 78, 91, 100–1
ecotheory 79–80, 82, 84–5, 90–2
  against human-centralism 79–80,
    84–5, 92
  and theology 91
Edip, Halide 45
  "Let Us Mind Our Own House" 44
Einboden, Jeffrey 29–30, 160 n.13
Emerson, Ralph Waldo 43, 55, 73
  and eastern mysticism 24–7, 29
  "Saadi" 26
Enlightenment, The
  and the commodification of nature 41
  in the Ottoman Empire 86–7
  and Romanticism 15
environmental ethics 64–5, 73, 78, 85, 94,
    97, 103. *See also* land
environmental movements 5–6, 38, 85,
    107, 123–4, 150–1. *See also* Gezi
    Park protest
  bioregionalism 69, 92, 96, 98
  and literary arts 1–2, 5, 7–8, 38–9, 44,
    58, 66, 106–7, 121, 154–7 (*See also*
    Ecopoetics)
  and the sublime 144–7
European White Stork
  cultural memory 7
  as "dead" metaphor 121–3
  migration patterns of 108–9, 113
  as poetic conceit 47, 105–6, 109–12,
    119–23, 125, 168 n.6
  threat to 108, 113–19, 121–5
  transnationalism 107, 124
Evernden, Neil
  The Social Creation of Nature 145
exceptionalism
  American 19–21, 23–5, 28
  human 86, 156, 158 n.2
  poetic 42

Finkelstein, Dorothee 26–7, 29, 32
Franchot, Jenny
  Melville's Traveling God 25–6
Frost, Robert 43

Gander, Forrest
  Redstart: An Ecological Poetics 122–3
Gezi Park protest 4–5, 38, 62, 164 n.17
  Romanticism of 39–40, 56
Göknar, Erdağ 18
Güler, Gülen 4, 165 n.1
Gülhane Park 56–8, 164 n.17
Gustafson, James 79, 91

Halman, Talat 17, 105
Hancock, James A.
  Storks, Ibises and Spoonbills of the World 115
Handley, George B.
  Postcolonial Ecologies 107
Haraway, Donna 94–5, 158 nn.1–3, 165–6 n.3
  The Companion Species Manifesto 96, 167 n.11
Heide, Markus
  "Herman Melville's 'Benito Cereno'" 20
Heisse, Ursula
  Sense of Place and Sense of Planet 155–6
Herpetology 8, 128, 137, 140, 150
Heyman, Peter 151–2
  Animality in British Romanticism 134–6, 139
Hikmet, Nâzım 164 n.14
  "About Mount Uludagh" 47–8
  Anatolian poems 44–7
  communism 39, 41–2, 46
  The Epic of Sheik Bedreddin 48–51
  The Epic of the War of Independence 54–6
  "First Look at Anatolia" 45
  imprisonment 38, 46–8, 51
  "Istanbul House of Detention" 46
  "Letter to My Son" 40
  Life's Good, Brother 41
  nature in poems 5–6, 40–1, 44–6, 51–3, 59
  modernist 43, 67, 162 n.8, 163 n.12
  popularity of 5, 43
  prison poems 46–8
  relevance to environmental movements 4–5, 7, 38–41, 44, 56, 58, 67, 74, 161 n.3, 164 n.17
  Romanticism of 5, 42–3, 45, 59
  Rubaiyat 41
  self-exile 38, 44, 51, 67
  Straw-blond 52–3
  Sufisim 41
  "Things I Didn't Know I Loved" 6–7, 67–73
  "To Chop Down the Plane Tree" 53–4
  trees 4–5, 38, 52–9
  "The Walnut Tree" 56–8, 164 n.17
Hillman, Brenda 106–7, 121
Hitt, Christopher
  "Toward an Ecological Sublime" 128, 136–7, 145–7, 153
humanism 135. *See also* post-humanism
  critiques of 80, 82
  human exceptionalism 85–7
  lives of animals in 79, 86–7, 90–1
hüzün 16, 34, 112
hydroelectric projects (HEPPS) 5
  environmental impact of 6, 61, 116
  resistance to 62–3, 161 n.2

Ilhan, Attila
  "Maria Missakian" 105–6
  "One Three Five" 105
Islam 13, 15, 48, 86, 161 n.4. *See also* Sufism
  in American literature 25–9, 32, 160 n.9, 160 n.13
  cultural 22, 82
  dogs 80–3, 87–8, 97, 100–1
  haram 81, 87
  human-centralism in 79, 82–3, 85, 101
  nationalism 19, 21–2, 31
  Westernization of 23, 85
Istanbul 1, 155, 164 n.17. *See also* Bosporus; Istanbul street dogs
  American writers in 2, 9, 13–14 (*See also* Melville, Herman; Twain, Mark)
  architecture of 3, 9, 32–3, 92
  "authenticity" of 23, 30
  megaprojects 4, 7, 107–8, 116–19, 125
  protests in 4–5, 63 (*See also* Gezi Park protest)
  religion in 13–17, 19–33 (*See also* Islam)
  trees of 2–5, 9, 32–4, 37–8, 40, 52–4, 56–9, 62
  Turkish writers in 9, 44–5 (*See also* Hikmet, Nazım; Kemal, Yahya; Tanpınar, Ahmet Hamdi)

as urban wilderness 2, 4, 9, 34 (*See also* European White Stork)
Westernization of 15–18, 22–4, 27–30, 34, 83–90, 97, 102
Istanbul Airport 118–19
Istanbul street dogs 4, 165 n.2
  abuse and exile of 83–4, 87–9, 97–9, 166 n.4
  domestication of 90, 94, 103, 166 n.3
  Islamic attitudes toward 82–3, 87–8, 97, 101–2
  literary accounts of 77, 95, 98–100
  as part of the urban ecosystem 78, 80, 82–3, 85, 91, 93–4, 96–100, 102–3
  protection of 84, 88–91, 102
  use-value of 85
  and Westernization 83–5, 87–97, 102

Kahl, M. Philip
  Storks, Ibises and Spoonbills of the World 115
Kahraman, Hasan Bülent
  "In Pursuit of Time Not Lost" 18–19, 22
Kant, Immanuel 137, 145, 151
  "The Analytic of the Sublime" 8, 128–9, 131–5, 138–9, 143, 152, 169 n.7
Karacaoğlu 120
Kemal, Yahya 15–17, 22, 24, 27, 165 n.1
Kimmerer, Robin Wall
  "Learning the Grammar of Animacy" 65, 69
Kinsella, John
  Redstart: An Ecological Poetics 122–3
Knickerbocker, Scott
  Ecopolitics: The Language of Nature, the Nature of Language 7, 73
Kruszyk, Robert
  "The Foraging of White Storks" 118
Kushlan, James A.
  Storks, Ibises and Spoonbills of the World 115

Land. *See also* environmental movements
  communal heritage and identity of 6, 13, 20, 26, 30, 32, 37–9, 44, 46–7, 50–1, 63, 155, 161 n.1
  ethics 6, 51, 59, 73–4, 92
  as poetic conceit 5, 9, 26, 32, 44–51, 53–4, 58, 68, 111, 130
  and resistance 47–8
  use-value of 6, 44, 62, 64–5, 68, 73–4, 158 n.2
Latour, Bruno
  "Politics of Nature: East and West Perspectives" 123–5, 168 n.7
Leopold, Aldo 69
  A Sand Country Almanac 64–5, 73, 92
Leroux, Jean-François
  "Wars for Oil: Moby-Dick, Orientalism, and Cold-War Criticism" 29
loggerhead. *See* sea turtles
Longinus 134, 146
  "On the Sublime" 8, 128–31, 137–9

Magnin, Gernant 124
  Important Bird Areas in Turkey 115–16
Manes, Christopher
  "Nature and Silence" 65–6
Marland, Pippa 151
Marr, Timothy
  "Without the Pale: Melville and Ethnic Cosmopolitanism" 19, 20, 27–8
McFague, Sallie 91
Melville, Herman 2, 18
  American Exceptionalism 19–21, 23–5, 28
metaphors
  "dead" 71, 121, 123
  as distortion 68
  human-centered 68, 71, 106
  and the natural world 34, 64, 73, 106, 110, 112, 123, 125, 138
Mevlana Orders 30–1, 34
Milne, Anne
  "Fully Mobile and AWAITING FURTHER INSTRUCTIONS" 96
modernism 67, 90, 96, 105, 162 n.8
  post- 134–5, 152
Moran, Berna
  "*Peace*, A Novel of Anxiety" 30–1
mysticism 3, 14, 20, 24–6, 28–9, 32, 34, 160 n.9
  Billy Budd 20
  Clarel 26, 160 n.9
  "The Continents" 34
  Moby-Dick 2, 14, 20–1, 24–5, 28–9, 32
  Near East Journal 2–3, 13–15, 32–4

Pequod 19
Typee 19–20
myth
   misappropriation of nature 7, 61–4, 66
   of national identity/origin 17, 19, 53, 57
   poetic 58, 73, 80–1, 120–1

nature. *See also* environmental movements; European White Stork; trees
   abuse and misappropriation of 7, 38, 40, 43, 59, 62–6, 93, 123, 149
   anthropocentric 5, 65–6, 69, 71, 130, 145
   and culture 2–3, 33–4, 44, 59, 121, 155
   feral 1, 4, 96 (*See also* Istanbul street dogs)
   human relationship with 2, 6–7, 40, 44, 58, 66–71, 73, 85, 92, 137
   intrinsic value of 1, 5, 8, 37, 40, 59, 72–3
   in Islamic mysticism 3, 32, 49, 78–9, 82
   language of 7, 64–6, 73, 95, 129, 145
   myth 61, 73
   and poetry 5, 7, 9, 28, 40–1, 43–4, 48, 52–6, 67–9, 72–4, 106, 122–3, 129, 138 (*See also* Ecopoetics)
   Romantic 5, 40, 152
   and social activism 5, 7, 38–40, 43–4, 49, 55–6, 58–9, 69, 74, 90–2, 106, 123–5
   and the sublime 8, 128–31, 133–9, 143–6, 152–3
   transnational approach to 8
   urban 1–3, 32–3, 37, 53, 56, 58, 93
   use-value of 5–7, 40–1, 44, 59, 64–5, 67–8, 71–2
nature writing 40, 44, 59, 154, 156. *See also* Ecopoetics; Transcendentalism
Neo-Classical movement 86

Orientalism 14, 19, 24–9, 32
ornithology 113, 114, 117
   and poetics 7, 110
Ottoman Empire 41
   American accounts of 13–14, 24 (*See also* Melville, Herman)
   decline of 15–18, 23, 37, 44, 87
   literary traditions of 43–4, 56
   national identity in 16–18, 23, 44
   romanticizing of 18, 22, 24, 27
   Westernization of 17, 23–4, 86–7

Pamuk, Orhan
   Istanbul: Memories and the City 15–18, 24, 27–8
pathetic fallacy 90
Platonism 24–5, 28, 32, 68, 157
Porter, James
   "The Sublime without Longinus" 129–31, 136, 146, 169 n.1
post-humanism 1, 8, 91, 158 n.2
   approach to nature 8, 79–80, 103, 155, 158 n.2
   ethics 92

Quran. *See also* Islam
   Hadith 81, 100
   status of animals in 79, 81–3, 88, 97, 100–1

Ra'ad, Basem L.
   Hidden Stories: Palestine and the Eastern Mediterranean 19–20, 158 n.1, 160 n.9
Rappole, John
   The Avian Migrant: The Biology of Bird Migration 114, 117
Reed, Peter
   "Man Apart: An Alternative to the Self-Realization Approach" 145–6
Reilly, Evelyn 107
renewable energy 61–2, 73, 100. *See also* hydroelectric projects (HEPPS)
Ritvo, Harriet
   "Animal Planet" 89–90
Romanticism 16, 39, 161 n.5
   and mysticism 15, 26, 28, 31
   of nature 90–1, 98
   and Orientalism 24, 27–8
   political objectives of 1, 5, 9, 37, 39–43, 45, 59
   and the sublime 134–5, 139, 145
Ruhsati, Aşık 119

Scott, David 26
sea turtles (loggerheads) (*Caretta caretta*) 168 n.6
   biology of 140, 147–8
   conservation of 8, 9, 148–51

encounter with 127–8, 133, 152–3
magnetic fields and migration 140–3
and the sublime 8, 128, 131–7, 139, 151–3
threats to 147–50
Sema, Sadri
Old Istanbul Memories 95
"Seven Sleepers" 81
Shepard, Paul
The Others: How Animals Made Us Human 77–8, 80, 84–6, 103
Sideris, Lisa
Environmental Ethics, Ecological Theory and Natural Selection 78–9, 82, 91–3, 103
Spanos, William 20
The Exceptionalist State and the State of Exception 20–1
speciesism 80, 82
sublime (The)
ecological 8, 128, 134, 137–8, 144–7, 152–3
fear in 8, 128–9, 132–3, 135–6, 137, 145, 153
feminine 130, 135, 137
Imagination 131–3, 136, 145, 151
poetic and rhetorical 45, 130–1, 133–5, 137
postmodern 134–5, 152
Reason 131–4, 137–9, 151
Romanticism 134–5, 139, 145
science 137–9, 143, 151
traditional definitions of 128–33 (*See also* Kant, Immanuel; Longinus)
and wonder 135–6, 142–3, 153
Sufism 41
American literary figures 3, 26–30, 34
as protest to modernity 15, 31, 33
street dogs 77, 100–1
symbiosis 9, 56, 64–5, 74, 91
poetic 32–3, 40, 68–9, 71

tadhlīl 100
Tanpınar, Ahmet Hamdi 9, 16, 59
As I Lived 19, 21–2
"Essential Differences Observed between East and West" 27
Five Cities (Beş Şehir) 2–3, 15–16, 22–4, 27–8, 30–1, 33–5
hüzün 16, 34

Huzur 16, 32
Islam 21–2, 28, 30–3
Romanticism 27–8
Those Outside the Scene 18
on trees 2–3, 33–4, 37
Turkish national identity 16–19, 21–4, 27–8, 30–5
Thoreau, Henry David 28, 43–4, 55, 73, 154
and Sufism 26, 29
Tlili, Serra
Animals in the Qur'an 79, 82–3, 100–1
Topçuoğlu, Ümit Sinan 84
Transcendentalism 24–5, 27
trees
as poetic conceit 52–9, 65, 67–9, 112
as political symbol 4–5, 37, 53–9, 62–3
urban 2–3, 4–5, 9, 33–4, 37–8, 40, 53–9, 62, 69
Turkish 43, 45, 163 n.12, 166 n.7
Twain, Mark 2, 19, 25
The Innocents Abroad 77, 98–9

Urry, John 143
Uyar, Turgut
"Reminiscence" 125

Wadiwell, Dinesh
The War Against Animals 150
Watson, David
"Melville, Interrupted" 25–6
Westernization
critiques of 17–18, 22–4, 30
of human–animal relationships 83–90, 93–4, 97–100, 102–3
and national identity 16, 23–4, 30, 34
Whitman, Walt 43, 50, 71, 164 n.14
"Song of Myself" 70
Witherington, Blair E. 150
Wordsworth, William 28, 42, 45, 152
"The Sublime and the Beautiful" 139

Yarar, Murat 124
Important Bird Areas in Turkey 115–16
Yavuz Sultan Selim Bridge 118

Zariç, Mahfuz
"From Cranes to Storks: Migratory Birds in Folk Poetry" 119–20
Zoroastrians 28, 80–1